Comprehensive Criminal Procedure
Fourth Edition

2019 Supplement

2019 Supplement

Comprehensive Criminal Procedure

Fourth Edition

Ronald Jay Allen

John Henry Wigmore Professor of Law
Northwestern University

(The Late) William J. Stuntz

Henry J. Friendly Professor of Law
Harvard University

Joseph L. Hoffmann

Harry Pratter Professor of Law
Indiana University Maurer School of Law

Debra A. Livingston

United States Circuit Judge, Second Circuit
Paul J. Kellner Professor of Law
Columbia University

Andrew D. Leipold

Edwin M. Adams Professor and Director,
Program in Criminal Law & Procedure
University of Illinois

Tracey L. Meares

Walton Hale Hamilton Professor of Law
Yale Law School

About Wolters Kluwer Legal & Regulatory U.S.

Wolters Kluwer Legal & Regulatory U.S. delivers expert content and solutions in the areas of law, corporate compliance, health compliance, reimbursement, and legal education. Its practical solutions help customers successfully navigate the demands of a changing environment to drive their daily activities, enhance decision quality and inspire confident outcomes.

Serving customers worldwide, its legal and regulatory portfolio includes products under the Aspen Publishers, CCH Incorporated, Kluwer Law International, ftwilliam. com and MediRegs names. They are regarded as exceptional and trusted resources for general legal and practice-specific knowledge, compliance and risk management, dynamic workflow solutions, and expert commentary.

Contents

PART FIVE   POSTTRIAL PROCEEDINGS

Table of Cases

Italics indicate principal cases.

PART ONE

THE CRIMINAL PROCESS

Chapter 2

The Idea of Due Process

A. Defining Due Process

Replace the second and third full sentences on page 74 with the following:

In the most recent cases to reach the issue, the Supreme Court, relying almost entirely on an historical analysis, concluded that the Second Amendment and the Excessive Fines Clause of the Eighth Amendment, respectively, are incorporated into the Due Process Clause. See McDonald v. City of Chicago, IL, 561 U.S. 742 (2010) (Second Amendment); Timbs v. Indiana, 586 U.S. ___ (2019) (Excessive Fines Clause). For more on these cases, see Note 5, at page 86, infra.

B. Incorporation

Replace the first sentence of Note 5 on page 86 with the following:

As mentioned above, in McDonald v. City of Chicago, IL, 561 U.S. 742 (2010), the Court concluded that the Second Amendment is implicit in the Due Process Clause.

Replace the last two sentences of Note 5 on page 86 with the following:

Meanwhile, in Timbs v. Indiana, 586 U.S. ___ (2019), the Court unanimously agreed that the Excessive Fines Clause of the Eighth Amendment is incorporated into the Due Process Clause and thus applies to the states. The case involved the civil forfeiture of a heroin dealer's $42,000 Land Rover—which he had used to carry out his drug deals—following his guilty plea to dealing in a controlled substance and conspiracy to commit theft. (The maximum fine for the offenses of conviction was $10,000.) Although the Court had no trouble reaching the incorporation conclusion, *Timbs* did not begin to address the more interesting question of whether the "excessiveness" of a civil forfeiture should be measured by comparison to the relevant crime (and the maximum authorized criminal punishment), or instead by the closeness of the relationship between the forfeited property and the crime. See Austin v. United States, 509 U.S. 602, 627-628 (1993) (Scalia, J., concurring in part and concurring in the judgment) (discussing this interesting question).

After *McDonald* and *Timbs*, only three of the specific provisions of the Bill of Rights remain unincorporated: the Third Amendment's protection against the quartering of soldiers; the grand jury provision dealt with in *Hurtado*; and the right to a civil jury in the Seventh Amendment.

PART TWO

THE RIGHT TO COUNSEL—
THE LINCHPIN OF
CONSTITUTIONAL
PROTECTION

Chapter 3

The Right to Counsel and Other Assistance

A. The Constitutional Requirements

1. The Right to the Assistance of Counsel at Trial

Insert the following Note after Note 5 on page 129:

6. Continuing the line of cases from *Nichols*, in United States v. Bryant, 579 U.S. ___ (2016), the Court concluded that the Sixth Amendment is not violated by a sentence enhancement based on prior uncounseled tribal-court convictions that were not themselves subject to the Sixth Amendment and that fully complied with the Indian Civil Rights Act. The Court explained that "convictions valid when entered—that is, those that, when rendered, did not violate the Constitution—retain that status when invoked in a subsequent proceeding."

B. Effective Assistance of Counsel

1. The Meaning of Effective Assistance

Insert the following paragraph at the end of Note 1 on page 177:

The Court seemed to answer this latter question "no" in McCoy v. Louisiana, 584 U.S. ___ (2018). The defendant in *McCoy* wanted to offer a "difficult to fathom" alibi that apparently almost literally made no sense. Still, according to the Court, his attorney did not "know" that he was going to commit perjury, and therefore was not obligated to refuse to present it—which may now mean no more than that the client has not so confided to his attorney. If so, *Nix v. Whiteside* is considerably reduced in importance. For more on *McCoy*, see infra at page 185, Note 5.

Insert the following Note after Note 4 on page 179:

5. As we have already seen, there are a small number of ineffective-assistance-of-counsel cases where deficient performance alone is sufficient to make out a violation, because prejudice is conclusively presumed. For example, if a defendant was denied a lawyer entirely during a critical stage of the trial, United States v. Cronic, 466 U.S. 648 (1984), the Sixth Amendment is violated without any showing of prejudice. See supra, at page 169. The same presumption of prejudice applies if the defendant was denied a lawyer on appeal, Penson v. Ohio, 488 U.S. 75 (1988). In addition, if the defendant specifically indicates that he wants to appeal his conviction, even from a guilty plea, and defense counsel does not file a notice of appeal, the *Strickland* test is satisfied — the failure to abide by the client's wishes in this context is professionally unreasonable, and because defendant was deprived an appeal that he otherwise would have taken, prejudice is again presumed. Roe v. Flores-Ortega, 528 U.S. 470 (2000).

But suppose the defendant not only pled guilty, but as part of the plea deal signed a waiver of his right to appeal. If the defendant later tells his lawyer to appeal anyway and the lawyer does not, is it still ineffective assistance of counsel? This question had divided lower courts, but in 2019, the Supreme Court held that even an appeal waiver does not relieve defense counsel of the obligation to abide by the client's wishes. Just as importantly, the Court concluded that the presumption of prejudice that attached to other failures to file an appeal continued to apply even when the defendant had signed an appeal waiver. Garza v. Idaho, 586 U.S. ___ (2019).

What explains the Court's willingness to dispense with the prejudice requirement in this setting? Shouldn't the defendant have to show that he had a valid, or at least plausible, claim on appeal — such that the loss of the right to appeal caused him some harm? Or is there some other justification for this presumption of prejudice, one that would not apply to the more common types of *Strickland* claims?

Insert the following Note after Note 4 on page 185:

4a. The Court's special concern about ineffective assistance in capital cases becomes even more heightened when race is also a significant factor. In Buck v. Davis, 580 U.S. ___ (2017), the Court held that a death-row inmate was entitled to appeal the denial of a Rule 60(b)(6) motion to reopen the trial judgment against him, in a federal habeas case involving alleged ineffective assistance of defense counsel for calling as a witness at capital sentencing a psychologist who testified that defendant's race increased the probability of future dangerousness, because the defendant had demonstrated a valid IAC claim and because the case presented "extraordinary" circumstances sufficient to justify granting exceptional relief under Rule 60(b)(6). Chief Justice Roberts, writing for the majority, explained: "Relying on race to impose a criminal sanction 'poisons public confidence' in the judicial process. It thus injures not just the defendant, but 'the law as an institution, . . . the community at large, and . . . the democratic ideal reflected in the processes of our courts.'" Id., at ___.

Insert the following paragraph at the end of Note 5 on page 185:

In *Nixon*, the defendant was unresponsive to his attorney's efforts to consult with him on trial strategy. While he did not consent to his attorney's actions, neither did he explicitly withhold consent. In McCoy v. Louisiana, 584 U.S. ___ (2018), by contrast, the defendant explicitly instructed his lawyer not to concede guilt and to rely on a "difficulty to fathom" alibi. The attorney believed the only hope was to concede that the defendant was the killer at the guilt stage, which would allow the defense to concentrate on mens rea and would be strategically helpful at the sentencing phase. Over a dissent by Justice Alito, the majority treated this as a case of an attorney conceding guilt (which has some support in the record), and held that conceding guilt of a charged crime over a defendant's objection is a structural violation of the Sixth Amendment necessitating a new trial.

3. Effective Assistance of Counsel and Plea Bargaining

Insert the following at the end of the carryover paragraph at the top of page 204:

In Lee v. United States, 582 U.S. ___ (2017), the Court clarified that "the inquiry . . . focuses on a defendant's decisionmaking, which may not turn solely on the likelihood of conviction after trial. . . . [T]he possibility of even a highly improbable result may be pertinent to the extent it would have affected [the defendant's] decisionmaking." Thus, even a defendant without any plausible legal defense may still prevail under *Hill*—if he can prove, based on "contemporaneous evidence to substantiate [his] expressed preferences," that with proper legal advice he would have rolled the dice and elected to go to trial.

C. Autonomy, Choice, and the Right to Counsel

2. The Right to Counsel of One's Choice

Insert the following Note after Note 1 on page 269:

1a. Refining the holding of *Caplin & Drysdale*, the Court held in Luis v. United States, 578 U.S. ___ (2016), that a person could not be restricted from using her own assets to pay for defense counsel. The critical distinction, according to the Court, is between "legitimate, untainted assets" and those that plausibly were obtained through criminal means.

PART THREE

THE RIGHT TO BE LET ALONE—AN EXAMINATION OF THE FOURTH AND FIFTH AMENDMENTS AND RELATED AREAS

Chapter 5

The Fourth Amendment

B. The Scope of the Fourth Amendment

1. The Meaning of "Searches"

c. Information, Privacy, and the Fourth Amendment

Add the following Note, main case, and additional Notes immediately after Note 5 on page 403. Delete the existing Notes 6 and 7 on pages 403 and 404:

6. The Supreme Court took up the question of CSLI sooner than some expected, granting certiorari in June 2017 to review the Sixth Circuit's decision in Carpenter v. United States, 819 F.3d 880 (6th Cir. 2016). Timothy Carpenter was convicted, inter alia, of six counts of aiding and abetting Hobbs Act robbery in violation of 18 U.S.C. § 1951(a), based, in part, on business records obtained from his wireless carriers. Seven accomplices testified at trial that Carpenter organized a string of armed robberies at Radio Shack and T-Mobile stores in and around Detroit, Michigan, and typically served as a lookout during the robberies from a stolen car across the street from the targeted location. CSLI obtained from providers showed that Carpenter's cell phone was within a half-mile to two miles of the locations of the robberies (which spanned a five-month period in 2010 and 2011) during the times they took place.

The Sixth Circuit in *Carpenter* declined to revisit the third-party doctrine as it applied to the CSLI records in this case. Pursuant to that doctrine, the cell site location information was reflected in business records in the hand of Carpenter's providers and could be obtained without implicating the Fourth Amendment. But recall that in her *Jones* concurrence, Justice Sotomayor raises the question whether "it may be necessary to reconsider the premise that an individual has no expectation of privacy in information voluntarily disclosed to third parties" on the ground that this approach is "ill suited to the digital age." Third-party records of various sorts (records traditionally deemed to fall *outside* Fourth Amendment concern) "contain information regarding virtually every aspect of our lives"—our interests and reading habits, our associates, finances, and medical conditions. Christopher Slobogin, Privacy at Risk 203 (2007). "Technology has made that information infinitely more easily aggregated and accessible." Id. In the following main case, consider how the Supreme Court addresses the subject of location information reflected in a wireless carrier's business records. What does the Court's decision say, more broadly, about the third-party doctrine in the digital age?

CARPENTER v. UNITED STATES
Certiorari to the United States Court of Appeals for the Sixth Circuit
585 U.S. ___ (2018)

CHIEF JUSTICE ROBERTS delivered the opinion of the Court.

This case presents the question whether the Government conducts a search under the Fourth Amendment when it accesses historical cell phone records that provide a comprehensive chronicle of the user's past movements. . . .

Cell phones continuously scan their environment looking for the best signal, which generally comes from the closest cell site. Most modern devices, such as smartphones, tap into the wireless network several times a minute whenever their signal is on, even if the owner is not using one of the phone's features. Each time the phone connects to a cell site, it generates a time-stamped record known as cell-site location information (CSLI). The precision of this information depends on the size of the geographic area covered by the cell site. . . .

Wireless carriers collect and store CSLI for their own business purposes, including finding weak spots in their network and applying "roaming" charges when another carrier routes data through their cell sites. In addition, wireless carriers often sell aggregated location records to data brokers, without individual identifying information of the sort at issue here. While carriers have long retained CSLI for the start and end of incoming calls, in recent years phone companies have also collected location information from the transmission of text messages and routine data connections. Accordingly, modern cell phones generate increasingly vast amounts of increasingly precise CSLI.

In 2011, police officers arrested four men suspected of robbing a series of Radio Shack and (ironically enough) T-Mobile stores in Detroit. One of the men confessed that, over the previous four months, the group (along with a rotating cast of getaway drivers and lookouts) had robbed nine different stores in Michigan and Ohio. The suspect identified 15 accomplices who had participated in the heists and gave the FBI some of their cell phone numbers; the FBI then reviewed his call records to identify additional numbers that he had called around the time of the robberies.

Based on that information, the prosecutors applied for court orders under the Stored Communications Act to obtain cell phone records for petitioner Timothy Carpenter and several other suspects. That statute, as amended in 1994, permits the Government to compel the disclosure of certain telecommunications records when it "offers specific and articulable facts showing that there are reasonable grounds to believe" that the records sought "are relevant and material to an ongoing criminal investigation." 18 U.S.C. § 2703(d). Magistrate Judges issued two orders directing Carpenter's wireless carriers—MetroPCS and Sprint—to disclose "cell/ site sector [information] for [Carpenter's] telephone[ ] at call origination and at call termination for incoming and outgoing calls" during the four-month period when the string of robberies occurred. The first order sought 152 days of cell-site records from MetroPCS, which produced records spanning 127 days. The second order requested seven days of CSLI from Sprint, which produced two days of records covering the period when Carpenter's phone was "roaming" in northeastern Ohio. Altogether the Government obtained 12,898 location points cataloging Carpenter's movements—an average of 101 data points per day.

Carpenter was charged with six counts of robbery and an additional six counts of carrying a firearm during a federal crime of violence. Prior to trial, Carpenter moved to suppress the cell-site data provided by the wireless carriers. . . . The District Court denied the motion.

At trial, seven of Carpenter's confederates pegged him as the leader of the operation. In addition, FBI agent Christopher Hess offered expert testimony about the cell-site data. Hess explained that each time a cell phone taps into the wireless network, the carrier logs a time-stamped record of the cell site and particular sector that were used. With this information, Hess produced maps that placed Carpenter's phone near four of the charged robberies. . . . Carpenter was convicted on all but one of the firearm counts and sentenced to more than 100 years in prison.

The Court of Appeals for the Sixth Circuit affirmed. . . . We granted certiorari.

. . . For much of our history, Fourth Amendment search doctrine was "tied to common-law trespass" and focused on whether the Government "obtains information by physically intruding on a constitutionally protected area." United States v. Jones, 565 U.S. 400, 405, 406 n. 3 (2012). More recently, the Court has recognized that "property rights are not the sole measure of Fourth Amendment violations." Soldal v. Cook County, 506 U.S. 56, 64 (1992). In Katz v. United States, 389 U.S. 347, 351 (1967), we established that "the Fourth Amendment protects people, not places," and expanded our conception of the Amendment to protect certain expectations of privacy as well. . . .

Although no single rubric definitively resolves which expectations of privacy are entitled to protection,[1] the analysis is informed by historical understandings "of what was deemed an unreasonable search and seizure when [the Fourth Amendment] was adopted." Carroll v. United States, 267 U.S. 132, 149 (1925). On this score, our cases have recognized some basic guideposts. First, that the Amendment seeks to secure "the privacies of life" against "arbitrary power." Boyd v. United States, 116 U.S. 616, 630 (1886). Second, and relatedly, that a central aim of the Framers was "to place obstacles in the way of a too permeating police surveillance." United States v. Di Re, 332 U.S. 581, 595 (1948). . . .

The case before us involves the Government's acquisition of wireless carrier cell-site records revealing the location of Carpenter's cell phone whenever it made or received calls. This sort of digital data—personal location information maintained by a third party—does not fit neatly under existing precedents. Instead, requests for cell-site records lie at the intersection of two lines of cases . . . .

The first set of cases addresses a person's expectation of privacy in his physical location and movements. In United States v. Knotts, 460 U.S. 276 (1983), we considered the Government's use of a "beeper" to aid in tracking a vehicle through traffic. . . . The Court concluded that the "augment[ed]" visual surveillance did not constitute a search because "[a] person traveling in an automobile on public thoroughfares has no reasonable expectation of privacy in his movements from one place to another." Id., at 281, 282. . . .

This Court in Knotts, however, was careful to distinguish between the rudimentary tracking facilitated by the beeper and more sweeping modes of surveillance. . . . Significantly, the Court reserved the question whether "different constitutional principles may be applicable" if "twenty-four hour surveillance of any citizen of this country [were] possible." Id., at 283-284.

. . . In United States v. Jones, FBI agents installed a GPS tracking device on Jones's vehicle and remotely monitored the vehicle's movements for 28 days. The Court decided the case based on the Government's physical

---

1. . . . Neither party has asked the Court to reconsider Katz in this case.

trespass of the vehicle. At the same time. . . [s]ince GPS monitoring of a vehicle tracks "every movement" a person makes in that vehicle, the concurring Justices concluded that "longer term GPS monitoring in investigations of most offenses impinges on expectations of privacy"—regardless whether those movements were disclosed to the public at large.

In a second set of decisions, the Court has drawn a line between what a person keeps to himself and what he shares with others. We have previously held that "a person has no legitimate expectation of privacy in information he voluntarily turns over to third parties." [Smith v. Maryland, 442 U.S. 735, 743-744 (1979).] That remains true "even if the information is revealed on the assumption that it will be used only for a limited purpose." United States v. Miller, 425 U.S. 435, 443 (1976). . . .

This third-party doctrine largely traces its roots to *Miller*. While investigating Miller for tax evasion, the Government subpoenaed his banks, seeking several months of canceled checks, deposit slips, and monthly statements. The Court rejected a Fourth Amendment challenge to the records collection. For one, Miller could "assert neither ownership nor possession" of the documents; they were "business records of the banks." Id., at 440. For another, the nature of those records confirmed Miller's limited expectation of privacy, because the checks were "not confidential communications but negotiable instruments to be used in commercial transactions," and the bank statements contained information "exposed to [bank] employees in the ordinary course of business." Id., at 442. The Court thus concluded that Miller had "take[n] the risk, in revealing his affairs to another, that the information [would] be conveyed by that person to the Government." Id., at 443.

Three years later, *Smith* applied the same principles in the context of information conveyed to a telephone company. The Court ruled that the Government's use of a pen register—a device that recorded the outgoing phone numbers dialed on a landline telephone—was not a search. Noting the pen register's "limited capabilities," the Court "doubt[ed] that people in general entertain any actual expectation of privacy in the numbers they dial." 442 U.S., at 742. Telephone subscribers know, after all, that the numbers are used by the telephone company "for a variety of legitimate business purposes," including routing calls. Id., at 743. And at any rate, the Court explained, such an expectation "is not one that society is prepared to recognize as reasonable." Ibid. . . .

The question we confront today is how to apply the Fourth Amendment to a new phenomenon: the ability to chronicle a person's past movements through the record of his cell phone signals. Such tracking partakes of many of the qualities of the GPS monitoring we considered in *Jones*. . . .

At the same time, the fact that the individual continuously reveals his location to his wireless carrier implicates the third-party principle of *Smith* and *Miller*. But while the third-party doctrine applies to telephone numbers and bank records, it is not clear whether its logic extends to the qualitatively different category of cell-site records. . . .

We decline to extend *Smith* and *Miller* to cover these novel circumstances. Given the unique nature of cell phone location records, the fact that the information is held by a third party does not by itself overcome the user's claim to Fourth Amendment protection. Whether the Government employs its own surveillance technology as in *Jones* or leverages the technology of a wireless carrier, we hold that an individual maintains a legitimate expectation of privacy in the record of his physical movements as captured through CSLI. The location information obtained from Carpenter's wireless carriers was the product of a search.[3] . . .

In fact, historical cell-site records present even greater privacy concerns than the GPS monitoring of a vehicle we considered in *Jones*. Unlike the bugged container in *Knotts* or the car in *Jones,* a cell phone—almost a "feature of human anatomy," [Riley v. California, 573 U.S. ___, at ___ (2014)], tracks nearly exactly the movements of its owner. . . . A cell phone faithfully follows its owner beyond public thoroughfares and into private residences, doctor's offices, political headquarters, and other potentially revealing locales. Accordingly, when the Government tracks the location of a cell phone it achieves near perfect surveillance, as if it had attached an ankle monitor to the phone's user.

Moreover, the retrospective quality of the data here gives police access to a category of information otherwise unknowable. In the past, attempts to reconstruct a person's movements were limited by a dearth of records and the frailties of recollection. With access to CSLI, the Government can now travel back in time to retrace a person's whereabouts, subject only to the retention policies of the wireless carriers, which currently maintain records for up to five years. Critically, because location information is continually logged for all of the 400 million devices in the United States—not just

---

3. The parties suggest as an alternative to their primary submissions that the acquisition of CSLI becomes a search only if it extends beyond a limited period. See Reply Brief 12 (proposing a 24-hour cutoff); Brief for United States 55-56 (suggesting a seven-day cutoff). As part of its argument, the Government treats the seven days of CSLI requested from Sprint as the pertinent period, even though Sprint produced only two days of records. Brief for United States 56. Contrary to Justice Kennedy's assertion, post, we need not decide whether there is a limited period for which the Government may obtain an individual's historical CSLI free from Fourth Amendment scrutiny, and if so, how long that period might be. It is sufficient for our purposes today to hold that accessing seven days of CSLI constitutes a Fourth Amendment search.

those belonging to persons who might happen to come under investigation — this newfound tracking capacity runs against everyone. . . .

The Government and Justice Kennedy contend, however, that the collection of CSLI should be permitted because the data is less precise than GPS information. . . .

[T]he rule the Court adopts "must take account of more sophisticated systems that are already in use or in development." *Kyllo*, 533 U.S., at 36. While the records in this case reflect the state of technology at the start of the decade, the accuracy of CSLI is rapidly approaching GPS-level precision. . . .

The Government's primary contention . . . is that the third-party doctrine governs this case. . . .

The Government's position fails to contend with the seismic shifts in digital technology that made possible the tracking of not only Carpenter's location but also everyone else's, not for a short period but for years and years. . . . There is a world of difference between the limited types of personal information addressed in *Smith* and *Miller* and the exhaustive chronicle of location information casually collected by wireless carriers today. . . .

The third-party doctrine partly stems from the notion that an individual has a reduced expectation of privacy in information knowingly shared with another. But the fact of "diminished privacy interests does not mean that the Fourth Amendment falls out of the picture entirely." *Riley*, 573 U.S., at ___. *Smith* and *Miller*, after all, did not rely solely on the act of sharing. Instead, they considered "the nature of the particular documents sought" to determine whether "there is a legitimate 'expectation of privacy' concerning their contents." *Miller*, 425 U.S., at 442. *Smith* pointed out the limited capabilities of a pen register . . . . *Miller* likewise noted that checks were "not confidential communications but negotiable instruments to be used in commercial transactions." 425 U.S., at 442. . . .

The Court has in fact already shown special solicitude for location information in the third-party context. In *Knotts*, the Court relied on *Smith* to hold that an individual has no reasonable expectation of privacy in public movements that he "voluntarily conveyed to anyone who wanted to look." *Knotts*, 460 U.S., at 281. But when confronted with more pervasive tracking, five Justices agreed that longer term GPS monitoring of even a vehicle traveling on public streets constitutes a search. *Jones*, 565 U.S., at 430 (Alito, J., concurring in judgment); id., at 415 (Sotomayor, J., concurring). . . .

Neither does the second rationale underlying the third-party doctrine — voluntary exposure — hold up when it comes to CSLI. Cell phone location information is not truly "shared" as one normally understands the term. In the first place, cell phones and the services they provide are "such a pervasive and insistent part of daily life" that carrying one is indispensable to participation in modern society. *Riley*, 573 U.S., at ___. Second, a cell phone logs a cell-site record by dint of its operation, without any affirmative act on the part of the user beyond powering up. . . .

We therefore decline to extend *Smith* and *Miller* to the collection of CSLI. Given the unique nature of cell phone location information, the fact that the Government obtained the information from a third party does not overcome Carpenter's claim to Fourth Amendment protection. The Government's acquisition of the cell-site records was a search within the meaning of the Fourth Amendment.

Our decision today is a narrow one. We do not express a view on matters not before us: real-time CSLI or "tower dumps" (a download of information on all the devices that connected to a particular cell site during a particular interval). We do not disturb the application of *Smith* and *Miller* or call into question conventional surveillance techniques and tools, such as security cameras. Nor do we address other business records that might incidentally reveal location information. Further, our opinion does not consider other collection techniques involving foreign affairs or national security. As Justice Frankfurter noted when considering new innovations in airplanes and radios, the Court must tread carefully in such cases, to ensure that we do not "embarrass the future." Northwest Airlines, Inc., v. Minnesota, 322 U.S. 292, 300 (1944).

Having found that the acquisition of Carpenter's CSLI was a search, we also conclude that the Government must generally obtain a warrant supported by probable cause before acquiring such records. . . .

The Government acquired the cell-site records pursuant to a court order issued under the Stored Communications Act, which required the Government to show "reasonable grounds" for believing that the records were "relevant and material to an ongoing investigation." 18 U.S.C. § 2703(d). That showing falls well short of the probable cause required for a warrant. . . .

Justice Alito contends that the warrant requirement simply does not apply when the Government acquires records using compulsory process. Unlike an actual search, he says, subpoenas for documents do not involve the direct taking of evidence; they are at most a "constructive search" conducted by the target of the subpoena. Given this lesser intrusion on personal privacy, Justice Alito argues that the compulsory production of records is not held to the same probable cause standard. . . .

But this Court has never held that the Government may subpoena third parties for records in which the suspect has a reasonable expectation of privacy. Almost all of the examples Justice Alito cites, contemplated requests for evidence implicating diminished privacy interests or for a corporation's own books. . . .

Justice Alito overlooks the critical issue. At some point, the dissent should recognize that CSLI is an entirely different species of business record—something that implicates basic Fourth Amendment concerns about arbitrary government power much more directly than corporate tax or payroll ledgers. . . .

If the choice to proceed by subpoena provided a categorical limitation on Fourth Amendment protection, no type of record would ever be protected by the warrant requirement. Under Justice Alito's view, private letters, digital contents of a cell phone—any personal information reduced to document form, in fact—may be collected by subpoena for no reason other than "official curiosity." United States v. Morton Salt Co., 338 U.S. 632, 652 (1950). . . .

This is certainly not to say that all orders compelling the production of documents will require a showing of probable cause. The Government will be able to use subpoenas to acquire records in the overwhelming majority of investigations. We hold only that a warrant is required in the rare case where the suspect has a legitimate privacy interest in records held by a third party.

Further, even though the Government will generally need a warrant to access CSLI, case-specific exceptions may support a warrantless search of an individual's cell-site records under certain circumstances. "One well-recognized exception applies when '"the exigencies of the situation" make the needs of law enforcement so compelling that [a] warrantless search is objectively reasonable under the Fourth Amendment.'" Kentucky v. King, 563 U.S. 452, 460 (2011) (quoting Mincey v. Arizona, 437 U.S. 385, 394 (1978)). Such exigencies include the need to pursue a fleeing suspect, protect individuals who are threatened with imminent harm, or prevent the imminent destruction of evidence. . . .

. . . Here the progress of science has afforded law enforcement a powerful new tool to carry out its important responsibilities. At the same time, this tool risks Government encroachment of the sort the Framers, "after consulting the lessons of history," drafted the Fourth Amendment to prevent. Di Re, 332 U.S., at 595.

We decline to grant the state unrestricted access to a wireless carrier's database of physical location information. In light of the deeply revealing nature of CSLI, its depth, breadth, and comprehensive reach, and the inescapable and automatic nature of its collection, the fact that such information is gathered by a third party does not make it any less deserving of Fourth Amendment protection. . . .

The judgment of the Court of Appeals is reversed, and the case is remanded for further proceedings consistent with this opinion.

JUSTICE KENNEDY, with whom JUSTICE THOMAS and JUSTICE ALITO join, dissenting.

. . . The Court has twice held that individuals have no Fourth Amendment interests in business records which are possessed, owned, and controlled by a third party. United States v. Miller, 425 U.S. 435 (1976); Smith v. Maryland, 442 U.S. 735 (1979). This is true even when the records contain personal and sensitive information. So when the Government uses a subpoena to obtain, for example, bank records, telephone records, and credit card statements from the businesses that create and keep these records, the Government does not engage in a search of the business's customers within the meaning of the Fourth Amendment.

In this case petitioner challenges the Government's right to use compulsory process to obtain a now-common kind of business record: cell-site records held by cell phone service providers. The Government acquired the records through an investigative process enacted by Congress. Upon approval by a neutral magistrate, and based on the Government's duty to show reasonable necessity, it authorizes the disclosure of records and information that are under the control and ownership of the cell phone service provider, not its customer. . . .

Cell-site records, however, are no different from the many other kinds of business records the Government has a lawful right to obtain by compulsory process. Customers like petitioner do not own, possess, control, or use the records, and for that reason have no reasonable expectation that they cannot be disclosed pursuant to lawful compulsory process.

The Court today disagrees. It holds for the first time that by using compulsory process to obtain records of a business entity, the Government has not just engaged in an impermissible action, but has conducted a search of the business's customer. The Court further concludes that the search in this case was unreasonable and the Government needed to get a warrant to obtain more than six days of cell-site records.

In concluding that the Government engaged in a search, the Court unhinges Fourth Amendment doctrine from the property-based concepts that have long grounded the analytic framework that pertains in these cases. In doing so it draws an unprincipled and unworkable line between cell-site records on the one hand and financial and telephonic records on the other. According to today's majority opinion, the Government can acquire a record of every credit card purchase and phone call a person makes over months or years without upsetting a legitimate expectation of privacy. But . . . the Government crosses a constitutional line when it obtains a court's approval to issue a subpoena for more than six days of cell-site records in order to determine whether a person was within several hundred city blocks of a crime scene. . . .

The location information revealed by cell-site records is imprecise, because an individual cell-site sector usually covers a large geographic area. The FBI agent who offered expert testimony about the cell-site records at issue here testified that a cell site in a city reaches between a half mile and two miles in all directions. . . . To put that in perspective, in urban areas cell-site records often would reveal the location of a cell phone user within an area covering between around a dozen and several hundred city blocks. In rural areas cell-site records can be up to 40 times more imprecise. By contrast, a Global Positioning System (GPS) can reveal an individual's location within around 15 feet.

Major cell phone service providers keep cell-site records for long periods of time. There is no law requiring them to do so. Instead, providers contract with their customers to collect and keep these records because they are valuable to the providers. Among other things, providers aggregate the records and sell them to third parties along with other information gleaned from cell phone usage. This data can be used, for example, to help a department store determine which of various prospective store locations is likely to get more foot traffic from middle-aged women who live in affluent zip codes. The market for cell phone data is now estimated to be in the billions of dollars.

Cell-site records also can serve an important investigative function, as the facts of this case demonstrate. . . .

. . . Here the only question necessary to decide is whether the Government searched anything of Carpenter's when it used compulsory process to obtain cell-site records from Carpenter's cell phone service providers. This Court's decisions in *Miller* and *Smith* dictate that the answer is no, as every Court of Appeals to have considered the question has recognized.

. . . *Miller* and *Smith* have been criticized as being based on too narrow a view of reasonable expectations of privacy. Those criticisms, however, are unwarranted. The principle established in *Miller* and *Smith* is correct for two reasons, the first relating to a defendant's attenuated interest in property owned by another, and the second relating to the safeguards inherent in the use of compulsory process.

First, *Miller* and *Smith* placed necessary limits on the ability of individuals to assert Fourth Amendment interests in property to which they lack a "requisite connection." Minnesota v. Carter, 525 U.S. 83, 99 (1998) (Kennedy, J., concurring). Fourth Amendment rights, after all, are personal. The Amendment protects "[t]he right of the people to be secure in *their* . . . persons, houses, papers, and effects"—not the persons, houses, papers, and effects of others. (Emphasis added.)

The concept of reasonable expectations of privacy, first announced in Katz v. United States, 389 U.S. 347 (1967), sought to look beyond the "arcane distinctions developed in property and tort law" in evaluating whether a person has a sufficient connection to the thing or place searched to assert Fourth Amendment interests in it. Rakas v. Illinois, 439 U.S. 128, 143 (1978). Yet "property concepts" are, nonetheless, fundamental "in determining the presence or absence of the privacy interests protected by that Amendment." Id., at 143-44, n. 12. . . .

Katz did not abandon reliance on property-based concepts. The Court in *Katz* analogized the phone booth used in that case to a friend's apartment, a taxicab, and a hotel room. So when the defendant "shu[t] the door behind him" and "pa[id] the toll," id., at 352, he had a temporary interest in the space and a legitimate expectation that others would not intrude, much like the interest a hotel guest has in a hotel room, or an overnight guest has in a host's home. . . .

Miller and *Smith* set forth an important and necessary limitation on the *Katz* framework. They rest upon the commonsense principle that the absence of property law analogues can be dispositive of privacy expectations. The defendants in those cases could expect that the third-party businesses could use the records the companies collected, stored, and classified as their own for any number of business and commercial purposes. The businesses were not bailees or custodians of the records, with a duty to hold the records for the defendants' use. The defendants could make no argument that the records were their own papers or effects. . . .

The second principle supporting *Miller* and *Smith* is the longstanding rule that the Government may use compulsory process to compel persons to disclose documents and other evidence within their possession and control. A subpoena is different from a warrant in its force and intrusive power. While a warrant allows the Government to enter and seize and make the examination itself, a subpoena simply requires the person to whom it is directed to make the disclosure. A subpoena, moreover, provides the recipient the "opportunity to present objections" before complying, which further mitigates the intrusion. Oklahoma Press Publishing Co. v. Walling, 327 U.S. 186, 195 (1946).

For those reasons this Court has held that a subpoena for records, although a "constructive" search subject to Fourth Amendment constraints, need not comply with the procedures applicable to warrants—even when challenged by the person to whom the records belong. Rather, a subpoena complies with the Fourth Amendment's reasonableness requirement so long as it is "'sufficiently limited in scope, relevant in purpose, and specific in directive so that compliance will not be unreasonably burdensome.'" Donovan v. Lone Steer, Inc., 464 U.S. 408, 415 (1984). Persons with no meaningful interests in the records sought by a subpoena, like the defendants in *Miller* and *Smith*, have no rights to object to the records' disclosure—much less to assert that the Government must obtain a warrant to compel disclosure of the records. . . .

Because Carpenter lacks a requisite connection to the cell-site records, he also may not claim a reasonable expectation of privacy in them. He could expect that a third party—the cell phone service provider—could use the information it collected, stored, and classified as its own for a variety of business and commercial purposes.

All this is not to say that *Miller* and *Smith* are without limits. *Miller* and *Smith* may not apply when the Government obtains the modern-day equivalents of an individual's own "papers" or "effects," even when those papers or effects are held by a third party. See Ex parte Jackson, 96 U.S. 727, 733 (1878) (letters held by mail carrier); United States v. Warshak, 631 F.3d 266, 283-288 (C.A.6 2010) (e-mails held by Internet service provider). As already discussed, however, this case does not involve property or a bailment of that sort. . . .

In my respectful view the majority opinion misreads this Court's precedents, old and recent, and transforms *Miller* and *Smith* into an unprincipled and unworkable doctrine. . . .

The Court errs at the outset by attempting to sidestep *Miller* and *Smith*. The Court frames this case as following instead from United States v. Knotts, 460 U.S. 276 (1983), and United States v. Jones, 565 U.S. 400 (2012). Those cases, the Court suggests, establish that "individuals have a reasonable expectation of privacy in the whole of their physical movements."

Knotts held just the opposite: "A person traveling in an automobile on public thoroughfares has no reasonable expectation of privacy in his movements from one place to another." 460 U.S., at 281. True, the Court in *Knotts* also suggested that "different constitutional principles may be applicable" to "dragnet-type law enforcement practices." Id., at 284. But by dragnet practices the Court was referring to "'twenty-four hour surveillance of any citizen of this country . . . without judicial knowledge or supervision.'" Id., at 283.

Those "different constitutional principles" mentioned in *Knotts*, whatever they may be, do not apply in this case. Here the Stored Communications Act requires a neutral judicial officer to confirm in each case that the Government has "reasonable grounds to believe" the cell-site records "are relevant and material to an ongoing criminal investigation." 18 U.S.C. § 2703(d). This judicial check mitigates the Court's concerns about "'a too permeating police surveillance.'" (quoting United States v. Di Re, 332 U.S. 581, 595 (1948)). . . .

The Court's reliance on *Jones* fares no better. In *Jones* the Government installed a GPS tracking device on the defendant's automobile. . . . [I]n *Jones* it was "not necessary to inquire about the target's expectation of privacy in his vehicle's movements." Grady v. North Carolina, 575 U.S. ___, ___ (2015) (per curiam).

Despite that clear delineation of the Court's holding in *Jones,* the Court today declares that *Jones* applied the "'different constitutional principles'" alluded to in *Knotts* to establish that an individual has an expectation of privacy in the sum of his whereabouts. For that proposition the majority relies on the two concurring opinions in *Jones,* one of which stated that "longer term GPS monitoring in investigations of most offenses impinges on expectations of privacy." 565 U.S., at 430 (Alito, J., concurring). But *Jones* involved direct governmental surveillance of a defendant's automobile without judicial authorization—specifically, GPS surveillance accurate within 50 to 100 feet. Even assuming that the different constitutional principles mentioned in *Knotts* would apply in a case like *Jones*—a proposition the Court was careful not to announce in *Jones*—those principles are inapplicable here. . . .

The Court appears, in my respectful view, to read *Miller* and *Smith* to establish a balancing test. For each "qualitatively different category" of information, the Court suggests, the privacy interests at stake must be weighed against the fact that the information has been disclosed to a third party. When the privacy interests are weighty enough to "overcome" the third-party disclosure, the Fourth Amendment's protections apply.

That is an untenable reading of *Miller* and *Smith.* As already discussed, the fact that information was relinquished to a third party was the entire basis for concluding that the defendants in those cases lacked a reasonable expectation of privacy. *Miller* and *Smith* do not establish the kind of category-by-category balancing the Court today prescribes.

But suppose the Court were correct to say that *Miller* and *Smith* rest on so imprecise a foundation. Still the Court errs, in my submission, when it concludes that cell-site records implicate greater privacy interests—and thus deserve greater Fourth Amendment protection—than financial records and telephone records.

Indeed, the opposite is true. A person's movements are not particularly private. . . . Millions of Americans choose to share their location on a daily basis, whether by using a variety of location-based services on their phones, or by sharing their location with friends and the public at large via social media.

And cell-site records, as already discussed, disclose a person's location only in a general area. . . . These records could not reveal where Carpenter lives and works, much less his "'familial, political, professional, religious, and sexual associations.'" (quoting *Jones*, supra, at 415 (Sotomayor, J., concurring)).

By contrast, financial records and telephone records do "'revea[l] . . . personal affairs, opinions, habits and associations.'" *Miller*, 425 U.S., at 451 (Brennan, J., dissenting). What persons purchase and to whom they talk might disclose how much money they make; the political and religious organizations to which they donate; whether they have visited a psychiatrist, plastic surgeon, abortion clinic, or AIDS treatment center; whether they go to gay bars or straight ones; and who are their closest friends and family members. The troves of intimate information the Government can and does obtain using financial records and telephone records dwarfs what can be gathered from cell-site records.

Still, the Court maintains, cell-site records are "unique" because they are "comprehensive" in their reach; allow for retrospective collection; are "easy, cheap, and efficient compared to traditional investigative tools"; and are not exposed to cell phone service providers in a meaningfully voluntary manner. But many other kinds of business records can be so described. . . .

Perhaps recognizing the difficulty of drawing the constitutional line between cell-site records and financial and telephonic records, the Court posits that the accuracy of cell-site records "is rapidly approaching GPS-level precision." That is certainly plausible in the era of cyber technology, yet the privacy interests associated with location information, which is often disclosed to the public at large, still would not outweigh the privacy interests implicated by financial and telephonic records.

Perhaps more important, those future developments are no basis upon which to resolve this case. In general, the Court "risks error by elaborating too fully on the Fourth Amendment implications of emerging technology before its role in society has become clear." Ontario v. Quon, 560 U.S. 746, 759 (2010). That judicial caution, prudent in most cases, is imperative in this one.

Technological changes involving cell phones have complex effects on crime and law enforcement. Cell phones make crimes easier to coordinate and conceal, while also providing the Government with new investigative tools that may have the potential to upset traditional privacy expectations. How those competing effects balance against each other, and how property norms and expectations of privacy form around new technology, often will be difficult to determine during periods of rapid technological change. In those instances, and where the governing legal standard is one of reasonableness, it is wise to defer to legislative judgments like the one embodied in § 2703(d) of the Stored Communications Act. . . .

The Court says its decision is a "narrow one." But its reinterpretation of *Miller* and *Smith* will have dramatic consequences for law enforcement, courts, and society as a whole.

Most immediately, the Court's holding that the Government must get a warrant to obtain more than six days of cell-site records limits the effectiveness of an important investigative tool for solving serious crimes. As this case demonstrates, cell-site records are uniquely suited to help the Government develop probable cause to apprehend some of the Nation's most dangerous criminals: serial killers, rapists, arsonists, robbers, and so forth. These records often are indispensable at the initial stages of investigations when the Government lacks the evidence necessary to obtain a warrant. And the long-term nature of many serious crimes, including serial crimes and terrorism offenses, can necessitate the use of significantly more than six days of cell-site records. The Court's arbitrary 6-day cutoff has the perverse effect of nullifying Congress' reasonable framework for obtaining cell-site records in some of the most serious criminal investigations.

The Court's decision also will have ramifications that extend beyond cell-site records to other kinds of information held by third parties, yet the Court fails "to provide clear guidance to law enforcement" and courts on key issues raised by its reinterpretation of *Miller* and *Smith.* Riley v. California, 573 U.S. ___, ___ (2014).

First, the Court's holding is premised on cell-site records being a "distinct category of information" from other business records. But the Court does not explain what makes something a distinct category of information. . . .

Second, the majority opinion gives courts and law enforcement officers no indication how to determine whether any particular category of information falls on the financial-records side or the cell-site-records side of its newly conceived constitutional line. The Court's multifactor analysis—considering intimacy, comprehensiveness, expense, retrospectivity, and voluntariness—puts the law on a new and unstable foundation.

Third, even if a distinct category of information is deemed to be more like cell-site records than financial records, courts and law enforcement officers will have to guess how much of that information can be requested before a warrant is required. The Court suggests that less than seven days of location information may not require a warrant. But the Court does not explain why that is so, and nothing in its opinion even alludes to the considerations that should determine whether greater or lesser thresholds should apply to information like IP addresses or website browsing history.

Fourth, by invalidating the Government's use of court-approved compulsory process in this case, the Court calls into question the subpoena practices of federal and state grand juries, legislatures, and other investigative bodies, as Justice Alito's opinion explains. . . .

This case should be resolved by interpreting accepted property principles as the baseline for reasonable expectations of privacy. Here the Government did not search anything over which Carpenter could assert ownership or control. Instead, it issued a court-authorized subpoena to a third party to disclose information it alone owned and controlled. That should suffice to resolve this case.

Having concluded, however, that the Government searched Carpenter when it obtained cell-site records from his cell phone service providers, the proper resolution of this case should have been to remand for the Court of Appeals to determine in the first instance whether the search was reasonable. . . . [T]he Court's reflexive imposition of the warrant requirement obscures important and difficult issues, such as the scope of Congress' power to authorize the Government to collect new forms of information using processes that deviate from traditional warrant procedures, and how the Fourth Amendment's reasonableness requirement should apply when the Government uses compulsory process instead of engaging in an actual, physical search.

These reasons all lead to this respectful dissent.

JUSTICE THOMAS, dissenting.

This case should not turn on "whether" a search occurred. It should turn, instead, on *whose* property was searched. The Fourth Amendment guarantees individuals the right to be secure from unreasonable searches of "*their* persons, houses, papers, and effects." (Emphasis added.) . . . By obtaining the cell-site records of MetroPCS and Sprint, the Government did not search Carpenter's property. He did not create the records, he does not maintain them, he cannot control them, and he cannot destroy them. Neither the terms of his contracts nor any provision of law makes the records his. The records belong to MetroPCS and Sprint.

The Court concludes that, although the records are not Carpenter's, the Government must get a warrant because Carpenter had a reasonable "expectation of privacy" in the location information that they reveal. I agree with Justice Kennedy, Justice Alito, Justice Gorsuch, and every Court of Appeals to consider the question that this is not the best reading of our precedents.

The more fundamental problem with the Court's opinion, however, is its use of the "reasonable expectation of privacy" test, which was first articulated by Justice Harlan in Katz v. United States, 389 U.S. 347, 360-361 (1967) (concurring opinion). . . .

Katz was the culmination of a series of decisions applying the Fourth Amendment to electronic eavesdropping. The first such decision was Olmstead v. United States, 277 U.S. 438 (1928), where federal officers had intercepted the defendants' conversations by tapping telephone lines near their homes. In an opinion by Chief Justice Taft, the Court concluded that this wiretap did not violate the Fourth Amendment. No "search" occurred, according to the Court, because the officers did not physically enter the defendants' homes. And neither the telephone lines nor the defendants' intangible conversations qualified as "persons, houses, papers, [or] effects" within the meaning of the Fourth Amendment. . . .

In the 1960's, however, the Court began to retreat from *Olmstead*. . . .

In *Katz*, the Court rejected *Olmstead's* . . . holding . . . that eavesdropping is not a search absent a physical intrusion into a constitutionally protected area. . . . The Court did not explain what should replace *Olmstead's* physical-intrusion requirement. It simply asserted that "the Fourth Amendment protects people, not places" and "what [a person] seeks to preserve as private . . . may be constitutionally protected." 389 U.S., at 351.

Justice Harlan's concurrence in *Katz* attempted to articulate the standard that was missing from the majority opinion. . . . Justice Harlan identified a "twofold requirement" to determine when the protections of the Fourth Amendment apply: "first that a person have exhibited an actual (subjective) expectation of privacy and, second, that the expectation be one that society is prepared to recognize as 'reasonable.'" [Id., at 361.]

Justice Harlan did not cite anything for this "expectation of privacy" test, and the parties did not discuss it in their briefs. The test appears to have been presented for the first time at oral argument by one of the defendant's lawyers. The lawyer, a recent law-school graduate, apparently had an "[e]piphany" while preparing for oral argument. He conjectured that, like the "reasonable person" test from his Torts class, the Fourth Amendment should turn on "whether a reasonable person . . . could have expected his communication to be private." [Schneider, Katz v. United States:

The Untold Story, 40 McGeorge L. Rev. 13, 19 (2009).] The lawyer presented his new theory to the Court at oral argument. After some questioning from the Justices, the lawyer conceded that his test should also require individuals to subjectively expect privacy. With that modification, Justice Harlan seemed to accept the lawyer's test almost verbatim in his concurrence.

Although the majority opinion in *Katz* had little practical significance after Congress enacted the Omnibus Crime Control and Safe Streets Act of 1968, Justice Harlan's concurrence profoundly changed our Fourth Amendment jurisprudence. . . .

. . . The *Katz* test distorts the original meaning of "searc[h]" — the word in the Fourth Amendment that it purports to define. Under the *Katz* test, the government conducts a search anytime it violates someone's "reasonable expectation of privacy." That is not a normal definition of the word "search." . . .

The *Katz* test strays even further from the text by focusing on the concept of "privacy." The word "privacy" does not appear in the Fourth Amendment (or anywhere else in the Constitution for that matter). Instead, the Fourth Amendment references "[t]he right of the people to be secure." It then qualifies that right by limiting it to "persons" and three specific types of property: "houses, papers, and effects." By connecting the right to be secure to these four specific objects, "[t]he text of the Fourth Amendment reflects its close connection to property." [United States v. Jones, 565 U.S. 400, 405 (2012).] "[P]rivacy," by contrast, "was not part of the political vocabulary of the [founding]. Instead, liberty and privacy rights were understood largely in terms of property rights." Cloud, Property Is Privacy: Locke and Brandeis in the Twenty-First Century, 55 Am. Crim. L. Rev. 37, 42 (2018).

Those who ratified the Fourth Amendment were quite familiar with the notion of security in property. Security in property was a prominent concept in English law. See, e.g., 3 W. Blackstone, Commentaries on the Laws of England 288 (1768) ("[E]very man's house is looked upon by the law to be his castle"); 3 E. Coke, Institutes of Laws of England 162 (6th ed. 1680) ("[F]or a man[']s house is his Castle, & domus sua cuique est tutissimum refugium [each man's home is his safest refuge]"). The political philosophy of John Locke, moreover, "permeated the 18th-century political scene in America." Obergefell v. Hodges, 576 U.S. ___, ___ (2015) (Thomas, J., dissenting). . . .

The concept of security in property recognized by Locke and the English legal tradition appeared throughout the materials that inspired the Fourth Amendment. In Entick v. Carrington, 19 How. St. Tr. 1029 (C.P. 1765) — a

heralded decision that the founding generation considered "the true and
ultimate expression of constitutional law," Boyd v. United States, 116 U.S.
616, 626 (1886) — Lord Camden explained that "[t]he great end, for which
men entered into society, was to secure their property." 19 How. St. Tr., at
1066. The American colonists echoed this reasoning in their "widespread
hostility" to the Crown's writs of assistance . . . .

Of course, the founding generation understood that, by securing their
property, the Fourth Amendment would often protect their privacy as well.
But the Fourth Amendment's attendant protection of privacy does not
justify *Katz's* elevation of privacy as the *sine qua non* of the Amendment. As
the majority opinion in *Katz* recognized, the Fourth Amendment "cannot
be translated into a general constitutional 'right to privacy,'" as its protections "often have nothing to do with privacy at all." 389 U.S., at 350.
Justice Harlan's focus on privacy in his concurrence — an opinion that was
issued between Griswold v. Connecticut, 381 U.S. 479 (1965), and Roe
v. Wade, 410 U.S. 113 (1973) — reflects privacy's status as the organizing
constitutional idea of the 1960's and 1970's. The organizing constitutional
idea of the founding era, by contrast, was property.

In shifting the focus of the Fourth Amendment from property to privacy,
the *Katz* test also reads the words "persons, houses, papers, and effects"
out of the text. . . . The Court today, for example, does not ask whether
cell-site location records are "persons, houses, papers, [or] effects" within
the meaning of the Fourth Amendment. Yet "persons, houses, papers, and
effects" cannot mean "anywhere" or "anything." . . .

"[P]ersons, houses, papers, and effects" are not the only words that the
Katz test reads out of the Fourth Amendment. The Fourth Amendment
specifies that the people have a right to be secure from unreasonable
searches of "their" persons, houses, papers, and effects. Although phrased
in the plural, "[t]he obvious meaning of ['their'] is that *each* person has
the right to be secure against unreasonable searches and seizures in *his
own* person, house, papers, and effects." [Minnesota v. Carter, 525 U.S. 83,
92 (1998) (opinion of Scalia, J.)] . . . Until today, our precedents have
not acknowledged that individuals can claim a reasonable expectation of
privacy in someone else's business records. . . .

That the *Katz* test departs so far from the text of the Fourth Amendment
is reason enough to reject it. But the *Katz* test also has proved unworkable
in practice. . . .

Justice Harlan's original formulation of the *Katz* test appears to ask
a descriptive question: Whether a given expectation of privacy is "one
that society is prepared to recognize as 'reasonable.'" 389 U.S., at 361.

As written, the *Katz* test turns on society's actual, current views about the reasonableness of various expectations of privacy.

But this descriptive understanding presents several problems. For starters, it is easily circumvented. If, for example, "the Government were suddenly to announce on nationwide television that all homes henceforth would be subject to warrantless entry," individuals could not realistically expect privacy in their homes. [Smith v. Maryland, 442 U.S. 735, 740, n. 5 (1979)]. A purely descriptive understanding of the *Katz* test also risks "circular[ity]." *Kyllo*, 533 U.S., at 34. . . .

To address this circularity problem, the Court has insisted that expectations of privacy must come from outside its Fourth Amendment precedents, "either by reference to concepts of real or personal property law or to understandings that are recognized and permitted by society." Rakas v. Illinois, 439 U.S. 128, 144, n. 12 (1978). But the Court's supposed reliance on "real or personal property law" rings hollow. The whole point of *Katz* was to "'discredi[t]'" the relationship between the Fourth Amendment and property law, 389 U.S., at 353, and this Court has repeatedly downplayed the importance of property law under the *Katz* test. Today, for example, the Court makes no mention of property law, except to reject its relevance.

As for "understandings that are recognized or permitted in society," this Court has never answered even the most basic questions about what this means. . . .

Here, for example, society might prefer a balanced regime that prohibits the Government from obtaining cell-site location information unless it can persuade a neutral magistrate that the information bears on an ongoing criminal investigation. That is precisely the regime Congress created under the Stored Communications Act and Telecommunications Act. . . .

Truth be told, this Court does not treat the *Katz* test as a descriptive inquiry. Although the *Katz* test is phrased in descriptive terms about society's views, this Court treats it like a normative question—whether a particular practice *should* be considered a search under the Fourth Amendment. . . . "[T]he only thing the past three decades have established about the *Katz* test" is that society's expectations of privacy "bear an uncanny resemblance to those expectations of privacy that this Court considers reasonable." *Carter*, 525 U.S., at 97 (opinion of Scalia, J.). Yet, "[t]hough we know ourselves to be eminently reasonable, self-awareness of eminent reasonableness is not really a substitute for democratic election." Sosa v. Alvarez-Machain, 542 U.S. 692, 750 (2004) (Scalia, J., concurring in part and concurring in judgment). . . .

Because the *Katz* test is a failed experiment, this Court is dutybound to reconsider it. Until it does, I agree with my dissenting colleagues' reading of our precedents. Accordingly, I respectfully dissent.

JUSTICE ALITO, with whom JUSTICE THOMAS joins, dissenting.

I share the Court's concern about the effect of new technology on personal privacy, but I fear that today's decision will do far more harm than good. The Court's reasoning fractures two fundamental pillars of Fourth Amendment law . . . .

First, the Court ignores the basic distinction between an actual search (dispatching law enforcement officers to enter private premises and root through private papers and effects) and an order merely requiring a party to look through its own records and produce specified documents. The former, which intrudes on personal privacy far more deeply, requires probable cause; the latter does not. Treating an order to produce like an actual search, as today's decision does, is revolutionary. It violates both the original understanding of the Fourth Amendment and more than a century of Supreme Court precedent. Unless it is somehow restricted to the particular situation in the present case, the Court's move will cause upheaval. Must every grand jury subpoena *duces tecum* be supported by probable cause? If so, investigations of terrorism, political corruption, white-collar crime, and many other offenses will be stymied. And what about subpoenas and other document-production orders issued by administrative agencies?

Second, the Court allows a defendant to object to the search of a third party's property. This also is revolutionary. The Fourth Amendment protects "[t]he right of the people to be secure in *their* persons, houses, papers, and effects" (emphasis added), not the persons, houses, papers, and effects of others. Until today, we have been careful to heed this fundamental feature of the Amendment's text. This was true when the Fourth Amendment was tied to property law, and it remained true after Katz v. United States, 389 U.S. 347 (1967), broadened the Amendment's reach.

By departing dramatically from these fundamental principles, the Court destabilizes long-established Fourth Amendment doctrine. We will be making repairs—or picking up the pieces—for a long time to come.

. . . The Court's holding is based on the premise that the order issued in this case was an actual "search" within the meaning of the Fourth Amendment, but that premise is inconsistent with the original meaning of the Fourth Amendment and with more than a century of precedent.

The order in this case was the functional equivalent of a subpoena for documents, and there is no evidence that these writs were regarded as "searches" at the time of the founding. Subpoenas *duces tecum* and other forms of compulsory document production were well known to the founding generation. Blackstone dated the first writ of subpoena to the reign of King Richard II in the late 14th century, and by the end of the 15th century, the use of such writs had "become the daily practice of the [Chancery] court." 3 W. Blackstone, Commentaries on the Laws of England 53 (G. Tucker ed. 1803) (Blackstone). Over the next 200 years, subpoenas would grow in prominence and power in tandem with the Court of Chancery, and by the end of Charles II's reign in 1685, two important innovations had occurred.

First, the Court of Chancery developed a new species of subpoena. Until this point, subpoenas had been used largely to compel attendance and oral testimony from witnesses; these subpoenas correspond to today's subpoenas *ad testificandum*. But the Court of Chancery also improvised a new version of the writ that tacked onto a regular subpoena an order compelling the witness to bring certain items with him. By issuing these so-called subpoenas *duces tecum*, the Court of Chancery could compel the production of papers, books, and other forms of physical evidence, whether from the parties to the case or from third parties. Such subpoenas were sufficiently commonplace by 1623 that a leading treatise on the practice of law could refer in passing to the fee for a "*Sub pœna of Ducas tecum*" (seven shillings and two pence) without needing to elaborate further. T. Powell, The Attourneys Academy 79 (1623). Subpoenas *duces tecum* would swell in use over the next century as the rules for their application became ever more developed and definite.

Second, although this new species of subpoena had its origins in the Court of Chancery, it soon made an appearance in the work of the common-law courts as well. One court later reported that "[t]he Courts of Common law . . . employed the same or similar means . . . from the time of Charles the Second at least." Amey v. Long, 9 East. 473, 484, 103 Eng. Rep. 653, 658 (K.B. 1808).

By the time Blackstone published his Commentaries on the Laws of England in the 1760's, the use of subpoenas *duces tecum* had bled over substantially from the courts of equity to the common-law courts. Admittedly, the transition was still incomplete: In the context of jury trials, for example, Blackstone complained about "the want of a compulsive power for the production of books and papers belonging to the parties." Blackstone 381; see also, e.g., Entick v. Carrington, 19 State Trials 1029, 1073 (K.B. 1765) ("I wish some cases had been shewn, where the law forceth evidence out of the owner's custody by process. [But] where the adversary has by force or fraud got possession of your own proper evidence, there is no way to get it back but by action"). But Blackstone found some comfort in the fact that at least those documents "[i]n the hands of third persons . . . can generally be obtained by rule of court, or by adding a clause of requisition to the writ of *subpoena*, which is then called a *subpoena duces tecum*." Blackstone 381. One of the primary questions outstanding, then, was whether common-law courts would remedy the "defect[s]" identified by the Commentaries, and allow parties to use subpoenas *duces tecum* not only with respect to third parties but also with respect to each other. Blackstone 381.

That question soon found an affirmative answer on both sides of the Atlantic. In the United States, the First Congress established the federal court system in the Judiciary Act of 1789. As part of that Act, Congress authorized "all the said courts of the United States . . . in the trial of actions at law, on motion and due notice thereof being given, to require the parties to produce books or writings in their possession or power, which contain evidence pertinent to the issue, in cases and under circumstances where they might be compelled to produce the same by the ordinary rules of proceeding in chancery." § 15, 1 Stat. 82. From that point forward, federal courts in the United States could compel the production of documents regardless of whether those documents were held by parties to the case or by third parties.

In Great Britain, too, it was soon definitively established that common-law courts, like their counterparts in equity, could subpoena documents held either by parties to the case or by third parties. . . .

The prevalence of subpoenas *duces tecum* at the time of the founding was not limited to the civil context. In criminal cases, courts and prosecutors were also using the writ to compel the production of necessary documents. . . .

[S]ubpoenas *duces tecum* were routine in part because of their close association with grand juries. Early American colonists imported the grand jury, like so many other common-law traditions, and they quickly flourished. Grand juries were empaneled by the federal courts almost as soon as the latter were established, and both they and their state counterparts actively exercised their wide-ranging common-law authority. See R. Younger, The People's Panel 47-55 (1963). . . .

Given the popularity and prevalence of grand juries at the time, the Founders must have been intimately familiar with the tools they used—including compulsory process—to accomplish their work. . . . Long before national independence was achieved, grand juries were already using their broad inquisitorial powers not only to present and indict criminal suspects but also to inspect public buildings, to levy taxes, to supervise the administration of the laws, to advance municipal reforms such as street repair and bridge maintenance, and in some cases even to propose legislation. Younger, supra, at 5-26. Of course, such work depended entirely on grand juries' ability to access any relevant documents.

Grand juries continued to exercise these broad inquisitorial powers up through the time of the founding. . . .

Talk of kings and common-law writs may seem out of place in a case about cell-site records and the protections afforded by the Fourth Amendment in the modern age. But this history matters, not least because it tells us what was on the minds of those who ratified the Fourth Amendment and how they understood its scope. . . .

The Fourth Amendment does not regulate all methods by which the Government obtains documents. Rather, it prohibits only those "searches and seizures" of "persons, houses, papers, and effects" that are "unreasonable." Consistent with that language, "at least until the latter half of the 20th century" "our Fourth Amendment jurisprudence was tied to common-law trespass." United States v. Jones, 565 U.S. 400, 405 (2012). So by its terms, the Fourth Amendment does not apply to the compulsory production of documents, a practice that involves neither any physical intrusion into private space nor any taking of property by agents of the state. . . .

Nor is there any reason to believe that the Founders intended the Fourth Amendment to regulate courts' use of compulsory process. American colonists rebelled against the Crown's physical invasions of their persons and their property, not against its acquisition of information by any and all means. . . .

General warrants and writs of assistance were noxious not because they allowed the Government to acquire evidence in criminal investigations, but because of the *means* by which they permitted the Government to acquire that evidence. Then, as today, searches could be quite invasive. . . .

. . . A subpoena *duces tecum* permits a subpoenaed individual to conduct the search for the relevant documents himself, without law enforcement officers entering his home or rooting through his papers and effects. As a result, subpoenas avoid the many incidental invasions of privacy that necessarily accompany any actual search. And it was *those* invasions of privacy—which, although incidental, could often be extremely intrusive and damaging—that led to the adoption of the Fourth Amendment.

Neither this Court nor any of the parties have offered the slightest bit of historical evidence to support the idea that the Fourth Amendment originally applied to subpoenas *duces tecum* and other forms of compulsory process. That is telling, for as I have explained, these forms of compulsory process were a feature of criminal (and civil) procedure well known to the Founders. The Founders would thus have understood that holding the compulsory production of documents to the same standard as actual searches and seizures would cripple the work of courts in civil and criminal cases alike. It would be remarkable to think that, despite that knowledge, the Founders would have gone ahead and sought to impose such a requirement. It would be even more incredible to believe that the Founders would have imposed that requirement through the inapt vehicle of an amendment directed at different concerns. But it would blink reality entirely to argue that this entire process happened without anyone saying *the least thing about it*—not during the drafting of the Bill of Rights, not during any of the subsequent ratification debates, and not for most of the century that followed. If the Founders thought the Fourth Amendment applied to the compulsory production of documents, one would imagine that there would be *some* founding-era evidence of the Fourth Amendment being applied to the compulsory production of documents. Yet none has been brought to our attention.

Of course, our jurisprudence has not stood still since 1791. We now evaluate subpoenas *duces tecum* and other forms of compulsory document production under the Fourth Amendment, although we employ a reasonableness standard that is less demanding than the requirements for a warrant. But the road to that doctrinal destination was anything but smooth, and our initial missteps—and the subsequent struggle to extricate ourselves from their consequences—should provide an object lesson for today's majority about the dangers of holding compulsory process to the same standard as actual searches and seizures.

For almost a century after the Fourth Amendment was enacted, this Court said and did nothing to indicate that it might regulate the compulsory production of documents. But that changed temporarily when the Court decided Boyd v. United States, 116 U.S. 616 (1886), the first—and, until today, the only—case in which this Court has ever held the compulsory production of documents to the same standard as actual searches and seizures.

The *Boyd* Court held that a court order compelling a company to produce potentially incriminating business records violated both the Fourth and the Fifth Amendments. The Court acknowledged that "certain aggravating incidents of actual search and seizure, such as forcible entry into a man's house and searching amongst his papers, are wanting" when the Government relies on compulsory process. Id., at 622. But it nevertheless asserted that the Fourth Amendment ought to "be liberally construed," id., at 635, and further reasoned that compulsory process "effects the sole object and purpose of search and seizure" by "forcing from a party evidence against himself," id., at 622. "In this regard," the Court concluded, "the Fourth and Fifth Amendments run almost into each other." Id., at 630. Having equated compulsory process with actual searches and seizures and having melded the Fourth Amendment with the Fifth, the Court then found the order at issue unconstitutional because it compelled the production of property to which the Government did not have superior title. . . .

Although *Boyd* was replete with stirring rhetoric, its reasoning was confused from start to finish in a way that ultimately made the decision unworkable. Over the next 50 years, the Court would gradually roll back *Boyd's* erroneous conflation of compulsory process with actual searches and seizures.

That effort took its first significant stride in Hale v. Henkel, 201 U.S. 43 (1906), where the Court found it "quite clear" and "conclusive" that "the search and seizure clause of the Fourth Amendment was not intended to interfere with the power of courts to compel, through a subpoena duces tecum, the production, upon a trial in court, of documentary evidence." Id., at 73. . . .

Hale, however, did not entirely liberate subpoenas duces tecum from Fourth Amendment constraints. While refusing to treat such subpoenas as the equivalent of actual searches, Hale concluded that they must not be unreasonable. . . . The *Hale* Court . . . left two critical questions unanswered: Under the Fourth Amendment, what makes the compulsory production of documents "reasonable," and how does that standard differ from the one that governs actual searches and seizures?

The Court answered both of those questions definitively in Oklahoma Press Publishing Co. v. Walling, 327 U.S. 186 (1946), where we held that the Fourth Amendment regulates the compelled production of documents, but less stringently than it does full-blown searches and seizures. . . .

. . . When it comes to "the production of corporate or other business records," the Court held that the Fourth Amendment "at the most guards against abuse only by way of too much indefiniteness or breadth in the things required to be 'particularly described,' if also the inquiry is one the demanding agency is authorized by law to make and the materials specified are relevant." *Oklahoma Press*, supra, at 208. Notably, the Court held that a showing of probable cause was not necessary so long as "the investigation is authorized by Congress, is for a purpose Congress can order, and the documents sought are relevant to the inquiry." Id., at 209. . . .

Today, however, the majority inexplicably ignores the settled rule of *Oklahoma Press* in favor of a resurrected version of *Boyd*. That is mystifying. This should have been an easy case regardless of whether the Court looked to the original understanding of the Fourth Amendment or to our modern doctrine.

As a matter of original understanding, the Fourth Amendment does not regulate the compelled production of documents at all. . . .

As a matter of modern doctrine, this case is equally straightforward. As Justice Kennedy explains, no search or seizure of Carpenter or his property occurred in this case. But even if the majority were right that the Government "searched" Carpenter, it would at most be a "figurative or constructive search" governed by the *Oklahoma Press* standard, not an "actual search" controlled by the Fourth Amendment's warrant requirement.

And there is no doubt that the Government met the *Oklahoma Press* standard here. . . . The Stored Communications Act allows a court to issue the relevant type of order "only if the governmental entity offers specific and articulable facts showing that there are reasonable grounds to believe that . . . the records . . . sough[t] are relevant and material to an ongoing criminal investigation." 18 U.S.C. § 2703(d). And the court "may quash or modify such order" if the provider objects that the "records requested are unusually voluminous in nature or compliance with such order otherwise would cause an undue burden on such provider." Ibid. No such objection was made in this case, and Carpenter does not suggest that the orders contravened the *Oklahoma Press* standard in any other way.

That is what makes the majority's opinion so puzzling. It decides that a "search" of Carpenter occurred within the meaning of the Fourth Amendment, but then it leaps straight to imposing requirements that—until this point—have governed only *actual* searches and seizures. Lost in its race to the finish is any real recognition of the century's worth of precedent it jeopardizes. . . .

Against centuries of precedent and practice, all that the Court can muster is the observation that "this Court has never held that the Government may subpoena third parties for records in which the suspect has a reasonable expectation of privacy." Frankly, I cannot imagine a concession more damning to the Court's argument than that. As the Court well knows, the reason that we have never seen such a case is because—until today—defendants categorically had no "reasonable expectation of privacy" and no property interest in records belonging to third parties. By implying otherwise, the Court tries the nice trick of seeking shelter under the cover of precedents that it simultaneously perforates.

Not only that, but even if the Fourth Amendment permitted someone to object to the subpoena of a third party's records, the Court cannot explain why that individual should be entitled to *greater* Fourth Amendment protection than the party actually being subpoenaed. When parties are subpoenaed to turn over their records, after all, they will at most receive the protection afforded by *Oklahoma Press* even though they will own and have a reasonable expectation of privacy in the records at issue. Under the Court's decision, however, the Fourth Amendment will extend greater protections to someone else who is not being subpoenaed and does not own the records. That outcome makes no sense, and the Court does not even attempt to defend it. . . .

Holding that subpoenas must meet the same standard as conventional searches will seriously damage, if not destroy, their utility. . . . Grand juries, for example, have long "compel[led] the production of evidence" in order to determine "*whether* there is probable cause to believe a crime has been committed." United States v. Calandra, 414 U.S. 338, 343 (1974) (emphasis added). Almost by definition, then, grand juries will be unable at first to demonstrate "the probable cause required for a warrant." If they are required to do so, the effects are as predictable as they are alarming: Many investigations will sputter out at the start, and a host of criminals will be able to evade law enforcement's reach.

. . . For over a hundred years, we have understood that holding subpoenas to the same standard as actual searches and seizures "would stop much if not all of investigation in the public interest at the threshold of inquiry." *Oklahoma Press,* supra, at 213. Today a skeptical majority decides to put that understanding to the test.

Compounding its initial error, the Court also holds that a defendant has the right under the Fourth Amendment to object to the search of a third party's property. This holding flouts the clear text of the Fourth Amendment, and it cannot be defended under either a property-based interpretation of that Amendment or our decisions applying the reasonable-expectations-of-privacy test . . . . By allowing Carpenter to object to the search of a third party's property, the Court threatens to revolutionize a second and independent line of Fourth Amendment doctrine.

It bears repeating that the Fourth Amendment guarantees "[t]he right of the people to be secure in *their* persons, houses, papers, and effects." (Emphasis added.) The Fourth Amendment does not confer rights with respect to the persons, houses, papers, and effects of others. Its language makes clear that "Fourth Amendment rights are personal," Rakas v. Illinois, 439 U.S. 128, 140 (1978), and as a result, this Court has long insisted that they "may not be asserted vicariously," id., at 133. It follows that a "person who is aggrieved . . . only through the introduction of damaging evidence secured by a search of a third person's premises or property has not had any of his Fourth Amendment rights infringed." Id., at 134.

In this case, . . . the cell-site records obtained by the Government belong to Carpenter's cell service providers, not to Carpenter. Carpenter did not create the cell-site records. Nor did he have possession of them; at all relevant times, they were kept by the providers. Once Carpenter subscribed to his provider's service, he had no right to prevent the company from creating or keeping the information in its records. Carpenter also had no right to demand that the providers destroy the records, no right to prevent the providers from destroying the records, and, indeed, no right to modify the records in any way whatsoever (or to prevent the providers from modifying the records). Carpenter, in short, has no meaningful control over the cell-site records, which are created, maintained, altered, used, and eventually destroyed by his cell service providers. . . .

In the days when this Court followed an exclusively property-based approach to the Fourth Amendment, the distinction between an individual's Fourth Amendment rights and those of a third party was clear cut. We first asked whether the object of the search—say, a house, papers, or effects—belonged to the defendant, and, if it did, whether the Government had committed a "trespass" in acquiring the evidence at issue.

When the Court held in *Katz* that "property rights are not the sole measure of Fourth Amendment violations," Soldal v. Cook County, 506 U.S. 56, 64 (1992), the sharp boundary between personal and third-party rights was tested. . . .

Efforts to claim Fourth Amendment protection against searches of the papers and effects of others came to a head in *Miller*, [425 U.S. 435 (1976)], where the defendant sought the suppression of two banks' microfilm copies of his checks, deposit slips, and other records. . . . Turning to *Katz*, he . . . argued that he had a reasonable expectation of privacy in the banks' records regarding his accounts.

Acceptance of this argument would have flown in the face of the Fourth Amendment's text, and the Court rejected that development. . . . Later, in Smith v. Maryland, 442 U.S. 735 (1979), the Court reached a similar conclusion regarding a telephone company's records of a customer's calls. . . .

. . . Carpenter indisputably lacks any meaningful property-based connection to the cell-site records owned by his provider. Because the records are not Carpenter's in any sense, Carpenter may not seek to use the Fourth Amendment to exclude them.

By holding otherwise, the Court effectively allows Carpenter to object to the "search" of a third party's property, not recognizing the revolutionary nature of this change. The Court seems to think that *Miller* and *Smith* invented a new "doctrine"—"the third-party doctrine"—and the Court refuses to "extend" this product of the 1970's to a new age of digital communications. But the Court fundamentally misunderstands the role of *Miller* and *Smith*. Those decisions did not forge a new doctrine; instead, they rejected an argument that would have disregarded the clear text of the Fourth Amendment and a formidable body of precedent. . . .

Although the majority professes a desire not to "'embarrass the future,'" we can guess where today's decision will lead.

One possibility is that the broad principles that the Court seems to embrace will be applied across the board. All subpoenas *duces tecum* and all other orders compelling the production of documents will require a demonstration of probable cause, and individuals will be able to claim a protected Fourth Amendment interest in any sensitive personal information about them that is collected and owned by third parties. Those would be revolutionary developments indeed.

The other possibility is that this Court will face the embarrassment of explaining in case after case that the principles on which today's decision rests are subject to all sorts of qualifications and limitations that have not yet been discovered. If we take this latter course, we will inevitably end up "mak[ing] a crazy quilt of the Fourth Amendment." *Smith,* supra, at 745.

All of this is unnecessary. In the Stored Communications Act, Congress addressed the specific problem at issue in this case. The Act restricts the misuse of cell-site records by cell service providers, something that the Fourth Amendment cannot do. The Act also goes beyond current Fourth Amendment case law in restricting access by law enforcement. It permits law enforcement officers to acquire cell-site records only if they meet a heightened standard and obtain a court order. If the American people now think that the Act is inadequate or needs updating, they can turn to their elected representatives to adopt more protective provisions. Because the collection and storage of cell-site records affects nearly every American, it is unlikely that the question whether the current law requires strengthening will escape Congress's notice.

Legislation is much preferable to the development of an entirely new body of Fourth Amendment caselaw for many reasons, including the enormous complexity of the subject, the need to respond to rapidly changing technology, and the Fourth Amendment's limited scope. The Fourth Amendment restricts the conduct of the Federal Government and the States; it does not apply to private actors. But today, some of the greatest threats to individual privacy may come from powerful private companies that collect and sometimes misuse vast quantities of data about the lives of ordinary Americans. If today's decision encourages the public to think that this Court can protect them from this looming threat to their privacy, the decision will mislead as well as disrupt. And if holding a provision of the Stored Communications Act to be unconstitutional dissuades Congress from further legislation in this field, the goal of protecting privacy will be greatly disserved.

The desire to make a statement about privacy in the digital age does not justify the consequences that today's decision is likely to produce.

JUSTICE GORSUCH, dissenting.

In the late 1960s this Court suggested for the first time that a search triggering the Fourth Amendment occurs when the government violates an "expectation of privacy" that "society is prepared to recognize as 'reasonable.'" Katz v. United States, 389 U.S. 347, 361 (1967) (Harlan, J., concurring). Then, in a pair of decisions in the 1970s applying the Katz test, the Court held that a "reasonable expectation of privacy" doesn't attach to information shared with "third parties." See Smith v. Maryland, 442 U.S. 735, 743-744 (1979); United States v. Miller, 425 U.S. 435, 443 (1976). By these steps, the Court came to conclude, the Constitution does nothing to limit investigators from searching records you've entrusted to your bank, accountant, and maybe even your doctor.

What's left of the Fourth Amendment? Today we use the Internet to do most everything. Smartphones make it easy to keep a calendar, correspond with friends, make calls, conduct banking, and even watch the game. Countless Internet companies maintain records about us and, increasingly, for us. Even our most private documents—those that, in other eras, we would have locked safely in a desk drawer or destroyed—now reside on third party servers. Smith and Miller teach that the police can review all of this material, on the theory that no one reasonably expects any of it will be kept private. But no one believes that, if they ever did.

What to do? It seems to me we could respond in at least three ways. The first is to ignore the problem, maintain Smith and Miller, and live with the consequences. . . . The second choice is to set Smith and Miller aside and try again using the Katz "reasonable expectation of privacy" jurisprudence that produced them. The third is to look for answers elsewhere.

Start with the first option. . . . Today the Court suggests that Smith and Miller distinguish between kinds of information disclosed to third parties and require courts to decide whether to "extend" those decisions to particular classes of information, depending on their sensitivity. But as the Sixth Circuit recognized and Justice Kennedy explains, no balancing test of this kind can be found in Smith and Miller. Those cases announced a categorical rule: Once you disclose information to third parties, you forfeit any reasonable expectation of privacy you might have had in it. And even if Smith and Miller did permit courts to conduct a balancing contest of the kind the Court now suggests, it's still hard to see how that would help the petitioner in this case. Why is someone's location when using a phone so much more sensitive than who he was talking to (*Smith*) or what financial transactions he engaged in (*Miller*)? I do not know and the Court does not say.

The problem isn't with the Sixth Circuit's application of *Smith* and *Miller* but with the cases themselves. Can the government demand a copy of all your e-mails from Google or Microsoft without implicating your Fourth Amendment rights? Can it secure your DNA from 23andMe without a warrant or probable cause? *Smith* and *Miller* say yes it can—at least without running afoul of *Katz*. But that result strikes most lawyers and judges today—me included—as pretty unlikely. . . . The reasons are obvious. "As an empirical statement about subjective expectations of privacy," the doctrine is "quite dubious." Baude & Stern, The Positive Law Model of the Fourth Amendment, 129 Harv. L. Rev. 1821, 1872 (2016). People often *do* reasonably expect that information they entrust to third parties, especially information subject to confidentiality agreements, will be kept private. Meanwhile, if the third party doctrine is supposed to represent a normative assessment of when a person should expect privacy, the notion that the answer might be "never" seems a pretty unattractive societal prescription.

What, then, is the explanation for our third party doctrine? The truth is, the Court has never offered a persuasive justification. The Court has said that by conveying information to a third party you "'assum[e] the risk'" it will be revealed to the police and therefore lack a reasonable expectation of privacy in it. *Smith*, supra, at 744. But assumption of risk doctrine developed in tort law. It generally applies when "by contract or otherwise [one] expressly agrees to accept a risk of harm" or impliedly does so by "manifest[ing] his willingness to accept" that risk and thereby "take[s] his chances as to harm which may result from it." Restatement (Second) of Torts §§ 496B, 496C(1), and Comment *b* (1965). That rationale has little play in this context. Suppose I entrust a friend with a letter and he promises to keep it secret until he delivers it to an intended recipient. In what sense have I agreed to bear the risk that he will turn around, break his promise, and spill its contents to someone else? More confusing still, what have I done to "manifest my willingness to accept" the risk that the government will pry the document from my friend and read it *without* his consent? . . .

Some have suggested the third party doctrine is better understood to rest on consent than assumption of risk. . . . I confess I still don't see it. Consenting to give a third party access to private papers that remain my property is not the same thing as consenting to a *search of those papers by the government*. Perhaps there are exceptions, like when the third party is an undercover government agent. But otherwise this conception of consent appears to be just assumption of risk relabeled—you've "consented" to whatever risks are foreseeable.

Another justification sometimes offered for third party doctrine is clarity. You (and the police) know exactly how much protection you have in information confided to others: none. As rules go, "the king always wins" is admirably clear. But the opposite rule would be clear too: Third party disclosures *never* diminish Fourth Amendment protection (call it "the king always loses"). So clarity alone cannot justify the third party doctrine.

In the end, what do *Smith* and *Miller* add up to? A doubtful application of *Katz* that lets the government search almost whatever it wants whenever it wants. . . .

There's a second option. What if we dropped *Smith* and *Miller's* third party doctrine and retreated to the root *Katz* question whether there is a "reasonable expectation of privacy" in data held by third parties? Rather than solve the problem with the third party doctrine, I worry this option only risks returning us to its source: After all, it was *Katz* that produced *Smith* and *Miller* in the first place.

Katz's problems start with the text and original understanding of the Fourth Amendment, as Justice Thomas thoughtfully explains today. The Amendment's protections do not depend on the breach of some abstract "expectation of privacy" whose contours are left to the judicial imagination. Much more concretely, it protects your "person," and your "houses, papers, and effects.". . . Under its plain terms, the Amendment grants you the right to invoke its guarantees whenever one of your protected things (your person, your house, your papers, or your effects) is unreasonably searched or seized. Period.

History too holds problems for *Katz*. Little like it can be found in the law that led to the adoption of the Fourth Amendment or in this Court's jurisprudence until the late 1960s. . . .

Even taken on its own terms, *Katz* has never been sufficiently justified. In fact, we still don't even know what its "reasonable expectation of privacy" test *is*. Is it supposed to pose an empirical question (what privacy expectations do people *actually* have) or a normative one (what expectations *should* they have)? Either way brings problems. . . .

Resorting to *Katz* in data privacy cases threatens more of the same. Just consider. The Court today says that judges should use *Katz's* reasonable expectation of privacy test to decide what Fourth Amendment rights people have in cell-site location information, explaining that "no single rubric definitively resolves which expectations of privacy are entitled to protection." But then it offers a twist. Lower courts should be sure to add two special principles to their *Katz* calculus: the need to avoid "arbitrary power" and the importance of "plac[ing] obstacles in the way of a too permeating police surveillance." While surely laudable, these principles don't offer lower courts much guidance. The Court does not tell us, for example, how far to carry either principle or how to weigh them against the legitimate needs of law enforcement. At what point does access to electronic data amount to "arbitrary" authority? When does police surveillance become "too permeating"? And what sort of "obstacles" should judges "place" in law enforcement's path when it does? We simply do not know. . . .

Later still, the Court adds that it can't say whether the Fourth Amendment is triggered when the government collects "real-time CSLI or 'tower dumps' (a download of information on all the devices that connected to a particular cell site during a particular interval)." But what distinguishes historical data from real-time data, or seven days of a single person's data from a download of *everyone's* data over some indefinite period of time? Why isn't a tower dump the *paradigmatic* example of "too permeating police surveillance" and a dangerous tool of "arbitrary" authority—the touchstones of the majority's modified *Katz* analysis? On what possible basis could such mass data collection survive the Court's test while collecting a single person's data does not? Here again we are left to guess. At the same time, though, the Court offers some firm assurances. It tells us its decision does *not* "call into question conventional surveillance techniques and tools, such as security cameras." That, however, just raises more questions for lower courts to sort out about what techniques qualify as "conventional" and why those techniques would be okay *even if* they lead to "permeating police surveillance" or "arbitrary police power."

Nor is this the end of it. After finding a reasonable expectation of privacy, the Court says there's still more work to do. Courts must determine whether to "extend" *Smith* and *Miller* to the circumstances before them. So apparently *Smith* and *Miller* aren't quite left for dead; they just no longer have the clear reach they once did. How do we measure their new reach? The Court says courts now must conduct a *second Katz*-like balancing inquiry, asking whether the fact of disclosure to a third party outweighs privacy interests in the "category of information" so disclosed. But how are lower courts supposed to weigh these radically different interests? Or assign values to different categories of information? All we know is that historical cell-site location information (for seven days, anyway) escapes *Smith* and *Miller's* shorn grasp, while a lifetime of bank or phone records does not. As to any other kind of information, lower courts will have to stay tuned. . . .

There is another way. From the founding until the 1960s, the right to assert a Fourth Amendment claim didn't depend on your ability to appeal to a judge's personal sensibilities about the "reasonableness" of your expectations or privacy. It was tied to the law. The Fourth Amendment protects "the right of the people to be secure in their persons, houses, papers and effects, against unreasonable searches and seizures." True to those words and their original understanding, the traditional approach asked if a house, paper or effect was *yours* under law. . . .

Given the prominence *Katz* has claimed in our doctrine, American courts are pretty rusty at applying the traditional approach to the Fourth Amendment. We know that if a house, paper, or effect is yours, you have a Fourth Amendment interest in its protection. But what kind of legal interest is sufficient to make something *yours?* And what source of law determines that? Current positive law? The common law at 1791, extended by analogy to modern times? Both? Much work is needed to revitalize this area and answer these questions. I do not begin to claim all the answers today, but (unlike with *Katz*) at least I have a pretty good idea what the questions *are*. And it seems to me a few things can be said.

First, the fact that a third party has access to or possession of your papers and effects does not necessarily eliminate your interest in them. Ever hand a private document to a friend to be returned? Toss your keys to a valet at a restaurant? Ask your neighbor to look after your dog while you travel? You would not expect the friend to share the document with others; the valet to lend your car to his buddy; or the neighbor to put Fido up for adoption. Entrusting your stuff to others is a *bailment.* A bailment is the "delivery of personal property by one person (the *bailor*) to another (the *bailee*) who holds the property for a certain purpose." Black's Law Dictionary 169 (10th ed. 2014); J. Story, Commentaries on the Law of Bailments § 2, p. 2 (1832) ("a bailment is a delivery of a thing in trust for some special object or purpose, and upon a contract, expressed or implied, to conform to the object or purpose of the trust"). A bailee normally owes a legal duty to keep the item safe, according to the terms of the parties' contract if they have one, and according to the "implication[s] from their conduct" if they don't. 8 C.J.S., Bailments § 36, pp. 468-469 (2017). . . . This approach is quite different from *Smith* and *Miller's* (counter)-intuitive approach to reasonable expectations of privacy; where those cases extinguish Fourth Amendment interests once records are given to a third party, property law may preserve them.

Our Fourth Amendment jurisprudence already reflects this truth. In Ex parte Jackson, 96 U.S. 727 (1878), this Court held that sealed letters placed in the mail are "as fully guarded from examination and inspection, except as to their outward form and weight, as if they were retained by the parties forwarding them in their own domiciles." Id., at 733. The reason, drawn from the Fourth Amendment's text, was that "[t]he constitutional guaranty of the right of the people to be secure in their papers against unreasonable searches and seizures extends to *their papers,* thus closed against inspection, *wherever they may be.*" Ibid. (emphasis added). It did not matter that letters were bailed to a third party (the government, no less). The sender enjoyed the same Fourth Amendment protection as he does "when papers are subjected to search in one's own household." Ibid.

These ancient principles may help us address modern data cases too. Just because you entrust your data—in some cases, your modern-day papers and effects—to a third party may not mean you lose any Fourth Amendment interest in its contents. Whatever may be left of *Smith* and *Miller,* few doubt that e-mail should be treated much like the traditional mail it has largely supplanted—as a bailment in which the owner retains a vital and protected legal interest.

Second, I doubt that complete ownership or exclusive control of property is always a necessary condition to the assertion of a Fourth Amendment right. Where houses are concerned, for example, individuals can enjoy Fourth Amendment protection without fee simple title. Both the text of the Amendment and the common law rule support that conclusion. . . . That is why tenants and resident family members—though they have no legal title—have standing to complain about searches of the houses in which they live. . . .

Another point seems equally true: just because you *have* to entrust a third party with your data doesn't necessarily mean you should lose all Fourth Amendment protections in it. Not infrequently one person comes into possession of someone else's property without the owner's consent. Think of the finder of lost goods or the policeman who impounds a car. The law recognizes that the goods and the car still belong to their true owners, for "where a person comes into lawful possession of the personal property of another, even though there is no formal agreement between the property's owner and its possessor, the possessor will become a constructive bailee when justice so requires." Christensen v. Hoover, 643 P.2d 525, 529 (Colo.1982) (en banc). At least some of this Court's decisions have already suggested that use of technology is functionally compelled by the demands of modern life, and in that way the fact that we store data with third parties may amount to a sort of involuntary bailment too.

Third, positive law may help provide detailed guidance on evolving technologies without resort to judicial intuition. State (or sometimes federal) law often creates rights in both tangible and intangible things. In the context of the Takings Clause we often ask whether those state-created rights are sufficient to make something someone's property for constitutional purposes. A similar inquiry may be appropriate for the Fourth Amendment. . . .

Fourth, while positive law may help establish a person's Fourth Amendment interest there may be some circumstances where positive law cannot be used to defeat it. *Ex parte Jackson* reflects that understanding. There this Court said that "[n]o law of Congress" could authorize letter carriers "to invade the secrecy of letters." 96 U.S., at 733. So the post office couldn't impose a regulation dictating that those mailing letters surrender all legal interests in them once they're deposited in a mailbox. If that is right, *Jackson* suggests the existence of a constitutional floor below which Fourth Amendment rights may not descend. Legislatures cannot pass laws declaring your house or papers to be your property except to the extent the police wish to search them without cause. . . . Nor does this mean protecting only the specific rights known at the founding; it means protecting their modern analogues too. So, for example, while thermal imaging was unknown in 1791, this Court has recognized that using that technology to look inside a home constitutes a Fourth Amendment "search" of that "home" no less than a physical inspection might.

Fifth, this constitutional floor may, in some instances, bar efforts to circumvent the Fourth Amendment's protection through the use of subpoenas. No one thinks the government can evade *Jackson*'s prohibition on opening sealed letters without a warrant simply by issuing a subpoena to a postmaster for "all letters sent by John Smith" or, worse, "all letters sent by John Smith concerning a particular transaction." So the question courts will confront will be this: What other kinds of records are sufficiently similar to letters in the mail that the same rule should apply?

It may be that, as an original matter, a subpoena requiring the recipient to produce records wasn't thought of as a "search or seizure" by the government implicating the Fourth Amendment, see ante, opinion of Alito, J., but instead as an act of compelled self-incrimination implicating the Fifth Amendment. But the common law of searches and seizures does not appear to have confronted a case where private documents equivalent to a mailed letter were entrusted to a bailee and then subpoenaed. . . . Given that (perhaps insoluble) uncertainty, I am content to adhere to *Jackson* and its implications for now.

To be sure, we must be wary of returning to the doctrine of Boyd v. United States, 116 U.S. 616 [(1886)]. *Boyd* invoked the Fourth Amendment to restrict the use of subpoenas even for ordinary business records and, as Justice Alito notes, eventually proved unworkable. But if we were to overthrow *Jackson* too and deny Fourth Amendment protection to *any* subpoenaed materials, we would do well to reconsider the scope of the

Fifth Amendment while we're at it. Our precedents treat the right against self-incrimination as applicable only to testimony, not the production of incriminating evidence. But there is substantial evidence that the privilege against self-incrimination was also originally understood to protect a person from being forced to turn over potentially incriminating evidence.

What does all this mean for the case before us? To start, I cannot fault the Sixth Circuit for holding that *Smith* and *Miller* extinguish any *Katz*-based Fourth Amendment interest in third party cell-site data. That is the plain effect of their categorical holdings. Nor can I fault the Court today for its implicit but unmistakable conclusion that the rationale of *Smith* and *Miller* is wrong; indeed, I agree with that. . . . At the same time, I do not agree with the Court's decision today to keep *Smith* and *Miller* on life support and supplement them with a new and multilayered inquiry that seems to be only *Katz*-squared. Returning there, I worry, promises more trouble than help. Instead, I would look to a more traditional Fourth Amendment approach. Even if *Katz* may still supply one way to prove a Fourth Amendment interest, it has never been the only way. Neglecting more traditional approaches may mean failing to vindicate the full protections of the Fourth Amendment.

Our case offers a cautionary example. It seems to me entirely possible a person's cell-site data could qualify as *his* papers or effects under existing law. Yes, the telephone carrier holds the information. But 47 U.S.C. § 222 designates a customer's cell-site location information as "customer proprietary network information" (CPNI), § 222(h)(1)(A), and gives customers certain rights to control use of and access to CPNI about themselves. The statute generally forbids a carrier to "use, disclose, or permit access to individually identifiable" CPNI without the customer's consent, except as needed to provide the customer's telecommunications services. § 222(c)(1). It also requires the carrier to disclose CPNI "upon affirmative written request by the customer, to any person designated by the customer." § 222(c)(2). Congress even afforded customers a private cause of action for damages against carriers who violate the Act's terms. § 207. Plainly, customers have substantial legal interests in this information, including at least some right to include, exclude, and control its use. Those interests might even rise to the level of a property right.

The problem is that we do not know anything more. Before the district court and court of appeals, Mr. Carpenter pursued only a *Katz* "reasonable expectations" argument. He did not invoke the law of property or any analogies to the common law, either there or in his petition for certiorari. Even in his merits brief before this Court, Mr. Carpenter's discussion of his positive law rights in cell-site data was cursory. . . . In these circumstances,

I cannot help but conclude—reluctantly—that Mr. Carpenter forfeited perhaps his most promising line of argument. . . .

NOTES AND QUESTIONS

1. Chief Justice Roberts, in the majority opinion, emphasizes that the majority's decision "is a narrow one" and that the third-party doctrine is inapplicable because of the "unique nature" of CLSI, again underscoring the narrowness of the holding. But does the majority succeed in its effort to "tread carefully" so as not to "embarrass the future"? Justices Kennedy and Alito argue, in contrast, that the majority has "transform[ed] *Miller* and *Smith* into an unprincipled and unworkable doctrine" that threatens to make a "crazy quilt" of the Fourth Amendment. Who has the better of this argument?

2. For that matter, just what does the majority hold? Chief Justice Roberts insists that CSLI lies at the intersection of two lines of precedent—cases like *Jones*, in which the concurring Justices expressed privacy concerns with location tracking and cases like *Smith* and *Miller*, involving the third-party doctrine. The government's conduct in this case implicated the Fourth Amendment, notwithstanding cases like *Smith* and *Miller*. But in footnote 3, the majority declines to address "whether there is a limited period for which the Government may obtain an individual's historical CSLI free from Fourth Amendment scrutiny, and if so, how long that period may be." And the Court similarly expresses no view on whether the Fourth Amendment is implicated when the Government seeks to ascertain all the devices that connected to a particular cell site during a particular interval in a so-called "tower dump." "It is sufficient for our purposes today," the majority says, "to hold that accessing seven days of CSLI constitutes a Fourth Amendment search." But is this much help, in deciding future cases?

3. Consider, for example, the Court's statement that "[w]e do not . . . call into question conventional surveillance techniques and tools, such as security cameras." As Professor Sklansky has observed, the technologies for storing, aggregating, and analyzing information from the "increasingly unremarkable" cameras that are today to be found in both "public and semi-public places" grow "exponentially more powerful" with each passing year. David Alan Sklansky, Too Much Information: How Not to Think About Privacy and the Fourth Amendment, 102 Cal. L. Rev. 1069, 1085 (2014). Fears of terrorism prompted the British to install cameras on a wide scale beginning in the 1990s—so that cameras proliferate there not only in parks and on streets, but in lobbies, restaurants, schools and hospitals,

and "[b]y one estimate, the average Briton is now photographed by more than 300 separate cameras . . . in a single day." Jeffrey Rosen, The Naked Crowd 36-37 (2004). The United States is catching up very fast. But don't such cameras raise similar concerns to CSLI? Does the majority "embarrass the future" by simply assuming they do not?

4. Although the majority couches its analysis in terms of the uniqueness of CSLI and the narrowness of its holding, the third-party doctrine clearly does not apply categorically after *Carpenter*. Some assessment of both the character of the information the government seeks from a third party and the voluntariness of its exposure is presumably required, in determining whether the Fourth Amendment applies. But as Professor Sklansky has observed, even if "the explosive growth of digitized information requires rethinking traditional rules of search and seizure," a conception of Fourth Amendment privacy as control over personal information is, itself, inadequate: "The problem is that so much information is being collected and collated in so many different places, corporate as well as governmental. . . . We need some way to distinguish the data flows that are most problematic, and this is precisely what focusing on information alone cannot provide." See Sklansky, 102 Cal. L. Rev. at 1119. Is the majority opinion in *Carpenter* helpful along this dimension? Are you persuaded that CSLI is unique? Or at least sufficiently distinct from bank and telephone records to justify different Fourth Amendment treatment?

5. Consider the dissents by Justices Kennedy and Alito. Both stress the extent to which the majority threatens to upset traditional subpoena practice, including in the Grand Jury, by concluding that a search occurred vis-à-vis Carpenter when the government obtained business records from his wireless carriers. But is this a bad thing? No one denies that in the digital age, vast quantities of information concerning each of us are being collected, aggregated, and stored in a manner that was not conceivable in the past. Chief Justice Roberts suggests as much for location data, when he says that the government "can now travel back in time to retrace a person's whereabouts" in a manner never before possible. In a portion of the majority opinion not excerpted here, Chief Justice Roberts affirms, citing *Kyllo*, that as "technology has enhanced the Government's capacity to encroach upon areas normally guarded from inquisitive eyes," this Court has sought to 'assure [ ] preservation of that degree of privacy against government that existed when the Fourth Amendment was adopted.'" (quoting Kyllo v. United States, 533 U.S. 27, 34 (2001)). Could the advent of the digital age argue for a new approach? Or is the majority off on a fool's errand — an errand not sufficiently grounded in the Fourth Amendment's text and history?

6. Notice that Justice Alito's dissent in *Carpenter* is consistent with his observation in *Jones* that "the best solution to privacy concerns" in times of dramatic technological change "may be legislative." But he makes a new argument here as well: that in the digital age, privacy may be threatened by "powerful private companies that collect and sometimes misuse vast quantities of data about the lives of ordinary Americans," at least as much as by the government. Justice Alito warns that the majority's decision may mislead the public to think that the Court can "protect them from this looming [private] threat to their privacy." Do you agree? Is a focus on the government's ability to acquire information from these powerful companies potentially blinding us to the private sector's ability to collect, retain, and monetize this information free of significant regulatory control?

7. Justice Thomas, while joining in the dissents of Justices Kennedy and Alito, declares in his own dissent that *Katz* is a "failed experiment." Justice Gorsuch doubles down in his dissent and notes that he, too, has his problems with the reasonable-expectation-of-privacy test: "Under its plain terms, the [Fourth] Amendment grants you the right to invoke its guarantees whenever one of your protected things (your person, house, your papers, or your effects) is unreasonably searched or seized. Period." Justice Gorsuch argues that return to a traditional, property-based conception of the Fourth Amendment is the path forward, in addressing Fourth Amendment issues in the digital age. He also thinks that it is "entirely possible a person's cell-site data could qualify as *his* papers or effects under existing law." So why does Justice Gorsuch dissent? Is this really a 6-3 decision?

8. What do you think about Justice Gorsuch's proposal for a return to the "traditional" approach? Consider, for instance, whether Carpenter had some property or other positive law interest in the CSLI here, sufficient to raise a Fourth Amendment claim. Justice Gorsuch says maybe, because 47 U.S.C. § 222 gives customers certain rights of control over and access to location information about themselves. But as Justice Alito argues in a portion of his dissent not excerpted here, many statutes provide for the confidentiality of records of various sorts — educational, medical, financial — so as to give some measure of control over their dissemination to students, patients, clients and the like. Moreover, statutory disclosure requirements can be found in many statutes, including the Freedom of Information Act, the Privacy Act, the Fair Credit Reporting Act, and the Family Educational Rights and Privacy Act. We have not generally considered such provisions sufficient to give someone a property interest in the underlying records. Justice Gorsuch suggests that perhaps we should, at least for Fourth Amendment coverage purposes. At this

level of abstraction, however, does this focus on positive law, as Justice Gorsuch explains it, have any greater potential for providing guidance than the majority's analysis, which begins with *Katz*?

9. Note the continuing debate over the significance of *Boyd v. United States* on two different issues, a property-based understanding of the Fourth Amendment and the role of subpoenas. On the first issue, it seemed pretty clear that—in the light of cases like *Riley* and *Jones*—the promise of *Katz* to bury *Boyd* was greatly overstated, as should have been obvious from the beginning. It is all very well to protect people, not places, but people are protected *in* places. The Court seems to think that the location of the information somehow makes *Boyd* irrelevant, but remember that to the *Boyd* Court the real harm was the seizing of private papers to be used against the defendant. It does not take much of a stretch to see how that could have been applied to Carpenter.

But what of the difference between subpoena and search warrant? The *Boyd* Court equated a subpoena with a search, and concluded that the Fourth Amendment—in conjunction with the Fifth Amendment—resulted in the evidence being illegally seized and not usable at trial. But remember that the *Boyd* Court was operating without the complex machinery of modern criminal procedure, including a quasi-constitutional exclusionary rule and sophisticated interpretations of self-incrimination, that later developed.

If one steps back from all of this, perhaps the *Boyd* Court's perspective still has some power: Does the government have a superior property interest in these goods? If not, then the government has to get a search warrant, simple as that—subject to, as always, some exceptions like abandoned property, forms of disclosure that demonstrate no privacy interest such as putting things in the garbage, and so on. The inquiry would thus be of that sort—asking, for example, in *Smith*, how easily accessed bank documents are; and, in *Miller*, whether it is only machines that "know" of the phone numbers called. This suggests that *Smith* would come out the same way, as access to bank records by bank employees is ubiquitous; but *Miller* would come out differently. Operators no longer lurk on telephone calls, tracking numbers and listening to conversations.

Whatever you think of these suggestions, do not lose sight of the central problem here, and it is the one identified in Allen & Rosenberg, supra, at page 353, Note 3. A relatively short clause—the Fourth Amendment—is being used as the basis of regulating all the vast intricacies of modern life using a voting mechanism that is doomed to generate strange outcomes (majority voting on multiple possible outcomes). Perhaps this suggests the Court should stay out of this business almost entirely, and let it be handled by legislation or by common law in the lower courts.

C. *Justifying Searches and Seizures*

3. Justifying Searches and Seizures Without Warrants

a. *Exigent Circumstances*

Replace Note 3 on pages 467-468 with the following new Note 3:

3. Since *Welsh*, the Supreme Court has considered the subject of testing for blood alcohol content ("BAC") in a handful of drunk-driving cases in situations *not* involving entry into the home. In Missouri v. McNeely, 569 U.S. 141 (2013), McNeely was stopped for speeding and crossing the centerline. McNeely refused to take a field breathalyzer test and was arrested and taken to the hospital for blood testing. The officer did not obtain a warrant for this test, and Missouri argued for a *per se* rule in drunk-driving cases that "whenever an officer has probable cause to believe an individual has been driving under the influence of alcohol, exigent circumstances will necessarily exist," thus excusing the officer from the need to obtain a warrant for the testing itself, "because the BAC evidence is inherently evanescent." *McNeely*, 569 U.S. at 152. A majority of the Court, however, rejected Missouri's argument:

> In those drunk-driving investigations where police officers can reasonably obtain a warrant before a blood sample can be drawn without significantly undermining the efficacy of the search, the Fourth Amendment mandates that they do so. We do not doubt that some circumstances will make obtaining a warrant impractical such that dissipation of alcohol from the bloodstream will support an exigency justifying a properly conducted warrantless blood test. That, however, is a reason to decide each case on its facts as we did in *Schmerber*."

Three years after *McNeely*, the Court in Birchfield v. North Dakota, 579 U.S. ___ (2016), held that the Fourth Amendment permits warrantless breath tests—but not warrantless blood tests—incident to arrests for drunk driving. The Court concluded that such tests are permitted categorically, and not on a case-by-case basis, consistent with the "ancient" search incident to arrest doctrine (which we explore in greater detail in Section C.6.a. of this chapter). At issue in *Birchfield* was whether states may criminalize an individual's refusal to undergo BAC testing for drunk-driving. The Court concluded that states may do so in situations where the search incident to arrest doctrine would permit the search. *Birchfield* is discussed further in Note 4 at page 643.

Finally, in Mitchell v. Wisconsin, 588 U.S. ___ (2019), the Court considered the drunk-driving conviction of Gerald Mitchell, an arrestee who was subjected to a warrantless blood BAC test while he was unconscious. Despite the *McNeely* decision, Justice Alito—writing for a plurality—explained that the exigent circumstances exception to the Fourth Amendment's warrant requirement applied in drunk-driving cases involving someone who is unconscious, because that person is unable to perform a breath test and "evidence is literally disappearing by the minute" (an argument that sounds interestingly like "inherently evanescent" . . .). In reaching this conclusion, Justice Alito noted that the situation presented in *Mitchell* was more like that in *Schmerber*, where there was the extraordinary circumstance of a suspect who had sustained injuries in an automobile accident, in contrast to the more "ordinary" drunk-driving case presumably still governed by *McNeely*.

While Justice Alito emphasized the presence of a medical emergency in *Mitchell*, and suggested that community caretaking considerations (which we discuss further infra, at Note 7) demanded a result in *Mitchell* that clearly departed from the prior decision in *McNeely*, Justice Thomas, concurring in the judgment, likely supplied a more plausible interpretation—which is that the plurality drew the line between an "ordinary" drunk-driving case and one involving an unconscious arrestee in order to avoid overturning *McNeely*, a case in which Justice Thomas had dissented.

c. Automobiles

Insert the following Note after Note 4 on page 491:

4a. Although we might question the logic and consistency of the lines the Court has drawn with respect to containers in cars, in Collins v. Virginia, 584 U.S. ___ (2018), its most recent case on the automobile exception, the Court ruled in favor of the petitioner, whose tarp-covered motorcycle was parked in the driveway of his girlfriend's home. In an 8-1 decision, with Justice Alito dissenting, the Court held that the automobile exception did not confer on police the right to enter the curtilage of the home where Collins resided and lift a tarp to observe the motorcycle hidden underneath without first obtaining a warrant.

6. Evaluating Individualized Suspicion

a. Searches Incident to Arrest

Insert the following Note after Note 3 on page 643:

4. When a police officer arrests an individual upon probable cause of drunk driving, may the officer—without first obtaining a warrant—require the individual to submit to a breathalyzer, or administer a blood test, to confirm the precise level of the driver's blood alcohol content (BAC), which is the primary basis for state laws that prohibit drunk driving? That was the question placed before the Court in Birchfield v. North Dakota, 579 U.S. ___ (2016).

The question has important practical consequences. All states provide that obtaining a driver's license creates "implied consent" to BAC testing upon detention for suspected drunk driving; refusal leads to license suspension or revocation, and evidence of the refusal may be introduced in court to show likely intoxication. As criminal penalties for drunk driving have increased, however, so too has the incentive for stopped drivers—"implied consent" notwithstanding—to refuse to submit to BAC testing. According to NHTSA, in 2011, more than 20% of all drivers asked to undergo BAC testing refused to do so. Some states, including North Dakota and Minnesota, have therefore taken the further step of making refusal to be tested a separate crime. Danny Birchfield was convicted of this crime for refusing a blood test. In one of the two companion cases, William Bernard was convicted for refusing to submit to a breathalyzer. In the third case, Steve Beylund was told by the arresting officer that it would be a crime to refuse a blood test, and he submitted to the test; the results led to an administrative hearing at which Beylund's driver's license was suspended for two years.

The Court, per Justice Alito, examined the three cases using the same balancing approach as in *Riley*. On privacy side of the balance, the Court concluded that breath testing (of the kind that was threatened in *Bernard*) "does not implicate significant privacy concerns." Blood tests, however, "are a different matter" that involve "piercing the skin" and "extract a part of the subject's body." Moreover, blood tests "must be judged in light of the availability of the less invasive alternative of a breath test."

Turning to the government's interest, the Court agreed that the states have a "paramount interest" in traffic safety, including the prevention of drunk driving. Weighing that interest against the respective privacy interests at stake, the Court concluded that the warrantless use of breathalyzers was justified as a search incident to arrest—especially given that any warrant requirement in such a situation would likely provide little additional protection to privacy. With respect to the "significantly more intrusive" alternative of blood testing, however, the Court reached the opposite conclusion: "[The States] have offered no satisfactory justification for demanding the more intrusive alternative without a warrant. . . . Nothing prevents the police from seeking a warrant for a blood test when there is sufficient time to do so in the particular circumstances or from relying on the exigent circumstances exception to the warrant requirement when there is not. See *McNeely*, 569 U.S., at ___." Finally, the Court rejected the argument that "implied consent" is enough to justify warrantless blood testing. Noting that "implied consent" laws had been upheld in the past, the Court explained: "It is another matter . . . for the State not only to insist upon an intrusive blood test, but also to impose criminal penalties on the refusal to submit to such a test. There must be a limit to the consequences to which motorists may be deemed to have consented by virtue of a decision to drive on public roads."

In the end, the Court's decision meant that Birchfield had his conviction reversed; Bernard had his conviction affirmed; and Beylund's case was remanded to the lower courts to determine whether the (now unlawful) threat of criminal punishment for failing to submit to the blood test rendered his actual consent to the test involuntary.

Justice Sotomayor, joined by Justice Ginsburg, concurred in part and dissented in part, because she would have also reversed Bernard's conviction on the ground that breathalyzers, like blood tests, should require a warrant. Justice Thomas also concurred in part and dissented in part, because he would have found all three cases to be proper examples of the "exigent circumstance" exception to the warrant requirement.

D.   Reasonableness and Police Use of Force

Insert the following Note after the end of Note 4 on page 694:

5. Courts are often slow to address the realities of shaping work environments of police officers. *Graham* is especially unhelpful is this regard, as it directs that an officer's use of force be assessed for reasonableness under the "totality of the circumstances" while providing almost no guidance regarding how courts should assess the particulars of any one situation. A pair of cases decided by the Supreme Court in 2017 illustrates this problem well.

In White v. Pauly, 580 U.S. ___ (2017), an officer arriving late to the scene shot and killed Daniel Pauly a few seconds after hearing the occupants state to officers already present, "We have guns. . . ." The decedent's lawyer argued, and the lower court agreed, that the officer was required to refrain from shooting until he had announced his presence. Specifically, the lower court held that a reasonable person in the officer's position should have understood that Daniel Pauly would defend his home against unknown intruders. The Supreme Court vacated the lower court's judgment, concluding that the officer did not violate clearly established law by failing to warn Pauly before shooting.

County of Los Angeles v. Mendez, 581 U.S. ___ (2017), also concerned police use of deadly force in an encounter with an armed person. In *Mendez*, police entered the respondents' makeshift shelter without a warrant and without knocking and announcing their presence, in violation of the Fourth Amendment, but because respondent Mendez met police with a BB gun, the court held under *Graham* that the police use of deadly force was reasonable in light of the officers' belief that Mendez was armed and threatened their lives. The *Mendez* Court unanimously rejected the Ninth Circuit's "provocation rule," a doctrine instructing courts to look back in time to determine whether a Fourth Amendment violation different from the forceful seizure at issue could serve as the basis of an excessive force claim. Interestingly, the Court made explicit in a footnote that it was declining to consider whether unreasonable conduct prior to the use of force foreseeably created the need to use it. This question is becoming increasingly important, as incidents involving police and civilians populate social media and lead the public to question the behavior of police in situations that precipitate civilian deaths.

E. The Scope of the Exclusionary Rule

2. Standing

Insert the following Note after Note 4 on page 726:

4a. The Court most recently tackled the issue of who can invoke the exclusionary rule in Byrd v. United States, 584 U.S. ___ (2018). The issue there was "[w]hether a driver has a reasonable expectation of privacy in a rental car when he has the renter's permission to drive the car but is not listed as an authorized driver on the rental agreement." Byrd's fiancée, Latasha Reed, rented a car in New Jersey, while Byrd waited outside. Despite the fact that the rental agreement Reed signed did not permit unauthorized drivers, Reed handed the keys to the over to Byrd, who drove alone to Pittsburgh, where state troopers discovered 49 bricks of heroin during a search after stopping Byrd for driving in the left lane. The Third Circuit, like most lower courts, held that Byrd did not have a reasonable expectation of privacy in the rental car because his name was not on the rental car contract, but the Supreme Court unanimously disagreed with this position. The key issue, the Court said, was whether Byrd had "lawful possession" of the car, and the fact that his name was not on the agreement did not answer that question. Here is the key passage of Justice Kennedy's opinion for the Court:

> One who owns and possesses a car, like one who owns and possesses a house, almost always has a reasonable expectation of privacy in it. More difficult to define and delineate are the legitimate expectations of privacy of others. . . .
>
> Stripped to its essentials, the Government's position is that only authorized drivers of rental cars have expectations of privacy in those vehicles. . . .
>
> The Court sees no reason why the expectation of privacy that comes from lawful possession and control and the attendant right to exclude would differ depending on whether the car in question is rented or privately owned by someone other than the person in current possession of it, much as it did not seem to matter whether the friend of the defendant in *Jones* owned or leased the apartment he permitted the defendant to use in his absence. Both would have the expectation of privacy that comes with the right to exclude. Indeed, the Government conceded at oral argument that an unauthorized driver in sole possession of a rental car would be permitted to exclude third parties from it, such as a carjacker.

Id., at ___. Reed had lawful possession, so she was able to delegate her interest to Byrd. Left unresolved, however, was whether the government's allegation that Byrd asked Reed to procure the car for him knowing that he could not rent a car on his own somehow defeated his lawful interest in the car. Essentially the government suggested that Byrd had procured the car by fraud, which was akin to theft. The Court declined to reach the question because the government had not raised it, relying instead on the unauthorized driver rationale.

3. "Fruit of the Poisonous Tree" Doctrine

Insert the following Note and main case after Note 4 on page 740; renumber the existing Note 5 on page 740 as Note 4 after the Strieff *case:*

5. What if a police officer makes an illegal stop, and subsequently discovers that the stopped individual has an outstanding warrant—perhaps for

a relatively minor offense, such as a misdemeanor traffic violation—and then proceeds to make an arrest, which in turn leads to a search incident to arrest and the seizure of evidence of a crime? Does the officer's discovery of the outstanding warrant provide an "independent source" for the resulting seizure of evidence? Is this an "inevitable discovery"? Or does the existence of the outstanding warrant simply "attenuate" the illegality of the original stop, thus rendering the evidence admissible? These questions were raised by the following case:

UTAH v. STRIEFF
Certiorari to the United States Court of Appeals for the Tenth Circuit
579 U.S. ___ (2016)

JUSTICE THOMAS delivered the opinion of the Court.

. . . In some cases . . . the link between the unconstitutional conduct and the discovery of the evidence is too attenuated to justify suppression. The question in this case is whether this attenuation doctrine applies when an officer makes an unconstitutional investigatory stop; learns during that stop that the suspect is subject to a valid arrest warrant; and proceeds to arrest the suspect and seize incriminating evidence during a search incident to that arrest. We hold that the evidence the officer seized as part of the search incident to arrest is admissible because the officer's discovery of the arrest warrant attenuated the connection between the unlawful stop and the evidence seized incident to arrest.

I

This case began with an anonymous tip. In December 2006, someone called the South Salt Lake City police's drug-tip line to report "narcotics activity" at a particular residence. Narcotics detective Douglas Fackrell investigated the tip. Over the course of about a week, Officer Fackrell conducted intermittent surveillance of the home. He observed visitors who left a few minutes after arriving at the house. These visits were sufficiently frequent to raise his suspicion that the occupants were dealing drugs.

One of those visitors was respondent Edward Strieff. Officer Fackrell observed Strieff exit the house and walk toward a nearby convenience store. In the store's parking lot, Officer Fackrell detained Strieff, identified himself, and asked Strieff what he was doing at the residence.

As part of the stop, Officer Fackrell requested Strieff's identification, and Strieff produced his Utah identification card. Officer Fackrell relayed Strieff's information to a police dispatcher, who reported that Strieff had an outstanding arrest warrant for a traffic violation. Officer Fackrell then arrested Strieff pursuant to that warrant. When Officer Fackrell searched Strieff incident to the arrest, he discovered a baggie of methamphetamine and drug paraphernalia.

The State charged Strieff with unlawful possession of methamphetamine and drug paraphernalia. Strieff moved to suppress the evidence, arguing that the evidence was inadmissible because it was derived from an unlawful investigatory stop. At the suppression hearing, the prosecutor conceded that Officer Fackrell lacked reasonable suspicion for the stop but argued that the evidence should not be suppressed because the existence of a valid arrest warrant attenuated the connection between the unlawful stop and the discovery of the contraband.

The trial court agreed with the State and admitted the evidence. . . . Strieff conditionally pleaded guilty to reduced charges of attempted possession of a controlled substance and possession of drug paraphernalia, but reserved his right to appeal the trial court's denial of the suppression motion. The Utah Court of Appeals affirmed. . . .

The Utah Supreme Court reversed. It held that the evidence was inadmissible because only "a voluntary act of a defendant's free will (as in a confession or consent to search)" sufficiently breaks the connection between an illegal search and the discovery of evidence. . . . Because Officer Fackrell's discovery of a valid arrest warrant did not fit this description, the court ordered the evidence suppressed.

We granted certiorari to resolve disagreement about how the attenuation doctrine applies where an unconstitutional detention leads to the discovery of a valid arrest warrant. . . . We now reverse.

II

. . .

B

It remains for us to address whether the discovery of a valid arrest warrant was a sufficient intervening event to break the causal chain between the unlawful stop and the discovery of drug-related evidence on Strieff's person. The three factors articulated in Brown v. Illinois, 422 U.S. 590 (1975), guide our analysis. First, we look to the "temporal proximity" between the unconstitutional conduct and the discovery of evidence to determine how closely the discovery of evidence followed the unconstitutional search. Second, we consider "the presence of intervening circumstances." Third, and "particularly" significant, we examine "the purpose and flagrancy of the

official misconduct." In evaluating these factors, we assume without deciding (because the State conceded the point) that Officer Fackrell lacked
reasonable suspicion to initially stop Strieff. And, because we ultimately
conclude that the warrant breaks the causal chain, we also have no need
to decide whether the warrant's existence alone would make the initial
stop constitutional even if Officer Fackrell was unaware of its existence.

1

The first factor, temporal proximity between the initially unlawful stop
and the search, favors suppressing the evidence. Our precedents have
declined to find that this factor favors attenuation unless "substantial time"
elapses between an unlawful act and when the evidence is obtained. Here,
however, Officer Fackrell discovered drug contraband on Strieff's person
only minutes after the illegal stop. [S]uch a short time interval counsels
in favor of suppression. . . .

In contrast, the second factor, the presence of intervening circumstances, strongly favors the State. In Segura [v. United States], 468 U.S.
796 [(1984)], the Court addressed similar facts to those here and found
sufficient intervening circumstances to allow the admission of evidence. . . .
This Court deemed the evidence admissible notwithstanding the illegal
search because the information supporting the warrant was "wholly unconnected with the [arguably illegal] entry and was known to the agents well
before the initial entry."

Segura, of course, applied the independent source doctrine because
the unlawful entry "did not contribute in any way to discovery of the evidence seized under the warrant." But the *Segura* Court suggested that the
existence of a valid warrant favors finding that the connection between
unlawful conduct and the discovery of evidence is "sufficiently attenuated
to dissipate the taint." That principle applies here.

In this case, the warrant was valid, it predated Officer Fackrell's investigation, and it was entirely unconnected with the stop. And once Officer
Fackrell discovered the warrant, he had an obligation to arrest Strieff. "A
warrant is a judicial mandate to an officer to conduct a search or make
an arrest, and the officer has a sworn duty to carry out its provisions.". . .
Officer Fackrell's arrest of Strieff thus was a ministerial act that was inde-
pendently compelled by the pre-existing warrant. And once Officer Fackrell
was authorized to arrest Strieff, it was undisputedly lawful to search Strieff
as an incident of his arrest to protect Officer Fackrell's safety. . . .

Finally, the third factor, "the purpose and flagrancy of the official misconduct," *Brown,* supra, at 604, also strongly favors the State. . . . Officer

Fackrell was at most negligent. In stopping Strieff, Officer Fackrell made two good-faith mistakes. First, he had not observed what time Strieff entered the suspected drug house, so he did not know how long Strieff had been there. Officer Fackrell thus lacked a sufficient basis to conclude that Strieff was a short-term visitor who may have been consummating a drug transaction. Second, because he lacked confirmation that Strieff was a short-term visitor, Officer Fackrell should have asked Strieff whether he would speak with him, instead of demanding that Strieff do so. Officer Fackrell's stated purpose was to "find out what was going on [in] the house.". . . But these errors in judgment hardly rise to a purposeful or flagrant violation of Strieff's Fourth Amendment rights. . . .

Moreover, there is no indication that this unlawful stop was part of any systemic or recurrent police misconduct. To the contrary, all the evidence suggests that the stop was an isolated instance of negligence that occurred in connection with a bona fide investigation of a suspected drug house. . . .

Applying these factors, we hold that the evidence discovered on Strieff's person was admissible because the unlawful stop was sufficiently attenuated by the preexisting arrest warrant.

JUSTICE SOTOMAYOR, with whom JUSTICE GINSBURG joins as to Parts I, II, and III, dissenting.

The Court today holds that the discovery of a warrant for an unpaid parking ticket will forgive a police officer's violation of your Fourth Amendment rights. Do not be soothed by the opinion's technical language: This case allows the police to stop you on the street, demand your identification, and check it for outstanding traffic warrants—even if you are doing nothing wrong. If the officer discovers a warrant for a fine you forgot to pay, courts will now excuse his illegal stop and will admit into evidence anything he happens to find by searching you after arresting you on the warrant. Because the Fourth Amendment should prohibit, not permit, such misconduct, I dissent.

I

. . .

II

It is tempting in a case like this, where illegal conduct by an officer uncovers illegal conduct by a civilian, to forgive the officer. After all, his instincts, although unconstitutional, were correct. But a basic principle lies at the heart of the Fourth Amendment: Two wrongs don't make a right. . . .

[T]he officer in this case discovered Strieff's drugs by exploiting his own illegal conduct. . . . The officer did not ask Strieff to volunteer his name only to find out, days later, that Strieff had a warrant against him. The officer illegally stopped Strieff and immediately ran a warrant check. The officer's discovery of a warrant was not some intervening surprise that he could not have anticipated. Utah lists over 180,000 misdemeanor warrants in its database, and at the time of the arrest, Salt Lake County had a "backlog of outstanding warrants" so large that it faced the "potential for civil liability." . . . The officer's violation was also calculated to procure evidence. His sole reason for stopping Strieff, he acknowledged, was investigative—he wanted to discover whether drug activity was going on in the house Strieff had just exited.

The warrant check, in other words, was not an "intervening circumstance" separating the stop from the search for drugs. It was part and parcel of the officer's illegal "expedition for evidence in the hope that something might turn up." Under our precedents, because the officer found Strieff's drugs by exploiting his own constitutional violation, the drugs should be excluded.

III

A

. . .

B

Most striking about the Court's opinion is its insistence that the event here was "isolated," with "no indication that this unlawful stop was part of any systemic or recurrent police misconduct." Respectfully, nothing about this case is isolated.

Outstanding warrants are surprisingly common. When a person with a traffic ticket misses a fine payment or court appearance, a court will issue a warrant. . . . The States and Federal Government maintain databases with over 7.8 million outstanding warrants, the vast majority of which appear to be for minor offenses. Even these sources may not track the "staggering" numbers of warrants, "'drawers and drawers'" full, that many cities issue for traffic violations and ordinance infractions. The Department of Justice recently reported that in the town of Ferguson, Missouri, with a population of 21,000, 16,000 people had outstanding warrants against them.*

Justice Department investigations across the country have illustrated how these astounding numbers of warrants can be used by police to stop people without cause. In a single year in New Orleans, officers "made nearly 60,000 arrests, of which about 20,000 were of people with outstanding traffic or misdemeanor warrants from neighboring parishes for such infractions as unpaid tickets." In the St. Louis metropolitan area, officers "routinely" stop people—on the street, at bus stops, or even in court—for no reason other than "an officer's desire to check whether the subject had a municipal arrest warrant pending." In Newark, New Jersey, officers stopped 52,235 pedestrians within a 4-year period and ran warrant checks on 39,308 of them. . . .

I do not doubt that most officers act in "good faith" and do not set out to break the law. That does not mean these stops are "isolated instance[s] of negligence," however. . . . The Utah Supreme Court described as "'routine procedure' or 'common practice'" the decision of Salt Lake City police officers to run warrant checks on pedestrians they detained without reasonable suspicion. In the related context of traffic stops, one widely followed police manual instructs officers looking for drugs to "run at least a warrants check on all drivers you stop. Statistically, narcotics offenders are . . . more likely to fail to appear on simple citations, such as traffic or trespass violations, leading to the issuance of bench warrants. Discovery of an outstanding warrant gives you cause for an immediate custodial arrest and search of the suspect." C. Remsberg, Tactics for Criminal Patrol 205-206 (1995); C. Epp et al., Pulled Over 23, 33-36 (2014).

IV

Writing only for myself, and drawing on my professional experiences, I would add that unlawful "stops" have severe consequences much greater than the inconvenience suggested by the name. This Court has given officers an array of instruments to probe and examine you. When we condone officers' use of these devices without adequate cause, we give them reason to target pedestrians in an arbitrary manner. We also risk treating members of our communities as second-class citizens.

* The relevant Justice Department report states that there were 16,000 outstanding warrants in Ferguson; it is unclear how many different people were subject to those warrants.—EDS.

Although many Americans have been stopped for speeding or jaywalking, few may realize how degrading a stop can be when the officer is looking for more. This Court has allowed an officer to stop you for whatever reason he wants—so long as he can point to a pretextual justification after the fact. Whren v. United States, 517 U.S. 806 (1996). That justification must provide specific reasons why the officer suspected you were breaking the law, Terry [v. Ohio], 392 U.S. [1,] 21 [(1968)], but it may factor in your ethnicity, United States v. Brignoni-Ponce, 422 U.S. 873 (1975), where you live, Adams v. Williams, 407 U.S. 143, (1972), what you were wearing, United States v. Sokolow, 490 U.S. 1, 4-5 (1989), and how you behaved, Illinois v. Wardlow, 528 U.S. 119 (2000). The officer does not even need to know which law you might have broken so long as he can later point to any possible infraction—even one that is minor, unrelated, or ambiguous. Devenpeck v. Alford, 543 U.S. 146 (2004); Heien v. North Carolina, 574 U.S. ___ (2014).

The indignity of the stop is not limited to an officer telling you that you look like a criminal. See Epp, Pulled Over, at 5. The officer may next ask for your "consent" to inspect your bag or purse without telling you that you can decline. See Florida v. Bostick, 501 U.S. 429 (1991). Regardless of your answer, he may order you to stand "helpless, perhaps facing a wall with [your] hands raised." *Terry*, 392 U.S., at 17. If the officer thinks you might be dangerous, he may then "frisk" you for weapons. This involves more than just a pat down. As onlookers pass by, the officer may "'feel with sensitive fingers every portion of [your] body. A thorough search [may] be made of [your] arms and armpits, waistline and back, the groin and area about the testicles, and entire surface of the legs down to the feet.'"

The officer's control over you does not end with the stop. If the officer chooses, he may handcuff you and take you to jail for doing nothing more than speeding, jaywalking, or "driving [your] pickup truck . . . with [your] 3-year-old son and 5-year-old daughter . . . without [your] seatbelt fastened." Atwater v. Lago Vista, 532 U.S. 318 (2001). At the jail, he can fingerprint you, swab DNA from the inside of your mouth, and force you to "shower with a delousing agent" while you "lift [your] tongue, hold out [your] arms, turn around, and lift [your] genitals." Florence v. Board of Chosen Freeholders of County of Burlington, 566 U.S. (2012); Maryland v. King, 569 U.S. ___, ___ (2013). Even if you are innocent, you will now join the 65 million Americans with an arrest record and experience the "civil death" of discrimination by employers, landlords, and whoever else conducts a background check. And, of course, if you fail to pay bail or appear for court, a judge will issue a warrant to render you "arrestable on sight" in the future.

This case involves a suspicionless stop, one in which the officer initiated this chain of events without justification. As the Justice Department notes, many innocent people are subjected to the humiliations of these unconstitutional searches. The white defendant in this case shows that anyone's dignity can be violated in this manner. But it is no secret that people of color are disproportionate victims of this type of scrutiny. . . .

By legitimizing the conduct that produces this double consciousness, this case tells everyone, white and black, guilty and innocent, that an officer can verify your legal status at any time. It says that your body is subject to invasion while courts excuse the violation of your rights. It implies that you are not a citizen of a democracy but the subject of a carceral state, just waiting to be cataloged.

We must not pretend that the countless people who are routinely targeted by police are "isolated." They are the canaries in the coal mine whose deaths, civil and literal, warn us that no one can breathe in this atmosphere. They are the ones who recognize that unlawful police stops corrode all our civil liberties and threaten all our lives. Until their voices matter too, our justice system will continue to be anything but.

I dissent.

[The dissenting opinion of Justice Kagan, joined by Justice Ginsburg, is omitted.]

NOTES AND QUESTIONS

1. In a series of cases, the Court has noted that the exclusionary rule is strong medicine because its consequence is can be the release of a criminal offender without punishment. Thus, as Justice Kagan notes in her separate dissent in *Strieff:* "Our decisions have thus endeavored to strike a sound balance between those two competing considerations—rejecting the 'reflexive' impulse to exclude evidence every time an officer runs afoul of the Fourth Amendment, but insisting on suppression when it will lead to 'appreciable deterrence' of police misconduct, Herring v. United States, 555 U.S. 135, 141 (2009)."

The *Strieff* majority apparently believes the price of exclusion is too high for Officer Frackrell's negligence, but Justice Sotomayor disagrees. Much turns, doesn't it, on an understanding of how representative this case is of systematic police abuses? Given the facts reviewed in both opinions, and the materials we have already read in Section 5.C on Police Discretion and Street Policing, who do you think has the better side of the argument?

2. Some specific information about the prevalence of warrants may help you to answer the question posed in Note 1: A few years before *Strieff* was decided, a group of scholars signed an amicus brief in support of a petition for certiorari to the Eighth Circuit in support of a petitioner who was convicted of an offense on facts similar to those presented in *Strieff*.[**] The brief made three points. First, although the vast majority of stops are constitutional, substantial percentages in many places — 10-15% — result in very large numbers of individuals being wrongfully stopped. For example, one study of 2.2 million stops carried out between 2004 and 2009 in New York City conservatively estimated that about 150,000 of those stops were unconstitutional, and another 500,000 stops were constitutionally questionable. Second, there is a nationwide backlog of unserved warrants for minor offenses. For example, in spring 2011, more than half of approximately 50,000 unserved warrants in Prince George's County, Maryland, were for vehicle infractions; only 642 of the warrants were for serious felonies. Third, in many states these outstanding warrants are for very old violations. The aforementioned amicus brief noted that half of the warrants in Prince George's County were for violations that were more than 3 years old; and in North Carolina, an audit found thousands of warrants dating back to the 1970's.

3. Does the Court's decision in *Strieff*, especially when combined with the statistics about the prevalence of outstanding warrants reported in the immediately preceding Note, provide police officers with a strong incentive to make *Terry* stops even without "reasonable suspicion," based solely on a hunch? Or to err on the side of making a stop, even if the "articulable basis" for suspicion is borderline? What, if any, alternative remedies exist that could possibly deter such an overly aggressive use of *Terry* authority? How much should we care about the answers to these questions? Does your response depend on whether you believe you are more, or less, likely to be the frequent object of such police scrutiny?

[**] One of the authors of this casebook was a signatory; the case was United States v. Faulkner, 636 F.3d 1009 (8th Cir. 2011). — Eds.

Chapter 6

Criminal Investigations in the Fourth Amendment's Shadow

A. Electronic Surveillance and the Search of Digital Information

1. Wiretapping and Related Electronic Surveillance

Insert the following paragraph at the end of third full paragraph on page 758:

The Supreme Court returned to this issue in Dahda v. United States, 584 U.S. ___ (2018). The statute sets forth three grounds for suppression, and the Court held that *Giordano* only dealt with the first, "unlawfully intercepted." The second, an order which is "insufficient on its face" was involved in *Dahda* because the order inappropriately called for wiretaps of phones outside the territorial jurisdiction of the court by listening posts also outside its territorial jurisdiction. The defendant argued that this made the order "insufficient on its face." The Government agreed not to use any evidence obtained by such illegal means but argued that the interceptions within the territorial jurisdiction should not be excluded simply because other parts of the order were inappropriate, and the Court agreed.

2. The Search of Stored Electronic Information and Other Digital Information

Insert the following notes after Note 4 on page 774. Delete the material from the start of Note 5 on page 774 through the end of Note 5 on page 788, including the main case of United States v. Graham on page 775:

5. Given the traditionally robust protections afforded the contents of communications, *Warshak*, although it invalidated a central feature of the SCA's statutory scheme, was in many ways simply an application of

long-standing Fourth Amendment principles in a new context. In light of the SCA's own requirement of a warrant to obtain the contents of e-mails that have been in storage fewer than 180 days, moreover, *Warshak* was also largely consistent with Congress's efforts in the statute both "to provide privacy protections for new uses of computer technologies," see id., at 382, and to safeguard the ability of law enforcement to access evidence on reasonable terms.

Now think back to *Carpenter* and the Supreme Court's decision there, rejecting the legislative judgment embodied in § 2703(d) of the SCA and determining that to access seven days of historical cell site location information ("CSLI"), the government must obtain a warrant based on probable cause. See *Carpenter*, supra, at page 10 of this Supplement. "From a practical standpoint," commentators had observed prior to the *Carpenter* decision, § 2703(d) orders "facilitate[ ] law enforcement access to non-content records at the early stages of an investigation, when the government is unlikely to meet the higher probable cause standard." Stephanie K. Pell & Christopher Soghoian, Can You See Me Now?: Toward Reasonable Standards for Law Enforcement Access to Location Data that Congress Could Enact, 27 Berkeley Tech. L.J. 117, 151 (2012). The Sixth Circuit in *Carpenter* noted that Congress "is usually better equipped than courts are to answer the empirical questions" posed by new technologies, and that the SCA itself reflects Congress's view that the government must show reasonable grounds, but not probable cause, to obtain CSLI. Having now more broadly considered the interplay between courts and legislatures in the rapidly evolving area of digital information, what do you think about the Supreme Court's rejection of Congress's judgment in this context? Is it clear to you that CSLI is sufficiently similar to the contents of e-mails that the Court was correct to bring the acquisition of such information from wireless providers within the coverage of the Fourth Amendment?

5a. The preceding note may speak to the difficulty of discerning, among the "geometrically proliferating ways in which our movements, transactions, and conversations are subject to electronic monitoring," see David Alan Sklansky, Too Much Information: How Not to Think about Privacy and the Fourth Amendment, 102 Cal. L. Rev. 1069, 1119 (2014), and thus to the creation of electronic records, exactly which among such records may merit Fourth Amendment protection. Justice Alito opines in his *Carpenter* dissent that "[l]egislation is much preferable to the development of an entirely new body of Fourth Amendment caselaw" to deal with this and other challenges posed in the digital age "for many reasons, including the enormous complexity of the subject, the need to respond to rapidly changing technology, and the Fourth Amendment's limited scope" (in that it does not apply to powerful private companies now in the business of collecting data). But is this a sufficient answer to the position we find ourselves in? Consider the following:

> It is far from clear . . . that legislatures really are better than courts at fashioning privacy rules for new technologies—or even that this is a sensible comparison to draw. . . . [W]hile statutes theoretically can be revised at any time, without waiting for the proper case to arise and without regard for precedent, in practice Congress is often notoriously sluggish. The case-by-case method of decisionmaking can prompt reconsideration of rules that legislatures would never get around to amending. Surveying the regulation of law enforcement practices by federal statutes, Professor Erin Murphy finds: (1) "Congress does less leading and much more following when it comes to regulating privacy"; (2) "law enforcement . . . plays a critical role in shaping" statutory protections of privacy through its "clear and constant voice in the political process"; and (3) while privacy statutes are sometimes amended, Congress often has proven unwilling or unable to correct "obviously flawed and outdated provisions." In fact, Murphy concludes, many of the most successful privacy statutes have stayed current "largely because of vague terms that can be adapted by judicial officials to apply to changed circumstances."

David Alan Sklansky, Two More Ways Not to Think About Privacy and the Fourth Amendment, 82 U. Chi. L. Rev. 223, 227-228 (2015) (quoting Erin Murphy, The Politics of Privacy in the Criminal Justice System: Information Disclosure, the Fourth Amendment, and Statutory Law Enforcement Exemptions, 111 Mich. L. Rev. 485, 498, 503, 533-536 (2013)). What do *you* think is the appropriate role for courts and for legislatures in this rapidly evolving area?

Insert the following Note after Note 6 on page 789:

6a. The Second Circuit took up the issue of what standards should govern the seizure and search of computers in an en banc decision issued on May 27, 2016. United States v. Ganias, 824 F.3d 199 (2d Cir. 2016). In *Ganias*, government agents obtained a warrant authorizing the seizure of the computers of Stravros Ganias, an accountant doing work for an Army contractor suspected of misconduct. When the warrant was executed in November 2003, investigators, rather than seize Ganias's three hard drives, made forensic mirror images of the data on the three computers, thus minimizing intrusion on his business. Agents were thereafter careful to limit their off-site search of this material so as to avoid review, where possible, of material not responsive to the warrant. Based on analysis of paper files taken during the search, however, the investigators came to suspect that Ganias himself may have committed tax violations. The government obtained a second warrant in April 2006 (about two and one-half years after the mirrors were created) to search Ganias's personal financial records on the retained mirrors. A panel of the Second Circuit determined that the Fourth Amendment was violated when these agents seized and indefinitely retained the mirrors, which included much data that was not responsive to the original warrant. The en banc court declined to address the merits of this Fourth Amendment question, ruling that the agents had acted in good faith. The Second Circuit, however, in an apparent effort to provide guidance to future courts regarding the seizure and search of computer files, addressed the subject at some length, albeit in dicta:

> The district court concluded that the conduct of the agents in this case comported fully with the Fourth Amendment, and thus did not reach the question whether they also acted in good faith. Because we conclude that the agents acted in good faith, we need not decide whether a Fourth Amendment violation occurred. We thus affirm the district court on an alternate ground. Nevertheless, though we offer no opinion on the existence of a Fourth Amendment violation in this case, we make some observations bearing on the reasonableness of the agents' actions, both to illustrate the complexity of the questions in this significant Fourth Amendment context and to highlight the importance of careful consideration of the technological contours of digital search and seizure for future cases. . . .
>
> Ganias . . . argues that the Government violated the Fourth Amendment in this case, notwithstanding the two warrants that issued, by retaining complete forensic copies of his three hard drives during the pendency of its investigation.
>
> According to Ganias, when law enforcement officers execute a warrant for a hard drive or forensic mirror that contains data that, as here, cannot feasibly be sorted into responsive and non-responsive categories on-site, "the Fourth Amendment demands, at the very least, that the officers expeditiously complete their off-site search and then promptly return (or destroy) files outside the warrant's scope." Arguing that a culling process took place here and that it had concluded by, at the latest, January 2005, Ganias faults the Government for retaining the mirrored drives—including storing one forensic copy in an evidence locker for safekeeping. It was this retention, he argues, that constituted the Fourth Amendment violation—a violation that, in turn, made the 2006 search of the data itself unconstitutional as, but for this retention, the search could never have occurred.
>
> To support this argument, Ganias relies principally on United States v. Tamura, 694 F.2d 591 (9th Cir. 1982), a Ninth Circuit case involving the search and seizure of physical records. In *Tamura* (unlike the present case, in which a warrant specifically authorized the agents to seize hard drives and to search them off-site) officers armed only with a warrant authorizing

them to seize specific "records" instead seized numerous boxes of printouts, file drawers, and cancelled checks for off-site search and sorting. After the officers had clearly sorted the responsive paper documents from the non-responsive ones, they refused—despite request—to return the non-responsive paper files. The Ninth Circuit concluded that both the unauthorized seizure of voluminous material not specified in the warrant and the retention of the seized documents violated the Fourth Amendment.

Because we resolve this case on good faith grounds, we need not decide the relevance, if any, of *Tamura*. . . . We note, however, that there are reasons to doubt whether *Tamura* (to the extent we would indeed follow it) answers the questions before us. First, on its facts, *Tamura* is distinguishable from this case, insofar as the officers there seized for off-site review records that the warrant did not authorize them to seize, and retained those records even after their return was requested. Here, in contrast, the warrant authorized the seizure of the hard drives, not merely particular records, and Ganias did not request return or destruction of the mirrors (even after he was indisputably alerted to the Government's continued retention of them) by, for instance, filing a motion for such return pursuant to Federal Rule of Criminal Procedure 41(g). Second, and more broadly, even if the facts of *Tamura* were otherwise on point, Ganias's invocation of *Tamura*'s reasoning rests on an analogy between paper files intermingled in a file cabinet and digital data on a hard drive. Though we do not take any position on the ultimate disposition of the constitutional questions herein, we nevertheless pause to address the appropriateness of this analogy. . . .

The central premise of Ganias's reliance on *Tamura* is that the search of a digital storage medium is analogous to the search of a file cabinet. The analogy has some force, particularly as seen from the perspective of the affected computer user. Computer users—or at least, average users (in contrast to, say, digital forensics experts)—typically experience computers as filing cabinets, as that is precisely how user interfaces are designed to be perceived by such users. Given that the file cabinet analogy (at least largely) thus captures an average person's subjective experience with a computer interface, the analogy may shed light on a user's subjective expectations of privacy regarding data maintained on a digital storage device. Because we experience digital files as discrete items, and because we navigate through a computer as through a virtual storage space, we may expect the law similarly to treat data on a storage device as comprised of distinct, severable files, even if, in fact, "[s]torage media do not naturally divide into parts." Josh Goldfoot, The Physical Computer and the Fourth Amendment, 16 Berkeley J. Crim. L. 112, 131 (2011). . . .

That said, though it may have some relevance to our inquiry, the file cabinet analogy is only that—an analogy, and an imperfect one. Cf. James Boyle, The Public Domain 107 (2008) ("Analogies are only bad when they ignore the key difference between the two things being analyzed."). Though to a user a hard drive may seem like a file cabinet, a digital forensics expert reasonably perceives the hard drive simply as a coherent physical storage medium for digital data—data that is interspersed *throughout* the medium, which itself must be maintained and accessed with care, lest this data be altered or destroyed. See Goldfoot, supra, at 114 (arguing digital storage media are physical objects like "drugs, blood, or clothing"); Wayne Jekot, Computer Forensics, Search Strategies, and the Particularity Requirement, 7 U. Pitt. J. Tech. L. & Pol'y, art. 5, at 1, 30 (2007) ("[A] computer does not simply hold data, it is *composed* of data."). Even the most conventional "files"—word documents and spreadsheets such as those the Government searched in this case—are not maintained, like files in a file cabinet, in discrete physical locations separate and distinct from other files. They are in fact "fragmented" on a storage device, potentially across physical locations. Jekot, supra, at 13. "Because of the manner in which data is written to the hard drive, rarely will one file be stored intact in one place on a hard drive," id.; so-called "files" are stored in multiple locations and in multiple forms, see Goldfoot, supra, at 127-28. And as a corollary to this fragmentation, the computer stores unseen information about any given "file"—not only metadata about when the file was created or who created it, see Michael W. Graves, Digital Archaeology: The Art and Science of Digital Forensics 94-95 (2014), but also prior versions or edits that may still exist "in the document or associated temporary files on [the] disk"—further interspersing the data corresponding to that "file" across the physical storage medium, Eoghan Casey, Digital Evidence and Computer Crime 507 (3d ed. 2011).

"Files," in short, are not as discrete as they may appear to a user. Their interspersion throughout a digital storage medium, moreover, may affect the degree to which it is feasible, in a case involving search pursuant to a warrant, to fully extract and segregate responsive data from non-responsive data. To be clear, we do not suggest that it is impossible to do so in any particular or in every case; we emphasize only that in assessing the reasonableness, for Fourth Amendment purposes, of the search and seizure of digital evidence, we must be attuned to the technological features unique to digital media as a whole and to those relevant in a particular case—features that simply do not exist in the context of paper files.

These features include an additional complication affecting the validity of the file cabinet analogy: namely, that a good deal of the information that a forensic examiner may seek on a digital storage device (again, because it is a coherent and complex forensic object and not a file cabinet) does not even remotely fit into the typical user's conception of a "file." Forensic investigators may, inter alia, search for and discover evidence that a file was deleted as well as evidence sufficient to reconstruct a deleted file—evidence that can exist in so-called "unallocated" space on a hard drive. See Casey, supra, at 496; Orin S. Kerr, Searches and Seizures in a Digital World, 119 Harv. L. Rev. 531, 542, 545 (2005); Fed. Judicial Ctr., supra, at 40 ("A host of information can lie in the interstices between the allocated spaces."). They may seek responsive metadata about a user's activities, or the manner in which information has been stored, to show such things as knowledge or intent, or to create timelines as to when information was created or accessed. Forensic examiners will sometimes seek evidence on a storage medium that something *did not happen*: "If a defendant claims he is innocent because a computer virus committed the crime, the absence of a virus on his hard drive is 'dog that did not bark' negative evidence that disproves his story. . . .

To prove something is not on a hard drive, it is necessary to look at every place on the drive where it might be found and confirm it is not there." Goldfoot, supra, at 141; see also United States v. O'Keefe, 461 F.3d 1338, 1341 (11th Cir. 2006) ("[The government's expert] testified that the two viruses he found on [the defendant's] computer were not capable of 'downloading and uploading child pornography and sending out advertisements.'").

Finally, because of the complexity of the data thereon and the manner in which it is stored, the nature of digital storage presents potential challenges to parties seeking to preserve digital evidence, authenticate it at trial, and establish its integrity for a fact-finder—challenges that materially differ from those in the paper file context. First, the extraction of specific data files to some other medium can alter, omit, or even destroy portions of the information contained in the original storage medium. Preservation of the original medium or a complete mirror may therefore be necessary in order to safeguard the integrity of evidence that has been lawfully obtained or to authenticate it at trial. Graves, supra, at 95-96 ("[The investigator] must be able to prove that the information presented came from where he or she claims and was not altered in any way during examination, and that there was no opportunity for it to have been replaced or altered in the interim."); see also Casey, supra, at 480 ("Even after copying data from a computer or piece of storage media, digital investigators generally retain the original evidential item in a secure location for future reference."). The preservation of data, moreover, is not simply a concern for law enforcement. Retention of the original storage medium or its mirror may also be necessary to afford criminal defendants access to that medium or its forensic copy so that, relying on forensic experts of their own, they may challenge the authenticity or reliability of evidence allegedly retrieved. Defendants may also require access to a forensic copy to conduct an independent analysis of precisely what the government's forensic expert did—potentially altering evidence in a manner material to the case—or to locate exculpatory evidence that the government missed.

Notwithstanding any other distinctions between this case and *Tamura*, then, the Government plausibly argues that, because digital storage media constitute coherent forensic objects with contours more complex than—and materially distinct from—file cabinets containing interspersed paper documents, a digital storage medium or its forensic copy may need to be retained, during the course of an investigation and prosecution, to permit the accurate extraction of the primary evidentiary material sought pursuant to the warrant; to secure metadata and other probative evidence stored in the interstices of the storage medium; and to preserve, authenticate, and effectively present at trial the evidence thus lawfully obtained. To be clear, we do not decide the ultimate merit of this argument as applied to the circumstances of this case. Nor do we gainsay the privacy concerns implicated when the government retains a hard drive or forensic mirror containing personal information irrelevant to the ongoing investigation, even if such information is never viewed. We discuss the aptness and limitations of Ganias's analogy and the Government's response simply to highlight the complexity of the relevant questions for future cases and to underscore the importance, in answering such questions, of engaging with the technological specifics.

In emphasizing such specifics, we reiterate that we do not mean to thereby minimize or ignore the privacy concerns implicated when a hard drive or forensic mirror is retained, even pursuant to a warrant. The seizure of a computer hard drive, and its subsequent retention by the government, can give the government possession of a vast trove of personal information about the person to whom the drive belongs, much of which may be entirely irrelevant to the criminal investigation that led to the seizure. Indeed, another weakness of the file cabinet analogy is that no file cabinet has the capacity to contain as much information as the typical computer hard drive. In 2005, Professor Orin Kerr noted that the typical personal computer hard drive had a storage capacity of about eighty gigabytes, which he estimated could hold text files equivalent to the "information contained in the books on one floor of a typical academic library." Kerr, Searches and Seizures in a Digital World, supra, at 542. By 2011, computers were being sold with one terabyte of capacity—about twelve times the size of Professor Kerr's library floor. Paul Ohm, Response, Massive Hard Drives, General Warrants, and the Power of Magistrate Judges, 97 Va. L. Rev. In Brief 1, 6 (2011). The *New York Times* recently reported that commercially available storage devices can hold "16 petabytes of data, roughly equal to 16 billion thick books." Quentin Hardy, As a Data Deluge Grows, Companies Rethink Storage, N.Y. Times, Mar. 15, 2016, at B3.

Moreover, quantitative measures fail to capture the significance of the data kept by many individuals on their computers. Tax records, diaries, personal photographs, electronic books, electronic media, medical data, records of internet searches, banking and shopping information—all may be kept in the same device, interspersed among the evidentiary material that justifies the seizure or search. While physical searches for paper records or other evidence may require agents to rummage at least cursorily through much private material, the reasonableness of seizure and subsequent retention by the government of such vast quantities of irrelevant private material was rarely if ever presented in cases prior to the age of digital storage, and has never before been considered justified, or even practicable, in such cases. Even as we recognize that search and seizure of digital media is, in some ways, distinct from what has come before, we must remain mindful of the privacy interests that necessarily inform our analysis.

We note, however, that parties with an interest in retained storage media are not without recourse. As noted above, Ganias never sought the return of any seized material, either by negotiating with the Government or by motion to the court. Though negotiated stipulations regarding the admissibility or integrity of evidence may not always suffice to satisfy reasonable interests of the government in retention during the pendency of an investigation, such stipulations may make return feasible in a proper case, and can be explored.

A person from whom property is seized by law enforcement may move for its return under Federal Rule of Criminal Procedure 41(g). Rule 41(g) permits a defendant or any "person aggrieved" by either an unlawful or *lawful* deprivation of property, see United States v. Comprehensive Drug Testing,

Inc., 621 F.3d 1162, 1173 (9th Cir. 2010) (en banc) (per curiam), to move for its return, Fed. R. Crim. P. 41(g). Evaluating such a motion, a district court "must receive evidence on any factual issue necessary to decide the motion," and, in the event that the motion is granted, may "impose reasonable conditions to protect access to the property and its use in later proceedings." Id. Since we resolve this case on other grounds, we need not address whether Ganias's failure to make such a motion forfeited any Fourth Amendment objection he might otherwise have had to the Government's retention of the mirrors. But we agree with the district court that, as a pragmatic matter, such a motion "would have given a court the opportunity to consider 'whether the government's interest could be served by an alternative to retaining the property,' and perhaps to order the [mirrors] returned to Ganias, all while enabling the court to 'impose reasonable conditions to protect access to the property and its use in later proceedings.'" *Ganias*, 2011 WL 2532396, at *8 (citation omitted) (first quoting In re Smith, 888 F.2d 167, 168 (D.C. Cir. 1989) (per curiam); then quoting Fed. R. Crim. P. 41(g)).

Rule 41(g) thus provides a potential mechanism, in at least some contexts, for dealing with the question of retention at a time when the government may be expected to have greater information about the data it seeks and the best process through which to search and present that data in court. It is worth observing, then, that Rule 41(g) constitutes a statutory solution (as opposed to a purely judicially constructed one) to at least one facet of the retention problem. Statutory approaches, of course, do not relieve courts from their obligation to interpret the Constitution; nevertheless, such approaches have, historically, provided one mechanism for safeguarding privacy interests while, at the same time, addressing the needs of law enforcement in the face of technological change. . . .

If you were drafting a statute to address computer searches, what would it say? It is clear that agents executing a search warrant outside the context of computer searches do not generally "overseize," taking and retaining for lengthy periods of time material that is not responsive to the warrant. (Agents look through the documents in the file cabinet on site, and take only those that the warrant authorizes them to seize.) On the other hand, once an item has been properly seized as evidence (think of the blood-stained shirt recovered from the suspect's home), agents do not generally return such items until the case is over, and they take pains to preserve the integrity of the evidence, so as to be able to use it effectively in court, and to make it available to persons charged with crimes.

So is a hard drive more like a file cabinet or a blood-stained shirt? Or is it really like neither? If agents conducting computer searches must of necessity seize data not responsive to the warrant and then, over time, perform their search, should they also be able later to obtain a second warrant, when probable cause develops to suggest that evidence of another crime might be found among the seized data? Why or why not?

PART FOUR

THE ADJUDICATION PROCESS

Chapter 11

The Scope of the Prosecution

A. The Right to a Speedy Trial

Insert the following Note after Note 8 on page 1130:

8a. In the same vein, and using the same reasoning based on the text of the Sixth Amendment, the Court has unanimously concluded that the Sixth Amendment speedy trial guarantee does not apply to delays between a conviction and sentencing. As with pre-indictment delays, a defendant aggrieved by delays in imposing a sentence must look elsewhere for constitutional protection: "For inordinate delay in sentencing," said the Court, "although the Speedy Trial Clause does not govern, a defendant may have other recourse, including, in appropriate circumstances, tailored relief under the Due Process Clauses of the Fifth and Fourteenth Amendments." Betterman v. Montana, 578 U.S. ___ (2016).

C. Joinder and Severance

Insert the following Note after Note 3 on page 1178, immediately before the main case of Zafiro v. United States:

4. Suppose the defendant is successful in having his charges severed, and suppose also that he is acquitted in the first trial. Can the defendant now argue that the government is barred by the double jeopardy clause from relitigating in the second trial any of the issues resolved in his favor in the first trial?

Defendant Currier was accused of helping to steal a safe that contained guns and money, and he was indicted for burglary, larceny, and being a felon in possession of a firearm. Currier was in fact a convicted felon, and to keep the jury from hearing about his criminal record, he successfully moved to sever the felon-in-possession count from the other two charges.

At the first trial he was acquitted of burglary and larceny, and when the government proceeded to try him for being a felon in possession of a firearm, Currier moved to prevent or limit the second trial. He argued that the first jury necessarily concluded that he did *not* help steal the safe, and as a result, there was no evidence that he ever possessed a firearm (the only guns allegedly involved in the transaction were those in the safe). As a result, Currier argued, the second jury could not convict him without calling into question the first jury's decision, and thus the government should be barred from re-litigating defendant's alleged possession of the stolen guns.

The Supreme Court, by 5-4 with Justice Gorsuch writing for the majority, disagreed. It found that because Currier had consented to the severance of the charges, he had waived any double jeopardy protection associated with the second trial. The Court noted that if there had been no severance, the government would have been allowed to try all three counts in a single trial, and so "consenting to two trials when one would have avoided a double jeopardy problem precludes any constitutional violation associated with holding a second trial." Currier v. Virginia, 585 U.S. ___ (2018).

In a part of the opinion joined by only three other Justices, Justice Gorsuch warned that a contrary rule could have a negative effect on defendants as a group. "Today," he wrote, "some state courts grant severance motions liberally to benefit defendants." Imposing double jeopardy restrictions on the government's ability try multiple counts in separate trials would raise the cost of granting these severance motions, and "20 States appearing before us [as amici] have warned that [they] might respond to any decision increasing the costs of severed trials by making them less freely available." The plurality acknowledged that "[o]f course, that is only a prediction," but said "it would be a mistake to ignore the possibility that by making severances more costly we might wind up making them rarer too." Id. at ___ (plurality opinion of Gorsuch, J.).

Are the concerns expressed in the plurality portion of Justice Gorsuch's opinion legitimate? Severance is supposed to be granted to avoid unfairly prejudicing the accused—so is it appropriate for the States to suggest that, if their view of the Double Jeopardy protection were not adopted, the protection offered by severance might be "less freely available?" On the other hand, isn't it proper for the Court to consider the practical legal effects of its ruling on trials and defendants?

Chapter 12

Discovery and Disclosure

A. Disclosure by the Government

2. The Prosecutor's Constitutional Disclosure Obligations

Insert the following Note after Note 1 on page 1206:

1a. This disagreement over the ultimate goal of *Brady* may explain the Court's 2017 decision in Turner v. United States, 582 U.S. ___ (2017). In a case the majority called "legally simple but factually complex," seven defendants and several others were charged with a horrific murder that occurred in 1984. The government's theory was that all seven had participated in the beating that caused the death, and among the evidence the led to the convictions was the self-incriminating testimony of two of the participants as well as statements by disinterested witnesses. Many years after the convictions were final, the seven defendants argued a *Brady* violation, identifying seven pieces of evidence that the government had withheld. The evidence included evidence that could have impeached several of the witnesses, and information that was consistent with a single person committing the murder rather than a group killing. The government acknowledged that the information was "favorable" to the accused, but argued it was not "material." The lower court held a 16-day hearing on the Brady claim, and eventually agreed that the evidence was not material.

The Supreme Court, by 6-2 (Justice Gorsuch not participating), affirmed, finding that there was no reasonable probability that the outcome would have been different had the government turned over the information. Justice Breyer for the Court found the impeachment evidence largely cumulative of evidence that was already introduced at trial. And as for the withheld evidence suggesting that a single person was guilty of the crime rather than a group, the Court found that in the context of the entire record, the information was "too little, too weak, or too distant from the main evidentiary points to meet *Brady*'s standards."

In dissent, Justice Kagan, joined by Justice Ginsburg, argued that had the withheld information been disclosed "the whole tenor of the trial would have changed. Rather than relying on [their trial defense], all the defendants would have relentlessly impeached the Government's (thoroughly impeachable) witnesses and offered the jurors a way to view the crime in a different light. In my view, that could well have flipped one or more jurors—which is all *Brady* requires."

Chapter 13

Guilty Pleas and Plea Bargaining

A. The Guilty Plea

2. The Effect of a Guilty Plea

Replace all of the material in this subsection, at pages 1247-1251, with the following new material:

A guilty plea resolves the substantive charges against the accused, but it does much more than that. A guilty plea not only extinguishes the right to a trial and the trial-related rights set forth in Rule 11(b)(1) (see Section A.1 of this chapter, above), it also sweeps away most of the legal challenges a defendant either already has raised or would be entitled to raise if he proceeded to trial. If, for example, a defendant pled guilty but prior to that had raised challenges based on an illegal search, improper joinder, or a coerced confession, the plea will normally prevent the defendant from later filing an appeal on these grounds. In rejecting these claims, appellate courts will routinely cite the basic "rule" on this topic: an unconditional guilty plea waives all non-jurisdictional claims that the defendant could have raised.

Notice the qualification: the plea must be "unconditional." Imagine a drug prosecution in which the defendant claims that the key evidence against him is inadmissible because it was seized illegally. Assume the defendant unsuccessfully moved to suppress the evidence in the district court, but believes he may succeed on the issue in the court of appeals. If the defendant's challenge were to prevail, the drug charge would be dismissed because without the drugs there is no case. On the other hand, if the suppression claim were to fail, the defendant would want to plead guilty because the evidence of guilt is clear. The norm in criminal procedure is not to allow interlocutory appeals, so now both the defense and prosecution are in an awkward position. If a guilty plea waived all non-jurisdictional claims, defendant would have to give up his potentially-meritorious challenge to the seizure in order to get the benefit of a guilty plea. On the other hand, it would be unnecessary and wasteful to hold a full trial, where guilt is a foregone conclusion, just to preserve the suppression issue for appeal.

The answer is a conditional guilty plea. Under Rule 11(a)(2), the parties can agree that defendant will plead guilty, thus avoiding an unnecessary trial, while preserving in writing the right to appeal "an adverse determination of a specified pretrial motion." If the defendant loses on appeal, the guilty plea and resulting conviction stand. If the defendant wins, he is allowed to withdraw his guilty plea.

This combination of rules—an unconditional guilty plea waives all non-jurisdictional issues, while a conditional plea identifies those issues that are not waived—is sufficient to answer most of the questions about the effect of a guilty plea. But in a series of decisions culminating in the next case, the Court has made it clear that there are exceptions to these rules.

CLASS v. UNITED STATES
Certiorari to the United States Court of Appeals for the D.C. Circuit
583 U.S. ___ (2018)

Justice Breyer delivered the opinion of the Court.

Does a guilty plea bar a criminal defendant from later appealing his conviction on the ground that the statute of conviction violates the Constitution? In our view, a guilty plea by itself does not bar that appeal.

I

In September 2013, a federal grand jury indicted petitioner, Rodney Class, for possessing firearms in his locked jeep, which was parked in a lot on the grounds of the United States Capitol in Washington, D.C. See 40 U.S.C. § 5104(e)(1) ("An individual . . . may not carry . . . on the Grounds or in any of the Capitol Buildings a firearm"). Soon thereafter, Class, appearing *pro se*, asked the Federal District Court for the District of Columbia to dismiss the indictment. As relevant here, Class alleged that the statute, § 5104(e), violates the Second Amendment. He also raised a due process claim, arguing that he was denied fair notice that weapons were banned in the parking lot. Following a hearing, the District Court denied both claims.

Several months later, Class pleaded guilty to "Possession of a Firearm on U.S. Capitol Grounds, in violation of 40 U.S.C. § 5104(e)." The Government agreed to drop related charges.

A written plea agreement set forth the terms of Class' guilty plea, including several categories of rights that he expressly agreed to waive. Those express waivers included: (1) all defenses based upon the statute of limitations; (2) several specified trial rights; (3) the right to appeal a sentence at or below the judicially determined, maximum sentencing guideline range; (4) most collateral attacks on the conviction and sentence; and (5) various rights to request or receive information concerning the investigation and prosecution of his criminal case. At the same time, the plea agreement expressly enumerated categories of claims that Class could raise on appeal, including claims based upon (1) newly discovered evidence; (2) ineffective assistance of counsel; and (3) certain statutes providing for sentence reductions. Finally, the plea agreement stated under the heading "Complete Agreement":

> "No agreements, promises, understandings, or representations have been made by the parties or their counsel other than those contained in writing herein, nor will any such agreements . . . be made unless committed to writing and signed. . . ."

The agreement said nothing about the right to raise on direct appeal a claim that the statute of conviction was unconstitutional.

The District Court held a plea hearing during which it reviewed the terms of the plea agreement (with Class present and under oath) to ensure the validity of the plea. After providing Class with the required information and warnings, the District Court accepted his guilty plea. Class was sentenced to 24 days imprisonment followed by 12 months of supervised release.

Several days later, Class appealed his conviction to the Court of Appeals for the District of Columbia Circuit. . . . He repeated his constitutional claims, namely, that the statute violates the Second Amendment and the Due Process Clause because it fails to give fair notice of which areas fall within the Capitol Grounds where firearms are banned. The Court of Appeals held that Class could not raise his constitutional claims because, by pleading guilty, he had waived them. . . .

II

The question is whether a guilty plea by itself bars a federal criminal defendant from challenging the constitutionality of the statute of conviction on direct appeal. We hold that it does not. Class did not relinquish his right to appeal the District Court's constitutional determinations simply by pleading guilty. As we shall explain, this holding flows directly from this Court's prior decisions.

Fifty years ago this Court directly addressed a similar claim (a claim that the statute of conviction was unconstitutional). And the Court stated that a defendant's "plea of guilty did not . . . waive his previous [constitutional] claim." Haynes v. United States, 390 U.S. 85, 87, n.2 (1968). Though Justice Harlan's opinion for the Court in *Haynes* offered little explanation for this statement, subsequent decisions offered a rationale that applies here.

In Blackledge v. Perry, 417 U.S. 21 (1974), North Carolina indicted and convicted Jimmy Seth Perry on a misdemeanor assault charge. When Perry exercised his right under a North Carolina statute to a *de novo* trial in a higher court, the State reindicted him, but this time the State charged a felony, which carried a heavier penalty, for the same conduct. Perry pleaded guilty. He then sought habeas relief on the grounds that the reindictment amounted to an unconstitutional vindictive prosecution. The State argued that Perry's guilty plea barred him from raising his constitutional challenge. But this Court held that it did not.

The Court noted that a guilty plea bars appeal of many claims, including some "'antecedent constitutional violations'" related to events (say, grand jury proceedings) that had "'occurred prior to the entry of the guilty plea.'" Id., at 30 (quoting Tollett v. Henderson, 411 U.S. 258, 266-267 (1973)). While *Tollett* claims were "of constitutional dimension," the Court explained that "the nature of the underlying constitutional infirmity is markedly different" from a claim of vindictive prosecution, which implicates "the very power of the State" to prosecute the defendant. Accordingly, the Court wrote that "the right" Perry "asserts and that we today accept is the right not to be haled into court at all upon the felony charge" since "[t]he very initiation of the proceedings" against Perry "operated to deprive him due process of law." Id., at 30-31.

A year and a half later, in Menna v. New York, 423 U.S. 61 (1975) (per curiam), this Court repeated what it had said and held in *Blackledge*. After Menna served a 30-day jail term for refusing to testify before the grand jury on November 7, 1968, the State of New York charged him once again for (what Menna argued was) the same crime. Menna pleaded guilty, but subsequently appealed arguing that the new charge violated the Double Jeopardy Clause. The lower courts held that Menna's constitutional claim had been "waived" by his guilty plea.

This Court reversed. Citing *Blackledge*, the Court held that "a plea of guilty to a charge does not waive a claim that—judged on its face—the charge is one which the State may not constitutionally prosecute." *Menna*, 423 U.S., at 63, and n.2. Menna's claim amounted to a claim that "the

State may not convict" him "no matter how validly his factual guilt is established." Menna's "guilty plea, therefore, [did] not bar the claim." . . .

In more recent years, we have reaffirmed the *Menna-Blackledge* doctrine and refined its scope. In United States v. Broce, 488 U.S. 563 (1989), the defendants pleaded guilty to two separate indictments in a single proceeding which "on their face" described two separate bid-rigging conspiracies. They later sought to challenge their convictions on double jeopardy grounds, arguing that they had only admitted to one conspiracy. Citing *Blackledge* and *Menna*, this Court repeated that a guilty plea does not bar a claim on appeal "where on the face of the record the court had no power to enter the conviction or impose the sentence." 488 U.S., at 569. However, because the defendants could not "prove their claim by relying on those indictments and the existing record" and "without contradicting those indictments," this Court held that their claims were "foreclosed by the admissions inherent in their guilty pleas." Id., at 576.

Unlike the claims in *Broce*, Class' constitutional claims here, as we understand them, do not contradict the terms of the indictment or the written plea agreement. They are consistent with Class' knowing, voluntary, and intelligent admission that he did what the indictment alleged. Those claims can be "resolved without any need to venture beyond that record."

Nor do Class' claims focus upon case-related constitutional defects that "'occurred prior to the entry of the guilty plea.'" *Blackledge*, 417 U.S., at 30. They could not, for example, "have been 'cured' through a new indictment by a properly selected grand jury." Ibid. (citing *Tollett*, 411 U.S., at 267). Because the defendant has admitted the charges against him, a guilty plea makes the latter kind of constitutional claim "irrelevant to the constitutional validity of the conviction." Haring v. Prosise, 462 U.S. 306, 321 (1983). But the cases to which we have referred make clear that a defendant's guilty plea does not make irrelevant the kind of constitutional claim Class seeks to make.

In sum, the claims at issue here do not fall within any of the categories of claims that Class' plea agreement forbids him to raise on direct appeal. They challenge the Government's power to criminalize Class' (admitted) conduct. They thereby call into question the Government's power to "'constitutionally prosecute'" him. A guilty plea does not bar a direct appeal in these circumstances.

III

We are not convinced by the three basic arguments that the Government and the dissent make in reply. . . .

As an initial matter, a valid guilty plea "forgoes not only a fair trial, but also other accompanying constitutional guarantees." [United States v. Ruiz, 536 U.S. 622, 628-629 (2002)]. While those "simultaneously" relinquished rights include the privilege against compulsory self-incrimination, the jury trial right, and the right to confront accusers, they do not include "a waiver of the privileges which exist beyond the confines of the trial." Mitchell v. United States, 526 U.S. 314, 324 (1999). Here, Class' statutory right directly to appeal his conviction "cannot in any way be characterized as part of the trial." Lafler v. Cooper, 566 U.S. 156, 165 (2012).

A valid guilty plea also renders irrelevant—and thereby prevents the defendant from appealing—the constitutionality of case-related government conduct that takes place before the plea is entered. See, e.g., *Haring,* supra, at 320 (holding a valid guilty plea "results in the defendant's loss of any meaningful opportunity he might otherwise have had to challenge the admissibility of evidence obtained in violation of the Fourth Amendment"). Neither can the defendant later complain that the indicting grand jury was unconstitutionally selected. But, as we have said, those kinds of claims are not at issue here.

Finally, a valid guilty plea relinquishes any claim that would contradict the "admissions necessarily made upon entry of a voluntary plea of guilty." *Broce,* supra, at 573-574. But the constitutional claim at issue here is consistent with Class' admission that he engaged in the conduct alleged in the indictment. Unlike the defendants in *Broce,* Class' challenge does not in any way deny that he engaged in the conduct to which he admitted. Instead, like the defendants in *Blackledge* and *Menna,* he seeks to raise a claim which, "'judged on its face'" based upon the existing record, would extinguish the government's power to "'constitutionally prosecute'" the defendant if the claim were successful.

Second, the Government and the dissent point to Rule 11(a)(2) of the Federal Rules of Criminal Procedure, which governs "conditional" guilty pleas. The Rule states:

> "*Conditional Plea.* With the consent of the court and the government, a defendant may enter a conditional plea of guilty or nolo contendere, reserving in writing the right to have an appellate court review an adverse determination of a specified pretrial motion. A defendant who prevails on appeal may then withdraw the plea."

The Government and the dissent argue that Rule 11(a)(2) means that "a defendant who pleads guilty *cannot* challenge his conviction on appeal on a forfeitable or waivable ground that he either failed to present to the district court or failed to reserve in writing." Brief for United States 23; see also post (opinion of Alito, J.). They support this argument by pointing to the notes of the Advisory Committee that drafted the text of Rule 11(a)(2). See Advisory Committee's Notes on 1983 Amendments to Fed. Rule Crim. Proc. 11, (hereinafter Advisory Committee's Notes). In particular, the dissent points to the suggestion that an unconditional guilty plea constitutes a waiver of "nonjurisdictional defects," while the Government points to the drafters' statement that they intended the Rule's "conditional plea procedure . . . to conserve prosecutorial and judicial resources and advance speedy trial objectives," while ensuring "much needed uniformity in the federal system on this matter." . . .

The problem with this argument is that, by its own terms, the Rule itself does not say whether it sets forth the *exclusive* procedure for a defendant to preserve a constitutional claim following a guilty plea. At the same time, the drafters' notes acknowledge that the "Supreme Court has held that certain kinds of constitutional objections may be raised after a plea of guilty." The notes then specifically refer to the *"Menna-Blackledge* doctrine." They add that the Rule "should not be interpreted as either broadening or narrowing [that] doctrine or as establishing procedures for its application." And the notes state that Rule 11(a)(2) "has no application" to the "kinds of constitutional objections" that may be raised under that doctrine. . . . We therefore hold that Rule 11(a)(2) cannot resolve this case.

Third, the Government argues that Class "expressly waived" his right to appeal his constitutional claim. The Government concedes that the written plea agreement, which sets forth the "Complete Agreement" between Class and the Government does not contain this waiver. Rather, the Government relies on the fact that during the Rule 11 plea colloquy, the District Court Judge stated that, under the written plea agreement, Class was "giving up [his] right to appeal [his] conviction." And Class agreed.

We do not see why the District Court Judge's statement should bar Class' constitutional claims. It was made to ensure Class understood "the terms of any plea-agreement provision waiving the right to appeal or to collaterally attack the sentence." Fed. Rule Crim. Proc. 11(b)(1)(N). It does not expressly refer to a waiver of the appeal right here at issue. And if it is interpreted as expressly including that appeal right, it was wrong, as the Government acknowledged at oral argument. Under these circumstances, Class' acquiescence neither expressly nor implicitly waived his right to appeal his constitutional claims.

* * *

For these reasons, we hold that Rodney Class may pursue his consti-tutional claims on direct appeal. The contrary judgment of the Court of Appeals for the District of Columbia Circuit is reversed, and the case is remanded for further proceedings consistent with this opinion.

JUSTICE ALITO, with whom JUSTICE KENNEDY and JUSTICE THOMAS join, dissenting.

Roughly 95% of felony cases in the federal and state courts are resolved by guilty pleas. Therefore it is critically important that defendants, pros-ecutors, and judges understand the consequences of these pleas. In this case, the parties have asked us to identify the claims that a defendant can raise on appeal after entering an unconditional guilty plea. Regrettably, the Court provides no clear answer.

By my count, the Court identifies no fewer than five rules for ascertain-ing the issues that can be raised. According to the Court, a defendant who pleads guilty may assert on appeal (1) a claim that "implicates 'the very power of the State' to prosecute [him]," (2) a claim that does not contra-dict the facts alleged in the charging document, (3) a claim that "'the facts alleged and admitted do not constitute a crime,'" and (4) claims other than "case-related constitutional defects that 'occurred prior to the entry of the guilty plea'" (some internal quotation marks omitted). In addition, the Court suggests (5) that such a defendant may not be able to assert a claim that "contradict[s] the terms of . . . [a] written plea agreement," but whether this rule applies when the claim falls into one of the prior four categories is left unclear. How these rules fit together is anybody's guess. And to make matters worse, the Court also fails to make clear whether its holding is based on the Constitution or some other ground.

I

. . . Rule 11 of the Federal Rules of Criminal Procedure makes it clear that, with one exception that I will discuss below, a defendant who enters an unconditional plea waives all nonjurisdictional claims. Although the Rule does not say this expressly, that is the unmistakable implication of subdivision (a)(2), which allows a defendant, "[w]ith the consent of the court and the government," to "enter a conditional plea of guilty or nolo contendere, reserving in writing the right to have an appellate court review an adverse determination of a specified pretrial motion." "Where [a law] explicitly enumerates certain exceptions to a general prohibition, addi-tional exceptions are not to be implied, in the absence of evidence of a contrary . . . intent." Andrus v. Glover Constr. Co., 446 U.S. 608, 616-617

(1980). And here, there is strong evidence confirming that other exceptions were ruled out.

The Advisory Committee's Notes on Rule 11 make this clear, stating that an unconditional plea (with the previously mentioned exception) "constitutes a waiver of all nonjurisdictional defects." Notes on 1983 Amendments, 18 U.S.C. App., p. 911. Advisory Committee's Notes on a federal rule of procedure "provide a reliable source of insight into the meaning of a rule, especially when, as here, the rule was enacted precisely as the Advisory Committee proposed." United States v. Vonn, 535 U.S. 55, 64, n. 6 [(2002)]. . . .

II

A

I now turn to the one exception mentioned in the Advisory Committee's Notes on Rule 11—what the Notes, rather grandly, term the "*Menna-Blackledge* doctrine." This "doctrine" consists of Blackledge v. Perry, 417 U.S. 21 (1974), a thinly reasoned decision handed down 44 years ago, and Menna v. New York, 423 U.S. 61 (1975) (per curiam), a per curiam decision issued the next year. These cases hold that a defendant has the right under the Due Process Clause of the Fourteenth Amendment to contest certain issues on appeal even if the defendant entered an unconditional guilty plea. . . .

B

Blackledge and *Menna* represented marked departures from our prior decisions. Before they were handed down, our precedents were clear: When a defendant pleaded guilty to a crime, he relinquished his right to litigate all nonjurisdictional challenges to his conviction (except for the claim that his plea was not voluntary and intelligent), and the prosecution could assert this forfeiture to defeat a subsequent appeal. The theory was easy to understand. As we explained in *Tollett*, our view was that "a guilty plea represents a break in the chain of events which has preceded it in the criminal process." 411 U.S., at 267. . . .

III

Blackledge and *Menna* diverged from these prior precedents, but neither case provided a clear or coherent explanation for the departure.

A

In *Blackledge*, the Court held that a defendant who pleaded guilty could nevertheless challenge his conviction on the ground that his right to due process was violated by a vindictive prosecution. The Court asserted that this right was "markedly different" from the equal protection and Fifth Amendment rights at stake in *Tollett* and the *Brady* trilogy because it "went to the very power of the State to bring the defendant into court to answer the charge brought against him." The meaning of this distinction, however, is hard to grasp.

The most natural way to understand *Blackledge*'s reference to "the very power of the State" would be to say that an argument survives a guilty plea if it attacks the court's jurisdiction. After all, that is usually what we mean when we refer to the power to adjudicate. See, e.g., Arbaugh v. Y & H Corp., 546 U.S. 500, 514 (2006). But that cannot be what *Blackledge* meant.

First, the defendant in *Blackledge* had been tried in state court in North Carolina for a state-law offense, and the jurisdiction of state courts to entertain such prosecutions is purely a matter of state law (unless Congress validly and affirmatively ousts their jurisdiction—something that had not happened in that case). Second, a rule that jurisdictional defects alone survive a guilty plea would not explain the result in *Blackledge* itself. Arguments attacking a court's subject-matter jurisdiction can neither be waived nor forfeited. But the due process right at issue in *Blackledge* was perfectly capable of being waived or forfeited—as is just about every other right that is personal to a criminal defendant.

So if the "very power to prosecute" theory does not refer to jurisdiction, what else might it mean? The only other possibility that comes to mind is that it might mean that a defendant can litigate a claim if it asserts a right not to be tried, as opposed to a right not to be convicted. But we have said that "virtually all rights of criminal defendants" are "merely . . . right[s] not to be convicted," as distinguished from "right[s] not to be tried." Flanagan v. United States, 465 U.S. 259, 267 (1984). Even when a constitutional violation requires the dismissal of an indictment, that "does not mean that [the] defendant enjoy[ed] a 'right not to be tried'" on the charges. United States v. MacDonald, 435 U.S. 850, 860, n.7 (1978).

The rule could hardly be otherwise. Most constitutional defenses (and plenty of statutory defenses), if successfully asserted in a pretrial motion, deprive the prosecution of the "power" to proceed to trial or secure a conviction. If that remedial consequence converted them all into rights not to be prosecuted, *Blackledge* would have no discernible limit. . . .

The upshot is that the supposed "right not to be prosecuted" has no intelligible meaning in this context. And *Blackledge* identified no basis for this new right in the text of the Constitution or history or prior precedent. . . .

B

If the thinking behind *Blackledge* is hard to follow, *Menna* may be worse. In that case, the Court held that a defendant who pleaded guilty could challenge his conviction on double jeopardy grounds. The case was decided by a three-page per curiam opinion, its entire analysis confined to a single footnote. And the footnote, rather than elucidating what was said in *Blackledge*, substituted a different rationale. Arguing that *Tollett* and the other prior related cases did not preclude appellate review of the double jeopardy claim, the Court wrote:

> "[A] counseled plea of guilty is an admission of factual guilt so reliable that, where voluntary and intelligent, it *quite validly* removes the issue of factual guilt from the case. In most cases, factual guilt is a sufficient basis for the State's imposition of punishment. A guilty plea, therefore, simply renders irrelevant those constitutional violations not logically inconsistent with the valid establishment of factual guilt." *Menna*, 423 U.S., at 62-63, n.2.

The wording of the final sentence is not easy to parse, but I interpret the Court's reasoning as follows: A defendant who pleads guilty does no more than admit that he committed the essential conduct charged in the indictment; therefore a guilty plea allows the litigation on appeal of any claim that is not inconsistent with the facts that the defendant necessarily admitted. If that is the correct meaning, the sentence would overrule many of the cases that it purported to distinguish, including *Tollett*, which involved an unconstitutional grand jury claim. . . .

C

When the Court returned to *Blackledge* and *Menna* in United States v. Broce, 488 U.S. 563 (1989), the Court essentially repudiated the theories offered in those earlier cases. (The Court [in the current case] terms this a "reaffirm[ation].") Like *Menna*, *Broce* involved a defendant (actually two defendants) who pleaded guilty but then sought to attack their convictions on double jeopardy grounds. This time, however, the Court held that their guilty pleas prevented them from litigating their claims.

The Court began by specifically disavowing *Menna*'s suggestion that a guilty plea admits only "'factual guilt,'" meaning "the acts described in the indictments." *Broce,* 488 U.S., at 568-569. Instead, the Court explained, an unconditional guilty plea admits "all of the factual *and legal elements* necessary to sustain a binding, final judgment of guilt and a lawful sentence." Id., at 569 (emphasis added). "By entering a plea of guilty, the accused is not simply stating that he did the discrete acts described in the indictment; he is admitting guilt of a substantive crime." Id., at 570. Such "admissions," *Broce* continued, are "necessarily made upon entry of a voluntary plea of guilty." Id., at 573-574. And invoking *Tollett,* the Court added that it makes no difference whether the defendant "'may not have correctly appraised the constitutional significance of certain historical facts.'" 488 U.S., at 572 (quoting 411 U.S., at 267). Thus, the Court concluded, a defendant's decision to plead guilty necessarily extinguishes whatever "potential defense[s]" he might have asserted in an effort to show that it would be unlawful to hold him liable for his conduct. 488 U.S., at 573. So much for *Menna.*

As for *Blackledge,* by holding that the defendants' double jeopardy rights were extinguished by their pleas, *Broce* necessarily rejected the idea that a right not to be tried survives an unconditional guilty plea. . . .

* * *

In sum, the governing law in the present case is Rule 11 of the Federal Rules of Criminal Procedure. Under that Rule, an unconditional guilty plea waives all nonjurisdictional claims with the possible exception of the "*Menna-Blackledge* doctrine" created years ago by this Court. That doctrine is vacuous, has no sound foundation, and produces nothing but confusion. At a minimum, I would limit the doctrine to the particular types of claims involved in those cases. I certainly would not expand its reach.

I fear that today's decision will bedevil the lower courts. I respectfully dissent.

NOTES AND QUESTIONS

1. The holding in *Class* is clear—an unconditional guilty plea does not operate as a waiver of the right to challenge the constitutionality of the statute to which the defendant has pled guilty—but does the rationale give a satisfactory explanation for which issues are preserved after an unconditional plea? If you were a defense lawyer, how would you explain to a client what claims he would be giving up if he pleads guilty?

2. Part of the disagreement between the majority and the dissent is over the effect of Rule 11(a)(2), which governs conditional pleas. The majority is surely correct that "by its own terms, the Rule itself does not say whether it sets forth the *exclusive* procedure for a defendant to preserve a constitutional claim following a guilty plea." It is also correct that the Rules drafters recognized that Menna v. New York, 423 U.S. 61 (1975) and Blackledge v. Perry, 417 U.S. 21 (1974), created exceptions to the general waiver rule. But isn't the dissent right to suggest (implicitly) that conditional pleas *should* be the exclusive tool to preserve claims for appeal? Doesn't a written reservation of the issues to be appealed reduce the chances of confusion and mistake about what the defendant believes he is doing when he pleads guilty? Stated differently, what values are advanced by allowing a defendant like Class to challenge the constitutionality of the criminal statute even though he did not reserve the right to do so when he pled guilty? Does the fact that a prosecutor and the court must consent to any conditional plea of guilty affect your answer?

3. Perhaps the disagreement between the majority and the dissent will ultimately make little difference. Is there anything in the *Class* opinion that would prevent prosecutors from insisting on a waiver of the right to challenge the constitutionality of a controversial statute as part of a guilty plea? Even if the defendant were to receive a benefit from agreeing to this additional term in a plea deal, are there societal costs imposed in allowing a challenge to a potentially unconstitutional statute to be waived so easily?

B. Plea Bargaining

3. The Subject Matter of Plea Bargaining

Insert the following new paragraph at the end of Note 4 on page 1286:

In Garza v. Idaho, 586 U.S. ___ (2019), the Court held that even where the defendant signed a waiver of the right to appeal in connection with a plea bargain, the defendant's lawyer renders ineffective assistance—with a presumption of prejudice—if she refuses to file a notice of appeal upon the defendant's request. The *Garza* case is discussed further in Chapter 3, at page 179.

4. Plea Bargains as Contracts

c. *Remedies for Breach of Contract*

On page 1311, in Note 1, replace the first sentence of the second paragraph with the following new sentence:

On the other hand, *Santobello* is quite different from the "other" *Brady* decision, (Brady v. Maryland, 373 U.S. 73 (1963), discussed in Chapter 12, Section A.3), which requires prosecutors to disclose information favorable to the accused and material to guilt or punishment.

Insert the following new paragraph at the end of Note 5 on page 1313:

In 2017, the Supreme Court reaffirmed *Santobello*'s conclusion that the remedy for a prosecutor's breach of the plea agreement is a decision entrusted to the sound discretion of the trial court. The Court reversed a Ninth Circuit decision holding that a State court had acted "contrary to clearly established Supreme Court law" when it put the parties back in the position they were in before the breach, rather than order specific performance as the defendant had requested. "[N]o holdin[g] of this Court requires the remedy of specific performance under the circumstances present here." Kernan v. Cuero, 583 U.S. ___ (2017) (per curiam) (internal quotation marks omitted).

Chapter 14

The Jury and the Criminal Trial

B. Jury Composition

Insert the following after the first full paragraph on page 1375:

On the other hand, a third *Batson* case that follows *Miller-El* shows that complex statistical analysis is not always needed, and perhaps shows that the Supreme Court's patience with lower court acceptance of prosecutor's explanations is limited. In Foster v. Chatman, 578 U.S. ___ (2016), the Court, in a majority opinion by Chief Justice Roberts with only Justice Thomas dissenting, found a *Batson* violation in a 30-year old capital case. Reversing the state court's contrary conclusions, the Court found the prosecutor's voir dire notes highly suggestive: Those notes contained explicit information about exactly which jurors were Black, all six of the prospective Black jurors were marked "definite NO's," and the notes further indicated that jurors who belonged to a Black church were unacceptable ("NO. No Black Church"). The Court concluded that the prosecutor's alleged race-neutral explanations were inconsistent with the record (even referring to one of those explanations as "nonsense"). The prosecutor claimed, for example, that one Black juror was struck because she was divorced and too young at age 34, and while the trial judge accepted this explanation, the Court did not, noting that three of the four divorced white prospective jurors were allowed to serve, and eight white prospective jurors under age 36 were allowed to serve. The Court also rejected the prosecutor's claim that it was keeping detailed notes on race in order to defend against a prospective *Batson* challenge. That explanation, said the majority, "reeks of afterthought, having never before been made in the nearly 30-year history of this litigation."

For more of the same, see Flowers v. Mississippi, 588 U.S. ___ (2019), where the state (via the same prosecutor) persistently pursued, over six (!) trials, what any reasonable observer would conclude was a deliberately racist jury selection process. The Court reversed; Justice Thomas, in dissent, argued for overruling *Batson* on the ground that "race matters in the courtroom," and thus litigants should be allowed to use their peremptories freely "to combat prejudice in their cases."

E. Proof and Verdict Issues

4. Impeachment of the Verdict

Add the following paragraph, main case, and Notes after the last paragraph of Section E.4., on page 1457:

The interests in finality, and in jurors being left alone once the case was over, is surely a weighty one. But suppose evidence comes to light after a verdict that one or more of the jurors made their decision on the basis of racial stereotypes. This would seem to be an "internal" influence on the verdict, as it is the product of the jurors' own beliefs and experiences rather than the product of some outside force, and thus would seem barred by Federal Rule of Evidence 606(b) and cases like *Tanner*. But should racial bias during jury deliberations be different? The Court took up this issue in next case.

PEÑA-RODRIGUEZ v. COLORADO
Certiorari to the Supreme Court of Colorado
580 U.S. __ (2017)

JUSTICE KENNEDY delivered the opinion of the Court.

. . .

Like all human institutions, the jury system has its flaws, yet experience shows that fair and impartial verdicts can be reached if the jury follows the court's instructions and undertakes deliberations that are honest, candid, robust, and based on common sense. A general rule has evolved to give substantial protection to verdict finality and to assure jurors that, once their verdict has been entered, it will not later be called into question based on the comments or conclusions they expressed during deliberations. This principle, itself centuries old, is often referred to as the no-impeachment rule. The instant case presents the question whether there is an exception to the no-impeachment rule when, after the jury is discharged, a juror comes forward with compelling evidence that another juror made clear and explicit statements indicating that racial animus was a significant motivating factor in his or her vote to convict.

I

State prosecutors in Colorado brought criminal charges against petitioner, Miguel Angel Peña-Rodriguez, based on the following allegations. In 2007, in the bathroom of a Colorado horse-racing facility, a man sexually assaulted two teenage sisters. The girls told their father and identified the man as an employee of the racetrack. The police located and arrested petitioner. Each girl separately identified petitioner as the man who had assaulted her.

The State charged petitioner with harassment, unlawful sexual contact, and attempted sexual assault on a child.

. . .

After a 3-day trial, the jury found petitioner guilty of unlawful sexual contact and harassment, but it failed to reach a verdict on the attempted sexual assault charge.

. . .

Following the discharge of the jury, petitioner's counsel entered the jury room to discuss the trial with the jurors. As the room was emptying, two jurors remained to speak with counsel in private. They stated that, during deliberations, another juror had expressed anti-Hispanic bias toward petitioner and petitioner's alibi witness. Petitioner's counsel reported this to the court and, with the court's supervision, obtained sworn affidavits from the two jurors.

The affidavits by the two jurors described a number of biased statements made by another juror, identified as Juror H.C. According to the two jurors, H.C. told the other jurors that he "believed the defendant was guilty because, in [H.C.'s] experience as an ex-law enforcement officer, Mexican men had a bravado that caused them to believe they could do whatever they wanted with women." The jurors reported that H.C. stated his belief that Mexican men are physically controlling of women because of their sense of entitlement, and further stated, "'I think he did it because he's Mexican and Mexican men take whatever they want.'" According to the jurors, H.C. further explained that, in his experience, "nine times out of ten Mexican men were guilty of being aggressive toward women and young girls." Finally, the jurors recounted that Juror H.C. said that he did not find petitioner's alibi witness credible because, among other things, the witness was "'an illegal.'" (In fact, the witness testified during trial that he was a legal resident of the United States.)

After reviewing the affidavits, the trial court acknowledged H.C.'s apparent bias. But the court denied petitioner's motion for a new trial, noting that "[t]he actual deliberations that Proof and Verdict Issues",6,4?> occur among the jurors are protected from inquiry under [Colorado Rule of

Evidence] 606(b)." Id., at 90. Like its federal counterpart, Colorado's Rule 606(b) generally prohibits a juror from testifying as to any statement made during deliberations in a proceeding inquiring into the validity of the verdict. See Fed. Rule Evid. 606(b).

The verdict deemed final, petitioner was sentenced to two years' probation and was required to register as a sex offender. A divided panel of the Colorado Court of Appeals affirmed petitioner's conviction, agreeing that H.C.'s alleged statements did not fall within an exception to Rule 606(b) and so were inadmissible to undermine the validity of the verdict.

The Colorado Supreme Court affirmed by a vote of 4 to 3. The prevailing opinion relied on two decisions of this Court rejecting constitutional challenges to the federal no-impeachment rule as applied to evidence of juror misconduct or bias. See Tanner v. United States, 483 U.S. 107 (1987); Warger v. Shauers, 135 S. Ct. 521 (2014). After reviewing those precedents, the court could find no "dividing line between different *types* of juror bias or misconduct," and thus no basis for permitting impeachment of the verdicts in petitioner's trial, notwithstanding H.C.'s apparent racial bias. This Court granted certiorari to decide whether there is a constitutional exception to the no-impeachment rule for instances of racial bias.

Juror H.C.'s bias was based on petitioner's Hispanic identity, which the Court in prior cases has referred to as ethnicity, and that may be an instructive term here. Yet we have also used the language of race when discussing the relevant constitutional principles in cases involving Hispanic persons. Petitioner and respondent both refer to race, or to race and ethnicity, in this more expansive sense in their briefs to the Court. This opinion refers to the nature of the bias as racial in keeping with the primary terminology employed by the parties and used in our precedents.

II

A

[In this part of the opinion, the Court traces the history of the rule that prevents jurors from impeaching their own verdict, noting that the Federal Rules had adopted "a broad no-impeachment rule, with only limited exceptions," while some States adopted a more lenient rule. With respect to the Federal Rule, Fed. R. Evid. 606(b), the Court noted that "[t]his version of the no-impeachment rule has substantial merit. It promotes full and vigorous discussion by providing jurors with considerable assurance that after being discharged they will not be summoned to recount their deliberations, and they will not otherwise be harassed or annoyed by litigants seeking to challenge the verdict. The rule gives stability and finality to verdicts."—EDS.]

B

Some version of the no-impeachment rule is followed in every State and the District of Columbia. Variations make classification imprecise, but, as a general matter, it appears that 42 jurisdictions follow the Federal Rule, while 9 follow [a more lenient rule]. Within both classifications there is a diversity of approaches. Nine jurisdictions that follow the Federal Rule have codified exceptions other than those listed in Federal Rule 606(b).[1] At least 16 jurisdictions, 11 of which follow the Federal Rule, have recognized an exception to the no-impeachment bar under the circumstances the Court faces here: juror testimony that racial bias played a part in deliberations. According to the parties and *amici*, only one State other than Colorado has addressed this issue and declined to recognize an exception for racial bias. See Commonwealth v. Steele, 961 A.2d 786 (Pa. 2008).

. . .

C

In addressing the scope of the common-law no-impeachment rule before Rule 606(b)'s adoption, . . . Courts noted the possibility of an exception to the rule in the "gravest and most important cases." [See United States v. Reid, 12 How. 361, 366, 13 L. Ed. 1023 (1852); McDonald v. Pless, 238 U.S. 264, 269 (1915).] Yet since the enactment of Rule 606(b), the Court has addressed the precise question whether the Constitution mandates an exception to it in just two instances.

In its first case, *Tanner*, 483 U.S. 107, the Court rejected a Sixth Amendment exception for evidence that some jurors were under the influence of drugs and alcohol during the trial. Central to the Court's reasoning were the "long-recognized and very substantial concerns" supporting "the protection of jury deliberations from intrusive inquiry." The *Tanner* Court echoed *McDonald*'s concern that, if attorneys could use juror testimony to attack verdicts, jurors would be "harassed and beset by the defeated party," thus destroying "all frankness and freedom of discussion and conference." The Court was concerned, moreover, that attempts to impeach a verdict

---

1. [An appendix to the opinion listing the different state approaches has been omitted.—EDS.]

would "disrupt the finality of the process" and undermine both "jurors' willingness to return an unpopular verdict" and "the community's trust in a system that relies on the decisions of laypeople."

. . .

The second case to consider the general issue presented here was *Warger*, 135 S. Ct. 521. The Court again rejected the argument that, in the circumstances there, the jury trial right required an exception to the no-impeachment rule. *Warger* involved a civil case where, after the verdict was entered, the losing party sought to proffer evidence that the jury forewoman had failed to disclose prodefendant bias during *voir dire*. As in *Tanner*, the Court put substantial reliance on existing safeguards for a fair trial. The Court stated: "Even if jurors lie in *voir dire* in a way that conceals bias, juror impartiality is adequately assured by the parties' ability to bring to the court's attention any evidence of bias before the verdict is rendered, and to employ nonjuror evidence even after the verdict is rendered."

In *Warger*, however, the Court did reiterate that the no-impeachment rule may admit exceptions. As in *Reid* and *McDonald*, the Court warned of "juror bias so extreme that, almost by definition, the jury trial right has been abridged." 135 S. Ct., at 529, n. 3. "If and when such a case arises," the Court indicated it would "consider whether the usual safeguards are or are not sufficient to protect the integrity of the process."

. . .

III

It must become the heritage of our Nation to rise above racial classifications that are so inconsistent with our commitment to the equal dignity of all persons. This imperative to purge racial prejudice from the administration of justice was given new force and direction by the ratification of the Civil War Amendments.

"[T]he central purpose of the Fourteenth Amendment was to eliminate racial discrimination emanating from official sources in the States." McLaughlin v. Florida, 379 U.S. 184, 192 (1964). In the years before and after the ratification of the Fourteenth Amendment, it became clear that racial discrimination in the jury system posed a particular threat both to the promise of the Amendment and to the integrity of the jury trial. "Almost immediately after the Civil War, the South began a practice that would continue for many decades: All-white juries punished black defendants particularly harshly, while simultaneously refusing to punish violence by whites, including Ku Klux Klan members, against blacks and Republicans." Forman, Juries and Race in the Nineteenth Century, 113 Yale L.J. 895, 909-910 (2004).

To take one example, just in the years 1865 and 1866, all-white juries in Texas decided a total of 500 prosecutions of white defendants charged with killing African-Americans. All 500 were acquitted. Id., at 916. . . .

The duty to confront racial animus in the justice system is not the legislature's alone. Time and again, this Court has been called upon to enforce the Constitution's guarantee against state-sponsored racial discrimination in the jury system. Beginning in 1880, the Court interpreted the Fourteenth Amendment to prohibit the exclusion of jurors on the basis of race. Strauder v. West Virginia, 100 U.S. 303, 305-309 (1880). The Court has repeatedly struck down laws and practices that systematically exclude racial minorities from juries. See, e.g., Neal v. Delaware, 103 U.S. 370 (1881); Hollins v. Oklahoma, 295 U.S. 394 (1935) (per curiam); Avery v. Georgia, 345 U.S. 559 (1953); Hernandez v. Texas, 347 U.S. 475 (1954); Castaneda v. Partida, 430 U.S. 482 (1977). To guard against discrimination in jury selection, the Court has ruled that no litigant may exclude a prospective juror on the basis of race. Batson v. Kentucky, 476 U.S. 79 (1986); Edmonson v. Leesville Concrete Co., 500 U.S. 614 (1991); Georgia v. McCollum, 505 U.S. 42 (1992). In an effort to ensure that individuals who sit on juries are free of racial bias, the Court has held that the Constitution at times demands that defendants be permitted to ask questions about racial bias during voir dire. Ham v. South Carolina, 409 U.S. 524 (1973); Rosales-Lopez, 451 U.S. 182S; Turner v. Murray, 476 U.S. 28 (1986).

The unmistakable principle underlying these precedents is that discrimination on the basis of race, "odious in all aspects, is especially pernicious in the administration of justice." Rose v. Mitchell, 443 U.S. 545, 555 (1979).

IV

A

This case lies at the intersection of the Court's decisions endorsing the no-impeachment rule and its decisions seeking to eliminate racial bias in the jury system. The two lines of precedent, however, need not conflict.

Racial bias of the kind alleged in this case differs in critical ways from the compromise verdict in *McDonald*, the drug and alcohol abuse in *Tanner*, or the pro-defendant bias in *Warger*. The behavior in those cases is troubling and unacceptable, but each involved anomalous behavior from a single jury—or juror—gone off course. Jurors are presumed to follow their oath, and neither history nor common experience show that the jury system is rife with mischief of these or similar kinds. To attempt to rid the jury of every irregularity of this sort would be to expose it to unrelenting scrutiny.

"It is not at all clear . . . that the jury system could survive such efforts to perfect it." *Tanner,* 483 U.S., at 120.

The same cannot be said about racial bias, a familiar and recurring evil that, if left unaddressed, would risk systemic injury to the administration of justice. This Court's decisions demonstrate that racial bias implicates unique historical, constitutional, and institutional concerns. An effort to address the most grave and serious statements of racial bias is not an effort to perfect the jury but to ensure that our legal system remains capable of coming ever closer to the promise of equal treatment under the law that is so central to a functioning democracy.

Racial bias is distinct in a pragmatic sense as well. In past cases this Court has relied on other safeguards to protect the right to an impartial jury. Some of those safeguards, to be sure, can disclose racial bias. *Voir dire* at the outset of trial, observation of juror demeanor and conduct during trial, juror reports before the verdict, and nonjuror evidence after trial are important mechanisms for discovering bias. Yet their operation may be compromised, or they may prove insufficient.

The stigma that attends racial bias may make it difficult for a juror to report inappropriate statements during the course of juror deliberations. It is one thing to accuse a fellow juror of having a personal experience that improperly influences her consideration of the case, as would have been required in *Warger.* It is quite another to call her a bigot.

The recognition that certain of the *Tanner* safeguards may be less effective in rooting out racial bias than other kinds of bias is not dispositive. All forms of improper bias pose challenges to the trial process. But there is a sound basis to treat racial bias with added precaution. . . .

B

For the reasons explained above, the Court now holds that where a juror makes a clear statement that indicates he or she relied on racial stereotypes or animus to convict a criminal defendant, the Sixth Amendment requires that the no-impeachment rule give way in order to permit the trial court to consider the evidence of the juror's statement and any resulting denial of the jury trial guarantee.

Not every offhand comment indicating racial bias or hostility will justify setting aside the no-impeachment bar to allow further judicial inquiry. For the inquiry to proceed, there must be a showing that one or more jurors made statements exhibiting overt racial bias that cast serious doubt on the fairness and impartiality of the jury's deliberations and resulting verdict. To qualify, the statement must tend to show that racial animus was a significant motivating factor in the juror's vote to convict. Whether that threshold showing has been satisfied is a matter committed to the substantial discretion of the trial court in light of all the circumstances, including the content and timing of the alleged statements and the reliability of the proffered evidence.

The practical mechanics of acquiring and presenting such evidence will no doubt be shaped and guided by state rules of professional ethics and local court rules, both of which often limit counsel's post-trial contact with jurors. These limits seek to provide jurors some protection when they return to their daily affairs after the verdict has been entered. But while a juror can always tell counsel they do not wish to discuss the case, jurors in some instances may come forward of their own accord.

That is what happened here. In this case the alleged statements by a juror were egregious and unmistakable in their reliance on racial bias. Not only did juror H.C. deploy a dangerous racial stereotype to conclude petitioner was guilty and his alibi witness should not be believed, but he also encouraged other jurors to join him in convicting on that basis.

. . .

C

As the preceding discussion makes clear, the Court relies on the experiences of the 17 jurisdictions that have recognized a racial-bias exception to the no-impeachment rule—some for over half a century—with no signs of an increase in juror harassment or a loss of juror willingness to engage in searching and candid deliberations.

The experience of these jurisdictions, and the experience of the courts going forward, will inform the proper exercise of trial judge discretion in these and related matters. This case does not ask, and the Court need not address, what procedures a trial court must follow when confronted with a motion for a new trial based on juror testimony of racial bias. The Court also does not decide the appropriate standard for determining when evidence of racial bias is sufficient to require that the verdict be set aside and a new trial be granted.

[Subsection D of the Court's opinion is omitted.—EDS.]

* * *

The Nation must continue to make strides to overcome race-based discrimination. The progress that has already been made underlies the Court's insistence that blatant racial prejudice is antithetical to the functioning of the jury system and must be confronted in egregious cases like this one despite the general bar of the no-impeachment rule. It is the mark of a maturing legal system that it seeks to understand and to implement the lessons of history. The Court now seeks to strengthen the broader principle that society can and must move forward by achieving the thoughtful, rational dialogue at the foundation of both the jury system and the free society that sustains our Constitution.

The judgment of the Supreme Court of Colorado is reversed, and the case is remanded for further proceedings not inconsistent with this opinion.

JUSTICE THOMAS, dissenting.

. . . I agree with Justice Alito that the Court's decision is incompatible with the text of the Amendment it purports to interpret and with our precedents. I write separately to explain that the Court's holding also cannot be squared with the original understanding of the Sixth or Fourteenth Amendments.

[Justice Thomas's dissent next traces the history of the non-impeachment rule. He concludes:]

The Court today acknowledges that the States "adopted the [no-impeachment] rule as a matter of common law," but ascribes no significance to that fact. I would hold that it is dispositive. Our common-law history does not establish that—in either 1791 (when the Sixth Amendment was ratified) or 1868 (when the Fourteenth Amendment was ratified)—a defendant had the right to impeach a verdict with juror testimony of juror misconduct. In fact, it strongly suggests that such evidence was prohibited. In the absence of a definitive common-law tradition permitting impeachment by juror testimony, we have no basis to invoke a constitutional provision that merely "follow[s] out the established course of the common law in all trials for crimes," 3 Story §1785, at 662, to overturn Colorado's decision to preserve the no-impeachment rule.

* * *

Perhaps good reasons exist to curtail or abandon the no-impeachment rule. Some States have done so, . . . and others have not. Ultimately, that question is not for us to decide. It should be left to the political process described by Justice Alito. See post (dissenting opinion). In its attempt to stimulate a "thoughtful, rational dialogue" on race relations, the Court today ends the political process and imposes a uniform, national rule. The Constitution does not require such a rule. Neither should we.

I respectfully dissent.

JUSTICE ALITO, with whom CHIEF JUSTICE ROBERTS and JUSTICE THOMAS join, dissenting.

. . .

Jurors are ordinary people. They are expected to speak, debate, argue, and make decisions the way ordinary people do in their daily lives. Our Constitution places great value on this way of thinking, speaking, and deciding. The jury trial right protects parties in court cases from being judged by a special class of trained professionals who do not speak the language of ordinary people and may not understand or appreciate the way ordinary people live their lives. To protect that right, the door to the jury room has been locked, and the confidentiality of jury deliberations has been closely guarded.

Today, with the admirable intention of providing justice for one criminal defendant, the Court not only pries open the door; it rules that respecting the privacy of the jury room, as our legal system has done for centuries, violates the Constitution. This is a startling development, and although the Court tries to limit the degree of intrusion, it is doubtful that there are principled grounds for preventing the expansion of today's holding.

The Court justifies its decision on the ground that the nature of the confidential communication at issue in this particular case—a clear expression of what the Court terms racial bias—is uniquely harmful to our criminal justice system. And the Court is surely correct that even a tincture of racial bias can inflict great damage on that system, which is dependent on the public's trust. But until today, the argument that the Court now finds convincing has not been thought to be sufficient to overcome confidentiality rules like the one at issue here.

. . .

[Parts I and II of Justice Alito's dissent are omitted. — EDS.]

III

A

The real thrust of the majority opinion is that the Constitution is less tolerant of racial bias than other forms of juror misconduct, but it is hard to square this argument with the nature of the Sixth Amendment right on which petitioner's argument and the Court's holding are based. What the Sixth Amendment protects is the right to an "impartial jury." Nothing in the text or history of the Amendment or in the inherent nature of the jury trial right suggests that the extent of the protection provided by the Amendment depends on the nature of a jury's partiality or bias. As the Colorado Supreme Court aptly put it, it is hard to "discern a dividing line between different *types* of juror bias or misconduct, whereby one form of partiality would implicate a party's Sixth Amendment right while another would not."

Nor has the Court found any decision of this Court suggesting that the Sixth Amendment recognizes some sort of hierarchy of partiality or bias. The Court points to a line of cases holding that, in some narrow circumstances, the Constitution requires trial courts to conduct *voir dire* on the subject of race. Those decisions, however, were not based on a ranking of types of partiality but on the Court's conclusion that in certain cases racial bias was especially likely. See *Turner,* 476 U.S., at 38, n. 12 (plurality opinion) (requiring *voir dire* on the subject of race where there is "a particularly compelling need to inquire into racial prejudice" because of a qualitatively higher "risk of racial bias"). Thus, this line of cases does not advance the majority's argument.

It is undoubtedly true that "racial bias implicates unique historical, constitutional, and institutional concerns." Ante, at 868. But it is hard to see what that has to do with the scope of an *individual criminal defendant's* Sixth Amendment right to be judged impartially. The Court's efforts to reconcile its decision with *McDonald, Tanner,* and *Warger* illustrate the problem. The Court writes that the misconduct in those cases, while "troubling and unacceptable," was "anomalous." By contrast, racial bias, the Court says, is a "familiar and recurring evil" that causes "systemic injury to the administration of justice.

. . . If the Sixth Amendment requires the admission of juror testimony about statements or conduct during deliberations that show one type of juror partiality, then statements or conduct showing any type of partiality should be treated the same way.

B

Recasting this as an equal protection case would not provide a ground for limiting the holding to cases involving racial bias. At a minimum, cases involving bias based on any suspect classification—such as national origin or religion—would merit equal treatment. So, I think, would bias based on sex, or the exercise of the First Amendment right to freedom of expression or association. Indeed, convicting a defendant on the basis of any irrational classification would violate the Equal Protection Clause.

Attempting to limit the damage worked by its decision, the Court says that only "clear" expressions of bias must be admitted, but judging whether a statement is sufficiently "clear" will often not be easy. Suppose that the allegedly biased juror in this case never made reference to Peña-Rodriguez's race or national origin but said that he had a lot of experience with "this macho type" and knew that men of this kind felt that they could get their way with women. Suppose that other jurors testified that they were certain that "this macho type" was meant to refer to Mexican or Hispanic men. Many other similarly suggestive statements can easily be imagined, and under today's decision it will be difficult for judges to discern the dividing line between those that are "clear[ly]" based on racial or ethnic bias and those that are at least somewhat ambiguous.

IV

Today's decision—especially if it is expanded in the ways that seem likely—will invite the harms that no-impeachment rules were designed to prevent.

First, as the Court explained in *Tanner,* "postverdict scrutiny of juror conduct" will inhibit "full and frank discussion in the jury room." 483 U.S., at 120-121. Or, as the Senate Report put it: "[C]ommon fairness requires that absolute privacy be preserved for jurors to engage in the full and free debate necessary to the attainment of just verdicts. Jurors will not be able to function effectively if their deliberations are to be scrutinized in post-trial litigation." S. Rep., at 14.

Today's ruling will also prompt losing parties and their friends, supporters, and attorneys to contact and seek to question jurors, and this pestering may erode citizens' willingness to serve on juries. Many jurisdictions now have rules that prohibit or restrict post-verdict contact with jurors, but whether those rules will survive today's decision is an open question—as is the effect of this decision on privilege rules such as those noted at the outset of this opinion.

Where post-verdict approaches are permitted or occur, there is almost certain to be an increase in harassment, arm-twisting, and outright coercion. As one treatise explains, "[a] juror who reluctantly joined a verdict is likely to be sympathetic to overtures by the loser, and persuadable to the view that his own consent rested on false or impermissible considerations, and the truth will be hard to know." 3 C. Mueller & L. Kirkpatrick, Federal Evidence §6:16, p. 75 (4th ed. 2013).

The majority's approach will also undermine the finality of verdicts. "Public policy requires a finality to litigation." S. Rep., at 14. And accusations of juror bias—which may be "raised for the first time days, weeks, or months after the verdict"—can "seriously disrupt the finality of the process." *Tanner,* supra, at 120. This threatens to "degrad[e] the prominence of the trial itself" and to send the message that juror misconduct need not be dealt with promptly.

. . .

The Court's only response is that some jurisdictions already make an exception for racial bias, and the Court detects no signs of "a loss of juror willingness to engage in searching and candid deliberations." One wonders what sort of outward signs the Court would expect to see if jurors in these jurisdictions do not speak as freely in the jury room as their counterparts in jurisdictions with strict no-impeachment rules. Gathering and assessing evidence regarding the quality of jury deliberations in different jurisdictions would be a daunting enterprise, and the Court offers no indication that anybody has undertaken that task.

In short, the majority barely bothers to engage with the policy issues implicated by no-impeachment rules. But even if it had carefully grappled with those issues, it still would have no basis for exalting its own judgment over that of the many expert policymakers who have endorsed broad no-impeachment rules.

V

The Court's decision is well-intentioned. It seeks to remedy a flaw in the jury trial system, but as this Court said some years ago, it is questionable whether our system of trial by jury can endure this attempt to perfect it. *Tanner*, 483 U.S., at 120.

I respectfully dissent.

NOTES AND QUESTIONS

1. Justice Kennedy's majority opinion seems to stand for the proposition that "race is different," and that our desire to wipe out vestiges of discrimination justify overriding other interests, including finality and juror repose. If you agree that race should be treated differently—or perhaps, as in *Peña-Rodriguez*, race and ethnicity—should the case be limited to these groups, as the majority suggests? If a juror referred to a female defendant in derogatory terms, or made anti-Semitic comments about a Jewish defendant, should the verdict be subject to impeachment through juror testimony?

2. Suppose a defense lawyer interviewed the jurors after a conviction and discovered that the jury completely misunderstood the burden of proof—they weren't sure of the defendant's guilt, but thought that his story was so weak that he failed to convince them of his innocence. Rule 606(b), and cases like *Tanner* seem clear that evidence like this of what

the jurors discussed would be inadmissible in a post-verdict challenge. But is the Fourteenth Amendment's command to eliminate racial bias different in kind than the defendant's constitutional right to have the case proved against him beyond a reasonable doubt? Stated differently, is there any principled line to draw between the reasoning in *Peña-Rodriguez* and *any* other case where the (potentially innocent) defendant is convicted by a confused or biased jury?

3. It is unclear what Mr. Peña-Rodriguez has to prove on remand to overturn his conviction. Must he prove that the jury *as a whole* was influenced by the expressions of ethnic animus? Or is it enough to show that one juror was biased? If the former, these claims will probably be rare and very hard to prove; how many jurors are likely to admit that they were influenced by statements like those allegedly made by Mr. H.C.? Does the majority opinion help guide the lower courts on this issue?

PART FIVE

POSTTRIAL PROCEEDINGS

Chapter 15

Sentencing

C. Do the Rules of Constitutional Criminal Procedure Apply to Sentencing?

Insert the following after the end of the carryover paragraph at the top of page 1498:

In Montgomery v. Louisiana, 577 U.S. ___ (2016), the Court held that *Miller* applies retroactively—meaning that all juveniles serving mandatory sentences of life without parole, even if they were sentenced before *Miller* was decided, are entitled to resentencing. See also infra, at page 1634 (discussing generally the issue of retroactivity in federal habeas corpus).

Insert the following at the end of the paragraph at the bottom of page 1511:

The same rule was later applied to hold the Florida death penalty statute (which differed from Arizona's in that it provided for the jury to conduct a capital sentencing hearing and make a sentencing "recommendation" to the trial judge—but still required the trial judge to hold a separate hearing and ultimately determine whether sufficient aggravating circumstances existed to justify a death sentence) unconstitutional under the Sixth Amendment. Hurst v. Florida, 577 U.S. ___ (2016).

Insert the following at the end of Note 6 on page 1547:

On the other hand, in Beckles v. United States, 580 U.S. ___ (2017), a five-member majority of the Court (led by Justice Thomas, who was joined by Chief Justice Roberts and Justices Kennedy, Breyer, and Alito) held that the "void-for-vagueness" doctrine, under the Due Process Clause, does *not* apply to the Federal Sentencing Guidelines—because traditional criminal sentencing involved "unfettered discretion" and the Guidelines merely provide guidance to sentencing judges. The Court also opined that the "twin concerns" that underlie vagueness doctrine—providing fair notice and preventing arbitrary enforcement—are not implicated by the Guidelines.

Can *Peugh* and *Beckles* be reconciled? Justice Breyer apparently must think so, since he joined the majority in both cases.

Insert the following Note after Note 8 on page 1548:

9. In the first case after Justice Scalia's death to address the subject of appellate sentencing review under *Apprendi, Blakely,* and *Booker,* the Court held that a defendant who can show that the district court relied upon an incorrect Guideline range in determining his sentence—but whose sentence nevertheless ended up being within the bounds of the *correct* Guideline range—has successfully established a "reasonable probability of a different outcome," thus entitling him to claim "plain error" on appeal under Rule 52(b) of the Federal Rules of Criminal Procedure, even though he failed to object to the judge's error at the time it occurred. Molina-Martinez v. United States, 578 U.S. ___ (2016). As Justice Kennedy's majority opinion explained:

> [T]he Guidelines are not only the starting point for most federal sentencing proceedings but also the lodestar. The Guidelines inform and instruct the district court's determination of an appropriate sentence. In the usual case, then, the systemic function of the selected Guidelines range will affect the sentence. . . . From the centrality of the Guidelines in the sentencing process it must follow that, when a defendant shows that the district court used an incorrect range, he should not be barred from relief on appeal simply because there is no other evidence that the sentencing outcome would have been different had the correct range been used.

Justice Kennedy noted that there may be particular instances in which a "reasonable probability" of prejudice might not exist, such as where the district court had expressed the view that a particular sentence "was appropriate irrespective of the Guidelines range." But where the record is silent, then "the court's reliance on an incorrect range in most instances will suffice to show an effect on the defendant's rights."

Justice Alito, joined by Justice Thomas, concurred in part and concurred in the judgment, agreeing with the result but preferring not to "speculate" about how often the "reasonable probability" test might be satisfied in future cases.

Chapter 16

Double Jeopardy

A. "Twice Put in Jeopardy"

1. Acquittals

Insert the following Note after Note 3 on page 1562:

3a. What if a defendant is acquitted and convicted in simultaneous, "irreconcilably inconsistent" trial verdicts—and then the convictions get overturned on appeal, based on a legal error unrelated to the reasons for the inconsistency? Does *that* situation lead to Ashe v. Swenson preclusion? In Bravo-Fernandez v. United States, 580 U.S. ___ (2016), the Court held "no"—such a defendant is subject to retrial on all charges, because the inconsistent trial verdicts do not represent any kind of clear result in the defendant's favor, and the unrelated appellate reversal is not relevant to the issue at hand.

Insert the following Note after Note 4 on page 1563:

5. Notice that the Double Jeopardy protection provided by *Ashe* is waivable. In Currier v. Virginia, 585 U.S. ___ (2018), the defendant successfully moved to sever a felon-in-possession-of-a-firearm count from charges alleging burglary and larceny. At the first trial Currier was acquitted of the burglary and larceny charges, and when the government proceeded to a second trial on the felon-in-possession count, Currier moved to dismiss. Citing *Ashe*, he claimed that the first jury had necessarily found that he was not involved in the burglary and larceny, and therefore there could be no evidence that he possessed a firearm without having the second jury reconsider the first jury's findings.

The Supreme Court, by 5-4, disagreed. Justice Gorsuch, for the majority, concluded that even if Currier's second trial would otherwise be covered by *Ashe*, he had consented to the second trial when he moved to sever the counts. Given that all three of the counts could have been tried in a single proceeding without violating the Double Jeopardy Clause, said the Court, there is likewise no Fifth Amendment violation when the defendant consents to have the charges considered in two trials rather than one. The Court rejected the notion that there was something unfair about forcing Currier to choose between having a single trial where the jury would hear about his prior felony record and having to stand trial twice. "This Court has held repeatedly that difficult strategic choices like these are not the same as no choice, and the Constitution does not . . . forbid requiring a litigant to make them." Id. at ___ (internal quotations and citations omitted).

C.   Double Jeopardy and the "Dual Sovereignty" Doctrine

Insert the following Notes after Note 3 on page 1597:

4. Unsurprisingly, the Court in Gamble v. United States, 587 U.S. ___ (2019), rejected the defendant's request to overrule that part of the dual sovereignty exception that allows both the United States and individual states to separately prosecute a person for any crimes arising out of the same act.

5. Adding to the curious line of dual sovereignty cases, the Court held in Puerto Rico v. Sanchez Valle, 579 U.S. ___ (2016), that the doctrine does not apply to permit Puerto Rico to try a person for an offense for which that person has already been in jeopardy under federal law. The Court concluded that the rule requires looking to the "ultimate authority" justifying criminal prosecution, and in the case of Puerto Rico the "ultimate authority" is the United States. The Court distinguished Indian Tribes on the ground that they were independent nations prior to being conquered by the United States. It is a curious distinction. There is no reason to believe that Indian Tribes exercised any power remotely like prosecutorial power, and in any event Congress has plenary authority over Indian Tribes and thus can control them in their entirety.

Chapter 17

Appellate and Collateral Review

A. Appellate Review

1. The Defendant's Right to Appeal

Insert the following new paragraph at the end of Section A.1. on page 1615:

In Garza v. Idaho, 586 U.S. ___ (2019), the Court held that even where the defendant signed a waiver of the right to appeal in connection with a plea bargain, the defendant's lawyer renders ineffective assistance—with a presumption of prejudice—if she refuses to file a notice of appeal upon the defendant's request. The *Garza* case is discussed further in Chapter 3, at page 179.

5. Prejudice and Harmless Error

Insert the following Note after Note 4 on page 1626:

4a. Does the label "structural error"—which means that no prejudice must be shown in order for a defendant to prevail on direct appeal—also affect in the same way the "prejudice" prong of the *Strickland* test for ineffective assistance of counsel, which is generally litigated in collateral review? In Weaver v. Massachusetts, 582 U.S. ___ (2017), the Court held "no." The case involved exclusion of the public from jury selection, in violation of the defendant's Sixth Amendment right to a public trial. In a majority opinion written by Justice Kennedy, the Court explained:

> The precise reason why a particular error is not amenable to [harmless error] analysis—and thus the precise reason why the Court has deemed it structural—varies in a significant way from error to error. There appear to be at least three broad rationales.
>
> First, an error has been deemed structural in some instances if the right at issue is not designed to protect the defendant from erroneous conviction

but instead protects some other interest. This is true of the defendant's right to conduct his own defense, which, when exercised, "usually increases the likelihood of a trial outcome unfavorable to the defendant." McKaskle v. Wiggins, 465 U.S. 168, n. 8 (1984). That right is based on the fundamental legal principle that a defendant must be allowed to make his own choices about the proper way to protect his own liberty. See Faretta v. California, 422 U.S. 806, 834 (1975). Because harm is irrelevant to the basis underlying the right, the Court has deemed a violation of that right structural error. See United States v. Gonzalez-Lopez, 548 U.S. 140, n. 4 (2006).

Second, an error has been deemed structural if the effects of the error are simply too hard to measure. For example, when a defendant is denied the right to select his or her own attorney, the precise "effect of the violation cannot be ascertained." Ibid. (quoting Vasquez v. Hillery, 474 U.S. 254, 263 (1986)). Because the government will, as a result, find it almost impossible to show that the error was "harmless beyond a reasonable doubt," *Chapman*, at 24, the efficiency costs of letting the government try to make the showing are unjustified.

Third, an error has been deemed structural if the error always results in fundamental unfairness. For example, if an indigent defendant is denied an attorney or if the judge fails to give a reasonable-doubt instruction, the resulting trial is always a fundamentally unfair one. See Gideon v. Wainwright, 372 U.S. 335-345 (1963) (right to an attorney); Sullivan v. Louisiana, 508 U.S. 275 (1993) (right to a reasonable-doubt instruction). It therefore would be futile for the government to try to show harmlessness.

These categories are not rigid. In a particular case, more than one of these rationales may be part of the explanation for why an error is deemed to be structural. See e.g., id., at 280-282. For these purposes, however, one point is critical: An error can count as structural even if the error does not lead to fundamental unfairness in every case. See *Gonzalez-Lopez*, supra, at 149, n. 4 (rejecting as "inconsistent with the reasoning of our precedents" the idea that structural errors "always or necessarily render a trial fundamentally unfair and unreliable" (emphasis deleted)).

Id., at ___. According to the Court in *Weaver*, exclusion of the public from jury selection is a "structural error," but does not always lead to "fundamental unfairness." And if the error is not raised until habeas corpus, through the doctrine of ineffective assistance of trial counsel (for failing to object to the exclusion), then the defendant must show *Strickland* "prejudice" in order to obtain a new trial. Justice Alito, joined by Justice Gorsuch, concurred in the judgment, arguing that straightforward application of *Strickland* doctrine dictated the outcome. Justice Breyer, joined by Justice Kagan, dissented, arguing that the very nature of "structural error" means *both* that "harmless error" does not apply on direct appeal, *and* that "prejudice" need not be shown on collateral review.

Insert the following at the end of the carryover paragraph at the top of page 1630:

By the way, *if* a defendant manages to prevail on appeal, the Due Process Clause requires adequate procedures, under the Mathews v. Eldridge balancing test (see supra Chapter 2, at pages 87-95 and 100-111), for recovering property that has already been taken by the government as fees, costs, and restitution. Reliance on a statute generally authorizing compensation for exonerated persons is insufficient to satisfy this due process requirement. See Nelson v. Colorado, 581 U.S. ___ (2017).

B. Collateral Review

3. Procedural Issues in Federal Habeas

c. Procedural Default

Insert the following Note after Note 4 on page 1657:

4a. Does the equitable exception to procedural default, as established in Martinez v. Ryan, apply also to claims of ineffective assistance of *appellate* counsel? In Davila v. Davis, 582 U.S. ___ (2017), the Court—per Justice Thomas, joined by Chief Justice Roberts and Justices Kennedy, Alito, and Gorsuch—held that it does not. According to the majority, this result was largely dictated by the fact that there is no constitutional right to an appeal (see the previous discussion of McKane v. Durston in Chapter 3, at pages 150-152 and 174-175, and in the current chapter at page 1615):

> "The criminal trial enjoys pride of place in our criminal justice system in a way that an appeal from that trial does not. . . . The Court in *Martinez* made clear that it exercised its equitable discretion in view of the unique importance of protecting a defendant's trial rights, particularly the right to effective assistance of trial counsel. . . .
> Petitioner's rule also is not required to ensure that meritorious claims of trial error receive review by at least one state or federal court – the chief concern expressed by this Court in *Martinez*. . . . This is true regardless of whether trial counsel preserved the alleged error at trial. If trial counsel preserved the error by properly objecting, then that claim of trial error 'will have been addressed by . . . the trial court. . . .' If an unpreserved trial error was so obvious that appellate counsel was constitutionally required to raise it

on appeal, then trial counsel likely provided ineffective assistance by failing
to object to it in the first instance. In that circumstance, the prisoner likely
could invoke *Martinez* . . . to obtain review of trial counsel's failure to object.
Similarly, if the underlying, defaulted claim of trial error was ineffective
assistance of trial counsel premised on something other than the failure to
object, then *Martinez* . . . again already provide[s] a vehicle for obtaining
review of that error in most circumstances. Petitioner's proposed rule is
thus unnecessary for ensuring that trial errors are reviewed by at least one
court."

Id., at ___. Justice Breyer, joined by Justices Ginsburg, Sotomayor, and
Kagan, dissented, arguing that "[t]he basic legal principle that should
determine the outcome of this case is the principle that requires courts
to treat like cases alike." Id., at ___.

Selected Rules and Statutes

Federal Rules of Criminal Procedure

Rule 1. Scope; Definitions

(a) Scope.

(1) In General. These rules govern the procedure in all criminal proceedings in the United States district courts, the United States courts of appeals, and the Supreme Court of the United States.

(2) State or Local Judicial Officer. When a rule so states, it applies to a proceeding before a state or local judicial officer.

(3) Territorial Courts. These rules also govern the procedure in all criminal proceedings in the following courts:

(A) the district court of Guam;

(B) the district court for the Northern Mariana Islands, except as otherwise provided by law; and

(C) the district court of the Virgin Islands, except that the prosecution of offenses in that court must be by indictment or information as otherwise provided by law.

(4) Removed Proceedings. Although these rules govern all proceedings after removal from a state court, state law governs a dismissal by the prosecution.

(5) Excluded Proceedings. Proceedings not governed by these rules include:

(A) the extradition and rendition of a fugitive;

(B) a civil property forfeiture for violating a federal statute;

(C) the collection of a fine or penalty;

(D) a proceeding under a statute governing juvenile delinquency to the extent the procedure is inconsistent with the statute, unless Rule 20(d) provides otherwise;

(E) a dispute between seamen under 22 U.S.C. §§256-258; and

(F) a proceeding against a witness in a foreign country under 28 U.S.C. §1784.

(b) Definitions. The following definitions apply to these rules:

(1) "Attorney for the government" means:

(A) the Attorney General or an authorized assistant;

(B) a United States attorney or an authorized assistant;

(C) when applicable to cases arising under Guam law, the Guam Attorney General or other person whom Guam law authorizes to act in the matter; and

(D) any other attorney authorized by law to conduct proceedings under these rules as a prosecutor.

(2) "Court" means a federal judge performing functions authorized by law.

(3) "Federal judge" means:

(A) a justice or judge of the United States as these terms are defined in 28 U.S.C. §451;

(B) a magistrate judge; and

(C) a judge confirmed by the United States Senate and empowered by statute in any commonwealth, territory, or possession to perform a function to which a particular rule relates.

(4) "Judge" means a federal judge or a state or local judicial officer.

(5) "Magistrate judge" means a United States magistrate judge as defined in 28 U.S.C. §§631-639.

(6) "Oath" includes an affirmation.

(7) "Organization" is defined in 18 U.S.C. §18.

(8) "Petty offense" is defined in 18 U.S.C. §19.

(9) "State" includes the District of Columbia, and any commonwealth, territory, or possession of the United States.

(10) "State or local judicial officer" means:

(A) a state or local officer authorized to act under 18 U.S.C. §3041; and

(B) a judicial officer empowered by statute in the District of Columbia or in any commonwealth, territory, or possession to perform a function to which a particular rule relates.

(11) "Telephone" means any technology for transmitting live electronic voice communication.

(12) "Victim" means a "crime victim" as defined in 18 U.S.C. §3771(e).

(c) Authority of a Justice or Judge of the United States. When these rules authorize a magistrate judge to act, any other federal judge may also act.

Rule 3.   The Complaint

The complaint is a written statement of the essential facts constituting the offense charged. Except as provided in Rule 4.1, it must be made under oath before a magistrate judge or, if none is reasonably available, before a state or local judicial officer.

Rule 4.   Arrest Warrant or Summons on a Complaint

(a) **Issuance.** If the complaint or one or more affidavits filed with the complaint establish probable cause to believe that an offense has been committed and that the defendant committed it, the judge must issue an arrest warrant to an officer authorized to execute it. At the request of an attorney for the government, the judge must issue a summons, instead of a warrant, to a person authorized to serve it. A judge may issue more than one warrant or summons on the same complaint. If an individual defendant fails to appear in response to a summons, a judge may, and upon request of an attorney for the government must, issue a warrant. If an organizational defendant fails to appear in response to a summons, a judge may take any action authorized by United States law.

(b) **Form.**

(1) Warrant. A warrant must:

(A) contain the defendant's name or, if it is unknown, a name or description by which the defendant can be identified with reasonable certainty;

(B) describe the offense charged in the complaint;

(C) command that the defendant be arrested and brought without unnecessary delay before a magistrate judge or, if none is reasonably available, before a state or local judicial officer; and

(D) be signed by a judge.

(2) Summons. A summons must be in the same form as a warrant except that it must require the defendant to appear before a magistrate judge at a stated time and place.

(c) **Execution or Service, and Return.**

(1) By Whom. Only a marshal or other authorized officer may execute a warrant. Any person authorized to serve a summons in a federal civil action may serve a summons.

(2) Location. A warrant may be executed, or a summons served, within the jurisdiction of the United States or anywhere else a federal statute authorizes an arrest. A summons to an organization under Rule 4(c)(3)(D) may also be served at a place not within a judicial district of the United States.

(3) Manner.

(A) A warrant is executed by arresting the defendant. Upon arrest, an officer possessing the original or a duplicate original warrant must show it to the defendant. If the officer does not possess the warrant, the officer must inform the defendant of the warrant's existence and of the offense charged and, at the defendant's request, must show the original or a duplicate original warrant to the defendant as soon as possible.

(B) A summons is served on an individual defendant:

(i) by delivering a copy to the defendant personally; or

(ii) by leaving a copy at the defendant's residence or usual place of abode with a person of suitable age and discretion residing at that location and by mailing a copy to the defendant's last known address.

(C) A summons is served on an organization in a judicial district of the United States by delivering a copy to an officer, to a managing or general agent, or to another agent appointed or legally authorized to receive service of process. If the agent is one authorized by statute and the statute so requires, a copy must also be mailed to the organization.

(D) A summons is served on an organization not within a judicial district of the United States:

(i) by delivering a copy, in a manner authorized by the foreign jurisdiction's law, to an officer, to a managing or general agent, or to an agent appointed or legally authorized to receive service of process; or

(ii) by any other means that gives notice, including one that is:

(a) stipulated by the parties;

(b) undertaken by a foreign authority in response to a letter rogatory, a letter of request, or a request submitted under an applicable international agreement; or

(c) permitted by an applicable international agreement.

(4) Return.

(A) After executing a warrant, the officer must return it to the judge before whom the defendant is brought in accordance with Rule 5. The officer may do so by reliable electronic means. At the request of an attorney for the government, an unexecuted warrant must be brought back to and canceled by a magistrate judge or, if none is reasonably available, by a state or local judicial officer.

(B) The person to whom a summons was delivered for service must return it on or before the return day.

(C) At the request of an attorney for the government, a judge may deliver an unexecuted warrant, an unserved summons, or a copy of the warrant or summons to the marshal or other authorized person for execution or service.

(d) Warrant by Telephone or Other Reliable Electronic Means. In accordance with Rule 4.1, a magistrate judge may issue a warrant or summons based on information communicated by telephone or other reliable electronic means.

Rule 4.1. Complaint, Warrant, or Summons by Telephone or Other Reliable Electronic Means

(a) In General. A magistrate judge may consider information communicated by telephone or other reliable electronic means when reviewing a complaint or deciding whether to issue a warrant or summons.

(b) Procedures. If a magistrate judge decides to proceed under this rule, the following procedures apply:

(1) Taking Testimony Under Oath. The judge must place under oath—and may examine—the applicant and any person on whose testimony the application is based.

(2) Creating a Record of the Testimony and Exhibits.

(A) Testimony Limited to Attestation. If the applicant does no more than attest to the contents of a written affidavit submitted by reliable electronic means, the judge must acknowledge the attestation in writing on the affidavit.

(B) Additional Testimony or Exhibits. If the judge considers additional testimony or exhibits, the judge must:

(i) have the testimony recorded verbatim by an electronic recording device, by a court reporter, or in writing;

(ii) have any recording or reporter's notes transcribed, have the transcription certified as accurate, and file it;

(iii) sign any other written record, certify its accuracy, and file it; and

(iv) make sure that the exhibits are filed.

(3) Preparing a Proposed Duplicate Original of a Complaint, Warrant, or Summons. The applicant must prepare a proposed duplicate original of a complaint, warrant, or summons, and must read or otherwise transmit its contents verbatim to the judge.

(4) Preparing an Original Complaint, Warrant, or Summons. If the applicant reads the contents of the proposed duplicate original, the judge must enter those contents into an original complaint, warrant, or summons. If the applicant transmits the contents by reliable electronic means, the transmission received by the judge may serve as the original.

(5) Modification. The judge may modify the complaint, warrant, or summons. The judge must then:

(A) transmit the modified version to the applicant by reliable electronic means; or

(B) file the modified original and direct the applicant to modify the proposed duplicate original accordingly.

(6) Issuance. To issue the warrant or summons, the judge must:

(A) sign the original documents;

(B) enter the date and time of issuance on the warrant or summons; and

(C) transmit the warrant or summons by reliable electronic means to the applicant or direct the applicant to sign the judge's name and enter the date and time on the duplicate original.

(c) Suppression Limited. Absent a finding of bad faith, evidence obtained from a warrant issued under this rule is not subject to suppression on the ground that issuing the warrant in this manner was unreasonable under the circumstances.

Rule 5. Initial Appearance

(a) In General.

(1) Appearance Upon an Arrest.

(A) A person making an arrest within the United States must take the defendant without unnecessary delay before a magistrate judge, or before a state or local judicial officer as Rule 5(c) provides, unless a statute provides otherwise.

(B) A person making an arrest outside the United States must take the defendant without unnecessary delay before a magistrate judge, unless a statute provides otherwise.

(2) Exceptions.

(A) An officer making an arrest under a warrant issued upon a complaint charging solely a violation of 18 U.S.C. §1073 need not comply with this rule if:

(i) the person arrested is transferred without unnecessary delay to the custody of appropriate state or local authorities in the district of arrest; and

(ii) an attorney for the government moves promptly, in the district where the warrant was issued, to dismiss the complaint.

(B) If a defendant is arrested for violating probation or supervised release, Rule 32.1 applies.

(C) If a defendant is arrested for failing to appear in another district, Rule 40 applies.

(3) Appearance Upon a Summons. When a defendant appears in response to a summons under Rule 4, a magistrate judge must proceed under Rule 5(d) or (e), as applicable.

(b) Arrest Without a Warrant. If a defendant is arrested without a warrant, a complaint meeting Rule 4(a)'s requirement of probable cause must be promptly filed in the district where the offense was allegedly committed.

(c) Place of Initial Appearance; Transfer to Another District.

(1) Arrest in the District Where the Offense Was Allegedly Committed. If the defendant is arrested in the district where the offense was allegedly committed:

(A) the initial appearance must be in that district; and

(B) if a magistrate judge is not reasonably available, the initial appearance may be before a state or local judicial officer.

(2) Arrest in a District Other Than Where the Offense Was Allegedly Committed. If the defendant was arrested in a district other than where the offense was allegedly committed, the initial appearance must be:

(A) in the district of arrest; or

(B) in an adjacent district if:

(i) the appearance can occur more promptly there; or

(ii) the offense was allegedly committed there and the initial appearance will occur on the day of arrest.

(3) Procedures in a District Other Than Where the Offense Was Allegedly Committed. If the initial appearance occurs in a district

other than where the offense was allegedly committed, the following procedures apply:

 (A) the magistrate judge must inform the defendant about the provisions of Rule 20;

 (B) if the defendant was arrested without a warrant, the district court where the offense was allegedly committed must first issue a warrant before the magistrate judge transfers the defendant to that district;

 (C) the magistrate judge must conduct a preliminary hearing if required by Rule 5.1;

 (D) the magistrate judge must transfer the defendant to the district where the offense was allegedly committed if:

  (i) the government produces the warrant, a certified copy of the warrant, or a reliable electronic form of either; and

  (ii) the judge finds that the defendant is the same person named in the indictment, information, or warrant; and

 (E) when a defendant is transferred and discharged, the clerk must promptly transmit the papers and any bail to the clerk in the district where the offense was allegedly committed.

 (4) Procedure for Persons Extradited to the United States. If the defendant is surrendered to the United States in accordance with a request for the defendant's extradition, the initial appearance must be in the district (or one of the districts) where the offense is charged.

 (d) Procedure in a Felony Case.

 (1) Advice. If the defendant is charged with a felony, the judge must inform the defendant of the following:

 (A) the complaint against the defendant, and any affidavit filed with it;

 (B) the defendant's right to retain counsel or to request that counsel be appointed if the defendant cannot obtain counsel;

 (C) the circumstances, if any, under which the defendant may secure pretrial release;

 (D) any right to a preliminary hearing;

 (E) the defendant's right not to make a statement, and that any statement made may be used against the defendant; and

 (F) that a defendant who is not a United States citizen may request that an attorney for the government or a federal law enforcement official notify a consular officer from the defendant's country of nationality that the defendant has been arrested—but that even without the defendant's request, a treaty or other international agreement may require consular notification.

(2) Consulting with Counsel. The judge must allow the defendant reasonable opportunity to consult with counsel.

(3) Detention or Release. The judge must detain or release the defendant as provided by statute or these rules.

(4) Plea. A defendant may be asked to plead only under Rule 10.

(e) Procedure in a Misdemeanor Case. If the defendant is charged with a misdemeanor only, the judge must inform the defendant in accordance with Rule 58(b)(2).

(f) Video Teleconferencing. Video teleconferencing may be used to conduct an appearance under this rule if the defendant consents.

Rule 5.1. Preliminary Hearing

(a) In General. If a defendant is charged with an offense other than a petty offense, a magistrate judge must conduct a preliminary hearing unless:

(1) the defendant waives the hearing;

(2) the defendant is indicted;

(3) the government files an information under Rule 7(b) charging the defendant with a felony;

(4) the government files an information charging the defendant with a misdemeanor; or

(5) the defendant is charged with a misdemeanor and consents to trial before a magistrate judge.

(b) Selecting a District. A defendant arrested in a district other than where the offense was allegedly committed may elect to have the preliminary hearing conducted in the district where the prosecution is pending.

(c) Scheduling. The magistrate judge must hold the preliminary hearing within a reasonable time, but no later than 14 days after the initial appearance if the defendant is in custody and no later than 21 days if not in custody.

(d) Extending the Time. With the defendant's consent and upon a showing of good cause—taking into account the public interest in the prompt disposition of criminal cases—a magistrate judge may extend the time limits in Rule 5.1(c) one or more times. If the defendant does not consent, the magistrate judge may extend the time limits only on a showing that extraordinary circumstances exist and justice requires the delay.

(e) Hearing and Finding. At the preliminary hearing, the defendant may cross-examine adverse witnesses and may introduce evidence but may not object to evidence on the ground that it was unlawfully acquired. If the magistrate judge finds probable cause to believe an offense has been committed and the defendant committed it, the magistrate judge must promptly require the defendant to appear for further proceedings.

(f) Discharging the Defendant. If the magistrate judge finds no probable cause to believe an offense has been committed or the defendant committed it, the magistrate judge must dismiss the complaint and discharge the defendant. A discharge does not preclude the government from later prosecuting the defendant for the same offense.

(g) Recording the Proceedings. The preliminary hearing must be recorded by a court reporter or by a suitable recording device. A recording of the proceeding may be made available to any party upon request. A copy of the recording and a transcript may be provided to any party upon request and upon any payment required by applicable Judicial Conference regulations.

(h) Producing a Statement.

(1) In General. Rule 26.2(a)-(d) and (f) applies at any hearing under this rule, unless the magistrate judge for good cause rules otherwise in a particular case.

(2) Sanctions for Not Producing a Statement. If a party disobeys a Rule 26.2 order to deliver a statement to the moving party, the magistrate judge must not consider the testimony of a witness whose statement is withheld.

Rule 6.   The Grand Jury

(a) Summoning a Grand Jury.

(1) In General. When the public interest so requires, the court must order that one or more grand juries be summoned. A grand jury must have 16 to 23 members, and the court must order that enough legally qualified persons be summoned to meet this requirement.

(2) Alternate Jurors. When a grand jury is selected, the court may also select alternate jurors. Alternate jurors must have the same qualifications and be selected in the same manner as any other juror. Alternate jurors replace jurors in the same sequence in which the alternates were selected. An alternate juror who replaces a juror is

subject to the same challenges, takes the same oath, and has the same authority as the other jurors.

(b) Objection to the Grand Jury or to a Grand Juror.

(1) Challenges. Either the government or a defendant may challenge the grand jury on the ground that it was not lawfully drawn, summoned, or selected, and may challenge an individual juror on the ground that the juror is not legally qualified.

(2) Motion to Dismiss an Indictment. A party may move to dismiss the indictment based on an objection to the grand jury or on an individual juror's lack of legal qualification, unless the court has previously ruled on the same objection under Rule 6(b)(1). The motion to dismiss is governed by 28 U.S.C. §1867(e). The court must not dismiss the indictment on the ground that a grand juror was not legally qualified if the record shows that at least 12 qualified jurors concurred in the indictment.

(c) Foreperson and Deputy Foreperson. The court will appoint one juror as the foreperson and another as the deputy foreperson. In the foreperson's absence, the deputy foreperson will act as the foreperson. The foreperson may administer oaths and affirmations and will sign all indictments. The foreperson — or another juror designated by the foreperson — will record the number of jurors concurring in every indictment and will file the record with the clerk, but the record may not be made public unless the court so orders.

(d) Who May Be Present.

(1) While the Grand Jury Is in Session. The following persons may be present while the grand jury is in session: attorneys for the government, the witness being questioned, interpreters when needed, and a court reporter or an operator of a recording device.

(2) During Deliberations and Voting. No person other than the jurors, and any interpreter needed to assist a hearing-impaired or speech-impaired juror, may be present while the grand jury is deliberating or voting.

(e) Recording and Disclosing the Proceedings.

(1) Recording the Proceedings. Except while the grand jury is deliberating or voting, all proceedings must be recorded by a court reporter or by a suitable recording device. But the validity of a prosecution is not affected by the unintentional failure to make a recording. Unless the court orders otherwise, an attorney for the government will retain control of the recording, the reporter's notes, and any transcript prepared from those notes.

(2) Secrecy.

(A) No obligation of secrecy may be imposed on any person except in accordance with Rule 6(e)(2)(B).

(B) Unless these rules provide otherwise, the following persons must not disclose a matter occurring before the grand jury:

(i) a grand juror;

(ii) an interpreter;

(iii) a court reporter;

(iv) an operator of a recording device;

(v) a person who transcribes recorded testimony;

(vi) an attorney for the government; or

(vii) a person to whom disclosure is made under Rule 6(e)(3)(A)(ii) or (iii).

(3) Exceptions.

(A) Disclosure of a grand-jury matter—other than the grand jury's deliberations or any grand juror's vote—may be made to:

(i) an attorney for the government for use in performing that attorney's duty;

(ii) any government personnel—including those of a state, state subdivision, Indian tribe, or foreign government—that an attorney for the government considers necessary to assist in performing that attorney's duty to enforce federal criminal law; or

(iii) a person authorized by 18 U.S.C. §3322.

(B) A person to whom information is disclosed under Rule 6(e)(3)(A)(ii) may use that information only to assist an attorney for the government in performing that attorney's duty to enforce federal criminal law. An attorney for the government must promptly provide the court that impaneled the grand jury with the names of all persons to whom a disclosure has been made, and must certify that the attorney has advised those persons of their obligation of secrecy under this rule.

(C) An attorney for the government may disclose any grand-jury matter to another federal grand jury.

(D) An attorney for the government may disclose any grand-jury matter involving foreign intelligence, counterintelligence (as defined in 50 U.S.C. §3003), or foreign intelligence information (as defined in Rule 6(e)(3)(D)(iii)) to any federal law enforcement, intelligence, protective, immigration, national defense, or national security official to assist the official receiving the information in the performance of that official's duties. An attorney for the government may also disclose any grand-jury matter involving, within the United States or elsewhere, a threat of attack or other grave hostile acts of a foreign power or its agent, a threat of domestic or international sabotage or terrorism, or clandestine intelligence gathering activities by an intelligence service or network of a foreign power or by its agent, to any appropriate federal, state, state subdivision, Indian tribal, or foreign government official, for the purpose of preventing or responding to such threat or activities.

(i) Any official who receives information under Rule 6(e)(3)(D) may use the information only as necessary in the conduct of that person's official duties subject to any limitations on the unauthorized disclosure of such information. Any state, state subdivision, Indian tribal, or foreign government official who receives information under Rule 6(e)(3)(D) may use the information only in a manner consistent with any guidelines issued by the Attorney General and the Director of National Intelligence.

(ii) Within a reasonable time after disclosure is made under Rule 6(e)(3)(D), an attorney for the government must file, under seal, a notice with the court in the district where the grand jury convened stating that such information was disclosed and the departments, agencies, or entities to which the disclosure was made.

(iii) As used in Rule 6(e)(3)(D), the term "foreign intelligence information" means:

(a) information, whether or not it concerns a United States person, that relates to the ability of the United States to protect against—

- actual or potential attack or other grave hostile acts of a foreign power or its agent;
- sabotage or international terrorism by a foreign power or its agent; or
- clandestine intelligence activities by an intelligence service or network of a foreign power or by its agent; or

(b) information, whether or not it concerns a United States person, with respect to a foreign power or foreign territory that relates to—

- the national defense or the security of the United States; or
- the conduct of the foreign affairs of the United States.

(E) The court may authorize disclosure—at a time, in a manner, and subject to any other conditions that it directs—of a grand-jury matter:

(i) preliminarily to or in connection with a judicial proceeding;

(ii) at the request of a defendant who shows that a ground may exist to dismiss the indictment because of a matter that occurred before the grand jury;

(iii) at the request of the government, when sought by a foreign court or prosecutor for use in an official criminal investigation;

(iv) at the request of the government if it shows that the matter may disclose a violation of State, Indian tribal, or foreign criminal law, as long as the disclosure is to an appropriate state, state-subdivision, Indian tribal, or foreign government official for the purpose of enforcing that law; or

(v) at the request of the government if it shows that the matter may disclose a violation of military criminal law under the Uniform Code of Military Justice, as long as the disclosure is to an appropriate military official for the purpose of enforcing that law.

(F) A petition to disclose a grand-jury matter under Rule 6(e)(3)(E)(i) must be filed in the district where the grand jury convened. Unless the hearing is ex parte—as it may be when the government is the petitioner—the petitioner must serve the petition on, and the court must afford a reasonable opportunity to appear and be heard to:

(i) an attorney for the government;

(ii) the parties to the judicial proceeding; and

(iii) any other person whom the court may designate.

(G) If the petition to disclose arises out of a judicial proceeding in another district, the petitioned court must transfer the petition to the other court unless the petitioned court can reasonably determine whether disclosure is proper. If the petitioned court decides to transfer, it must send to the transferee court the material sought to be disclosed, if feasible, and a written evaluation of the need for continued grand-jury secrecy. The transferee court must afford those persons identified in Rule 6(e)(3)(F) a reasonable opportunity to appear and be heard.

(4) Sealed Indictment. The magistrate judge to whom an indictment is returned may direct that the indictment be kept secret until the defendant is in custody or has been released pending trial. The

clerk must then seal the indictment, and no person may disclose the indictment's existence except as necessary to issue or execute a warrant or summons.

(5) Closed Hearing. Subject to any right to an open hearing in a contempt proceeding, the court must close any hearing to the extent necessary to prevent disclosure of a matter occurring before a grand jury.

(6) Sealed Records. Records, orders, and subpoenas relating to grand-jury proceedings must be kept under seal to the extent and as long as necessary to prevent the unauthorized disclosure of a matter occurring before a grand jury.

(7) Contempt. A knowing violation of Rule 6, or of any guidelines jointly issued by the Attorney General and the Director of National Intelligence under Rule 6, may be punished as a contempt of court.

(f) Indictment and Return. A grand jury may indict only if at least 12 jurors concur. The grand jury—or its foreperson or deputy foreperson—must return the indictment to a magistrate judge in open court. To avoid unnecessary cost or delay, the magistrate judge may take the return by video teleconference from the court where the grand jury sits. If a complaint or information is pending against the defendant and 12 jurors do not concur in the indictment, the foreperson must promptly and in writing report the lack of concurrence to the magistrate judge.

(g) Discharging the Grand Jury. A grand jury must serve until the court discharges it, but it may serve more than 18 months only if the court, having determined that an extension is in the public interest, extends the grand jury's service. An extension may be granted for no more than 6 months, except as otherwise provided by statute.

(h) Excusing a Juror. At any time, for good cause, the court may excuse a juror either temporarily or permanently, and if permanently, the court may impanel an alternate juror in place of the excused juror.

(i) "Indian Tribe" Defined. "Indian tribe" means an Indian tribe recognized by the Secretary of the Interior on a list published in the Federal Register under 25 U.S.C. §479a-1.

Rule 7. The Indictment and the Information

(a) When Used.

(1) Felony. An offense (other than criminal contempt) must be prosecuted by an indictment if it is punishable:

(A) by death; or

(B) by imprisonment for more than one year.

(2) Misdemeanor. An offense punishable by imprisonment for one year or less may be prosecuted in accordance with Rule 58(b)(1).

(b) Waiving Indictment. An offense punishable by imprisonment for more than one year may be prosecuted by information if the defendant—in open court and after being advised of the nature of the charge and of the defendant's rights—waives prosecution by indictment.

(c) Nature and Contents.

(1) In General. The indictment or information must be a plain, concise, and definite written statement of the essential facts constituting the offense charged and must be signed by an attorney for the government. It need not contain a formal introduction or conclusion. A count may incorporate by reference an allegation made in another count. A count may allege that the means by which the defendant committed the offense are unknown or that the defendant committed it by one or more specified means. For each count, the indictment or information must give the official or customary citation of the statute, rule, regulation, or other provision of law that the defendant is alleged to have violated. For purposes of an indictment referred to in section 3282 of title 18, United States Code, for which the identity of the defendant is unknown, it shall be sufficient for the indictment to describe the defendant as an individual whose name is unknown, but who has a particular DNA profile, as that term is defined in section 3282.

(2) Citation Error. Unless the defendant was misled and thereby prejudiced, neither an error in a citation nor a citation's omission is a ground to dismiss the indictment or information or to reverse a conviction.

(d) Surplusage. Upon the defendant's motion, the court may strike surplusage from the indictment or information.

(e) Amending an Information. Unless an additional or different offense is charged or a substantial right of the defendant is prejudiced, the court may permit an information to be amended at any time before the verdict or finding.

(f) Bill of Particulars. The court may direct the government to file a bill of particulars. The defendant may move for a bill of particulars before or within 14 days after arraignment or at a later time if the court permits. The government may amend a bill of particulars subject to such conditions as justice requires.

Rule 8. Joinder of Offenses or Defendants

(a) Joinder of Offenses. The indictment or information may charge a defendant in separate counts with two or more offenses if the offenses charged—whether felonies or misdemeanors or both—are of the same or similar character, or are based on the same act or transaction, or are connected with or constitute parts of a common scheme or plan.

(b) Joinder of Defendants. The indictment or information may charge two or more defendants if they are alleged to have participated in the same act or transaction, or in the same series of acts or transactions, constituting an offense or offenses. The defendants may be charged in one or more counts together or separately. All defendants need not be charged in each count.

Rule 9. Arrest Warrant or Summons on an Indictment or Information

(a) Issuance. The court must issue a warrant—or at the government's request, a summons—for each defendant named in an indictment or named in an information if one or more affidavits accompanying the information establish probable cause to believe that an offense has been committed and that the defendant committed it. The court may issue more than one warrant or summons for the same defendant. If a defendant fails to appear in response to a summons, the court may, and upon request of an attorney for the government must, issue a warrant. The court must issue the arrest warrant to an officer authorized to execute it or the summons to a person authorized to serve it.

(b) Form.

(1) Warrant. The warrant must conform to Rule 4(b)(1) except that it must be signed by the clerk and must describe the offense charged in the indictment or information.

(2) Summons. The summons must be in the same form as a warrant except that it must require the defendant to appear before the court at a stated time and place.

(c) Execution or Service; Return; Initial Appearance.

(1) Execution or Service.

(A) The warrant must be executed or the summons served as provided in Rule 4(c)(1), (2), and (3).

(B) The officer executing the warrant must proceed in accordance with Rule 5(a)(1).

(2) Return. A warrant or summons must be returned in accordance with Rule 4(c)(4).

(3) Initial Appearance. When an arrested or summoned defendant first appears before the court, the judge must proceed under Rule 5.

Rule 10.   Arraignment

(a) In General. An arraignment must be conducted in open court and must consist of:

(1) ensuring that the defendant has a copy of the indictment or information;

(2) reading the indictment or information to the defendant or stating to the defendant the substance of the charge; and then

(3) asking the defendant to plead to the indictment or information.

(b) Waiving Appearance. A defendant need not be present for the arraignment if:

(1) the defendant has been charged by indictment or misdemeanor information;

(2) the defendant, in a written waiver signed by both the defendant and defense counsel, has waived appearance and has affirmed that the defendant received a copy of the indictment or information and that the plea is not guilty; and

(3) the court accepts the waiver.

(c) Video Teleconferencing. Video teleconferencing may be used to arraign a defendant if the defendant consents.

Rule 11.   Pleas

(a) Entering a Plea.

(1) In General. A defendant may plead not guilty, guilty, or (with the court's consent) nolo contendere.

(2) Conditional Plea. With the consent of the court and the government, a defendant may enter a conditional plea of guilty or nolo contendere, reserving in writing the right to have an appellate

court review an adverse determination of a specified pretrial motion. A defendant who prevails on appeal may then withdraw the plea.

(3) Nolo Contendere Plea. Before accepting a plea of nolo contendere, the court must consider the parties' views and the public interest in the effective administration of justice.

(4) Failure to Enter a Plea. If a defendant refuses to enter a plea or if a defendant organization fails to appear, the court must enter a plea of not guilty.

(b) Considering and Accepting a Guilty or Nolo Contendere Plea.

(1) Advising and Questioning the Defendant. Before the court accepts a plea of guilty or nolo contendere, the defendant may be placed under oath and the court must address the defendant personally in open court. During this address, the court must inform the defendant of, and determine that the defendant understands, the following:

(A) the government's right, in a prosecution for perjury or false statement, to use against the defendant any statement that the defendant gives under oath;

(B) the right to plead not guilty, or having already so pleaded, to persist in that plea;

(C) the right to a jury trial;

(D) the right to be represented by counsel—and, if necessary, have the court appoint counsel—at trial and at every other stage of the proceeding;

(E) the right at trial to confront and cross-examine adverse witnesses, to be protected from compelled self-incrimination, to testify and present evidence, and to compel the attendance of witnesses;

(F) the defendant's waiver of these trial rights if the court accepts a plea of guilty or nolo contendere;

(G) the nature of each charge to which the defendant is pleading;

(H) any maximum possible penalty, including imprisonment, fine, and term of supervised release;

(I) any mandatory minimum penalty;

(J) any applicable forfeiture;

(K) the court's authority to order restitution;

(L) the court's obligation to impose a special assessment;

(M) in determining a sentence, the court's obligation to calculate the applicable sentencing-guideline range and to consider that range, possible departures under the Sentencing Guidelines, and other sentencing factors under 18 U.S.C. §3553(a);

(N) the terms of any plea-agreement provision waiving the right to appeal or to collaterally attack the sentence; and

(O) that, if convicted, a defendant who is not a United States citizen may be removed from the United States, denied citizenship, and denied admission to the United States in the future.

(2) Ensuring That a Plea Is Voluntary. Before accepting a plea of guilty or nolo contendere, the court must address the defendant personally in open court and determine that the plea is voluntary and did not result from force, threats, or promises (other than promises in a plea agreement).

(3) Determining the Factual Basis for a Plea. Before entering judgment on a guilty plea, the court must determine that there is a factual basis for the plea.

(c) Plea Agreement Procedure.

(1) In General. An attorney for the government and the defendant's attorney, or the defendant when proceeding pro se, may discuss and reach a plea agreement. The court must not participate in these discussions. If the defendant pleads guilty or nolo contendere to either a charged offense or a lesser or related offense, the plea agreement may specify that an attorney for the government will:

(A) not bring, or will move to dismiss, other charges;

(B) recommend, or agree not to oppose the defendant's request, that a particular sentence or sentencing range is appropriate or that a particular provision of the Sentencing Guidelines, or policy statement, or sentencing factor does or does not apply (such a recommendation or request does not bind the court); or

(C) agree that a specific sentence or sentencing range is the appropriate disposition of the case, or that a particular provision of the Sentencing Guidelines, policy statement, or sentencing factor does or does not apply (such a recommendation or request binds the court once the court accepts the plea agreement).

(2) Disclosing a Plea Agreement. The parties must disclose the plea agreement in open court when the plea is offered, unless the court for good cause allows the parties to disclose the plea agreement in camera.

(3) Judicial Consideration of a Plea Agreement.

(A) To the extent the plea agreement is of the type specified in Rule 11(c)(1)(A) or (C), the court may accept the agreement, reject it, or defer a decision until the court has reviewed the pre-sentence report.

(B) To the extent the plea agreement is of the type specified in Rule 11(c)(l)(B), the court must advise the defendant that the defendant has no right to withdraw the plea if the court does not follow the recommendation or request.

(4) Accepting a Plea Agreement. If the court accepts the plea agreement, it must inform the defendant that to the extent the plea agreement is of the type specified in Rule 11(c)(1)(A) or (C), the agreed disposition will be included in the judgment.

(5) Rejecting a Plea Agreement. If the court rejects a plea agreement containing provisions of the type specified in Rule 11(c)(1)(A) or (C), the court must do the following on the record and in open court (or, for good cause, in camera):

(A) inform the parties that the court rejects the plea agreement;

(B) advise the defendant personally that the court is not required to follow the plea agreement and give the defendant an opportunity to withdraw the plea; and

(C) advise the defendant personally that if the plea is not withdrawn, the court may dispose of the case less favorably toward the defendant than the plea agreement contemplated.

(d) Withdrawing a Guilty or Nolo Contendere Plea. A defendant may withdraw a plea of guilty or nolo contendere:

(1) before the court accepts the plea, for any reason or no reason; or

(2) after the court accepts the plea but before it imposes sentence if:

(A) the court rejects a plea agreement under Rule 11(c)(5); or

(B) the defendant can show a fair and just reason for requesting the withdrawal.

(e) Finality of a Guilty or Nolo Contendere Plea. After the court imposes sentence, the defendant may not withdraw a plea of guilty or nolo contendere, and the plea may be set aside only on direct appeal or collateral attack.

(f) Admissibility or Inadmissibility of a Plea, Plea Discussions, and Related Statements. The admissibility or inadmissibility of a plea, a plea discussion, and any related statement is governed by Federal Rule of Evidence 410.

(g) Recording the Proceedings. The proceedings during which the defendant enters a plea must be recorded by a court reporter or by a suitable recording device. If there is a guilty plea or a nolo contendere plea, the record must include the inquiries and advice to the defendant required under Rule 11(b) and (c).

(h) Harmless Error. A variance from the requirements of this rule is harmless error if it does not affect substantial rights.

Rule 12.1.   Notice of an Alibi Defense

(a) Government's Request for Notice and Defendant's Response.

(1) Government's Request. An attorney for the government may request in writing that the defendant notify an attorney for the government of any intended alibi defense. The request must state the time, date, and place of the alleged offense.

(2) Defendant's Response. Within 14 days after the request, or at some other time the court sets, the defendant must serve written notice on an attorney for the government of any intended alibi defense. The defendant's notice must state:

(A) each specific place where the defendant claims to have been at the time of the alleged offense; and

(B) the name, address, and telephone number of each alibi witness on whom the defendant intends to rely.

(b) Disclosing Government Witnesses.

(1) Disclosure.

(A) In general. If the defendant serves a Rule 12.1(a)(2) notice, an attorney for the government must disclose in writing to the defendant or the defendant's attorney:

(i) the name, address, and telephone number of each witness the government intends to rely on to establish the defendant's presence at the scene of the alleged offense; and

(ii) each government rebuttal witness to the defendant's alibi defense.

(B) Victim's Address and Telephone Number. If the government intends to rely on a victim's testimony to establish that the defendant was present at the scene of the alleged offense and the defendant establishes a need for the victim's address and telephone number, the court may:

(i) order the government to provide the information in writing to the defendant or the defendant's attorney; or

(ii) fashion a reasonable procedure that allows preparation of the defense and also protects the victim's interests.

(2) Time to Disclose. Unless the court directs otherwise, an attorney for the government must give its Rule 12.1(b)(1) disclosure within 14 days after the defendant serves notice of an intended alibi defense under Rule 12.1(a)(2), but no later than 14 days before trial.

(c) Continuing Duty to Disclose.

(1) In General. Both an attorney for the government and the defendant must promptly disclose in writing to the other party the name of each additional witness—and the address and telephone number of each additional witness other than a victim—if:

(A) the disclosing party learns of the witness before or during trial; and

(B) the witness should have been disclosed under Rule 12.1(a) or (b) if the disclosing party had known of the witness earlier.

(2) Address and Telephone Number of an Additional Victim Witness. The address and telephone number of an additional victim witness must not be disclosed except as provided in Rule 12.1(b)(1)(B).

(d) Exceptions. For good cause, the court may grant an exception to any requirement of Rule 12.1(a)-(c).

(e) Failure to Comply. If a party fails to comply with this rule, the court may exclude the testimony of any undisclosed witness regarding the defendant's alibi. This rule does not limit the defendant's right to testify.

(f) Inadmissibility of Withdrawn Intention. Evidence of an intention to rely on an alibi defense, later withdrawn, or of a statement made in connection with that intention, is not, in any civil or criminal proceeding, admissible against the person who gave notice of the intention.

Rule 13.   Joint Trial of Separate Cases

The court may order that separate cases be tried together as though brought in a single indictment or information if all offenses and all defendants could have been joined in a single indictment or information.

Rule 14.   Relief from Prejudicial Joinder

(a) Relief. If the joinder of offenses or defendants in an indictment, an information, or a consolidation for trial appears to prejudice a defendant or the government, the court may order separate trials of counts, sever the defendants' trials, or provide any other relief that justice requires.

(b) Defendant's Statements. Before ruling on a defendant's motion to sever, the court may order an attorney for the government to deliver to the court for in camera inspection any defendant's statement that the government intends to use as evidence.

Rule 16.   Discovery and Inspection

(a) Government's Disclosure.

(1) Information Subject to Disclosure.

(A) Defendant's Oral Statement. Upon a defendant's request, the government must disclose to the defendant the substance of any relevant oral statement made by the defendant, before or after arrest, in response to interrogation by a person the defendant knew was a government agent if the government intends to use the statement at trial.

(B) Defendant's Written or Recorded Statement. Upon a defendant's request, the government must disclose to the defendant, and make available for inspection, copying, or photographing, all of the following:

(i) any relevant written or recorded statement by the defendant if:

- the statement is within the government's possession, custody, or control; and
- the attorney for the government knows—or through due diligence could know—that the statement exists;

(ii) the portion of any written record containing the substance of any relevant oral statement made before or after arrest if the defendant made the statement in response to interrogation by a person the defendant knew was a government agent; and

(iii) the defendant's recorded testimony before a grand jury relating to the charged offense.

(C) Organizational Defendant. Upon a defendant's request, if the defendant is an organization, the government must disclose to the defendant any statement described in Rule 16(a)(1)(A) and (B) if the government contends that the person making the statement:

(i) was legally able to bind the defendant regarding the subject of the statement because of that person's position as the defendant's director, officer, employee, or agent; or

(ii) was personally involved in the alleged conduct constituting the offense and was legally able to bind the defendant regarding that conduct because of that person's position as the defendant's director, officer, employee, or agent.

(D) Defendant's Prior Record. Upon a defendant's request, the government must furnish the defendant with a copy of the defendant's prior criminal record that is within the government's possession, custody, or control if the attorney for the government knows—or through due diligence could know—that the record exists.

(E) Documents and Objects. Upon a defendant's request, the government must permit the defendant to inspect and to copy or photograph books, papers, documents, data, photographs, tangible objects, buildings or places, or copies or portions of any of these items, if the item is within the government's possession, custody, or control and:

(i) the item is material to preparing the defense;

(ii) the government intends to use the item in its case-in-chief at trial; or

(iii) the item was obtained from or belongs to the defendant.

(F) Reports of Examinations and Tests. Upon a defendant's request, the government must permit a defendant to inspect and to copy or photograph the results or reports of any physical or mental examination and of any scientific test or experiment if:

(i) the item is within the government's possession, custody, or control;

(ii) the attorney for the government knows—or through due diligence could know—that the item exists; and

(iii) the item is material to preparing the defense or the government intends to use the item in its case-in-chief at trial.

(G) Expert Witnesses. At the defendant's request, the government must give to the defendant a written summary of any testimony that the government intends to use under Rules 702, 703, or 705 of the Federal Rules of Evidence during its case-in-chief at trial. If the government requests discovery under subdivision (b)(1)(C)(ii) and the defendant complies, the government must, at the defendant's request, give to the defendant a written summary of testimony that the government intends to use under Rules 702, 703, or 705 of the Federal Rules of Evidence as evidence at trial on the issue of the defendant's mental condition. The summary provided under this subparagraph must describe the witness's opinions, the bases and reasons for those opinions, and the witness's qualifications.

(2) Information Not Subject to Disclosure. Except as permitted by Rule 16(a)(1)(A)-(D), (F), and (G), this rule does not authorize the discovery or inspection of reports, memoranda, or other internal government documents made by an attorney for the government or other government agent in connection with investigating or prosecuting the case. Nor does this rule authorize the discovery or inspection of statements made by prospective government witnesses except as provided in 18 U.S.C. §3500.

(3) Grand Jury Transcripts. This rule does not apply to the discovery or inspection of a grand jury's recorded proceedings, except as provided in Rules 6, 12(h), 16(a)(l), and 26.2.

(b) Defendant's Disclosure.

(1) Information Subject to Disclosure.

(A) Documents and Objects. If a defendant requests disclosure under Rule 16(a)(1)(E) and the government complies, then the defendant must permit the government, upon request, to inspect and to copy or photograph books, papers, documents, data, photographs, tangible objects, buildings or places, or copies or portions of any of these items if:

(i) the item is within the defendant's possession, custody, or control; and

(ii) the defendant intends to use the item in the defendant's case-in-chief at trial.

(B) Reports of Examinations and Tests. If a defendant requests disclosure under Rule 16(a)(1)(F) and the government complies, the defendant must permit the government, upon request, to inspect and to copy or photograph the results or reports of any physical or mental examination and of any scientific test or experiment if:

(i) the item is within the defendant's possession, custody, or control; and

(ii) the defendant intends to use the item in the defendant's case-in-chief at trial, or intends to call the witness who prepared the report and the report relates to the witness's testimony.

(C) Expert Witnesses. The defendant must, at the government's request, give to the government a written summary of any testimony that the defendant intends to use under Rules 702, 703, or 705 of the Federal Rules of Evidence as evidence at trial, if—

(i) the defendant requests disclosure under subdivision (a)(1)(G) and the government complies; or

(ii) the defendant has given notice under Rule 12.2(b) of an intent to present expert testimony on the defendant's mental condition.

This summary must describe the witness's opinions, the bases and reasons for those opinions, and the witness's qualifications[.]

(2) Information Not Subject to Disclosure. Except for scientific or medical reports, Rule 16(b)(1) does not authorize discovery or inspection of:

(A) reports, memoranda, or other documents made by the defendant, or the defendant's attorney or agent, during the case's investigation or defense; or

(B) a statement made to the defendant, or the defendant's attorney or agent, by:

(i) the defendant;

(ii) a government or defense witness; or

(iii) a prospective government or defense witness.

(c) Continuing Duty to Disclose. A party who discovers additional evidence or material before or during trial must promptly disclose its existence to the other party or the court if:

(1) the evidence or material is subject to discovery or inspection under this rule; and

(2) the other party previously requested, or the court ordered, its production.

(d) Regulating Discovery.

(1) Protective and Modifying Orders. At any time the court may, for good cause, deny, restrict, or defer discovery or inspection, or grant other appropriate relief. The court may permit a party to show good cause by a written statement that the court will inspect ex parte. If relief is granted, the court must preserve the entire text of the party's statement under seal.

(2) Failure to Comply. If a party fails to comply with this rule, the court may:

(A) order that party to permit the discovery or inspection; specify its time, place, and manner; and prescribe other just terms and conditions;

(B) grant a continuance;

(C) prohibit that party from introducing the undisclosed evidence; or

(D) enter any other order that is just under the circumstances.

Rule 17. Subpoena

(a) Content. A subpoena must state the court's name and the title of the proceeding, include the seal of the court, and command the witness to attend and testify at the time and place the subpoena specifies. The clerk must issue a blank subpoena—signed and sealed—to the party requesting it, and that party must fill in the blanks before the subpoena is served.

(b) Defendant Unable to Pay. Upon a defendant's ex parte application, the court must order that a subpoena be issued for a named witness if the defendant shows an inability to pay the witness's fees and the necessity of the witness's presence for an adequate defense. If the court orders a subpoena to be issued, the process costs and witness fees will be paid in the same manner as those paid for witnesses the government subpoenas.

(c) Producing Documents and Objects.

(1) In General. A subpoena may order the witness to produce any books, papers, documents, data, or other objects the subpoena designates. The court may direct the witness to produce the designated items in court before trial or before they are to be offered in evidence. When the items arrive, the court may permit the parties and their attorneys to inspect all or part of them.

(2) Quashing or Modifying the Subpoena. On motion made promptly, the court may quash or modify the subpoena if compliance would be unreasonable or oppressive.

(3) Subpoena for Personal or Confidential Information About a Victim. After a complaint, indictment, or information is filed, a subpoena requiring the production of personal or confidential information about a victim may be served on a third party only by court order. Before entering the order and unless there are exceptional circumstances, the court must require giving notice to the victim

so that the victim can move to quash or modify the subpoena or otherwise object.

(d) Service. A marshal, a deputy marshal, or any nonparty who is at least 18 years old may serve a subpoena. The server must deliver a copy of the subpoena to the witness and must tender to the witness one day's witness-attendance fee and the legal mileage allowance. The server need not tender the attendance fee or mileage allowance when the United States, a federal officer, or a federal agency has requested the subpoena.

(e) Place of Service.

(1) In the United States. A subpoena requiring a witness to attend a hearing or trial may be served at any place within the United States.

(2) In a Foreign Country. If the witness is in a foreign country, 28 U.S.C. §1783 governs the subpoena's service.

(f) Issuing a Deposition Subpoena.

(1) Issuance. A court order to take a deposition authorizes the clerk in the district where the deposition is to be taken to issue a subpoena for any witness named or described in the order.

(2) Place. After considering the convenience of the witness and the parties, the court may order—and the subpoena may require—the witness to appear anywhere the court designates.

(g) Contempt. The court (other than a magistrate judge) may hold in contempt a witness who, without adequate excuse, disobeys a subpoena issued by a federal court in that district. A magistrate judge may hold in contempt a witness who, without adequate excuse, disobeys a subpoena issued by that magistrate judge as provided in 28 U.S.C. §636(e).

(h) Information Not Subject to a Subpoena. No party may subpoena a statement of a witness or of a prospective witness under this rule. Rule 26.2 governs the production of the statement.

Rule 18. Place of Prosecution and Trial

Unless a statute or these rules permit otherwise, the government must prosecute an offense in a district where the offense was committed. The court must set the place of trial within the district with due regard for the convenience of the defendant, any victim, and the witnesses, and the prompt administration of justice.

Rule 21.   Transfer for Trial

(a) For Prejudice. Upon the defendant's motion, the court must transfer the proceeding against that defendant to another district if the court is satisfied that so great a prejudice against the defendant exists in the transferring district that the defendant cannot obtain a fair and impartial trial there.

(b) For Convenience. Upon the defendant's motion, the court may transfer the proceeding, or one or more counts, against that defendant to another district for the convenience of the parties, any victim, and the witnesses, and in the interest of justice.

(c) Proceedings on Transfer. When the court orders a transfer, the clerk must send to the transferee district the file, or a certified copy, and any bail taken. The prosecution will then continue in the transferee district.

(d) Time to File a Motion to Transfer. A motion to transfer may be made at or before arraignment or at any other time the court or these rules prescribe.

Rule 23.   Jury or Nonjury Trial

(a) Jury Trial. If the defendant is entitled to a jury trial, the trial must be by jury unless:
    (1) the defendant waives a jury trial in writing;
    (2) the government consents; and
    (3) the court approves.
(b) Jury Size.
    (1) In General. A jury consists of 12 persons unless this rule provides otherwise.
    (2) Stipulation for a Smaller Jury. At any time before the verdict, the parties may, with the court's approval, stipulate in writing that:
        (A) the jury may consist of fewer than 12 persons; or
        (B) a jury of fewer than 12 persons may return a verdict if the court finds it necessary to excuse a juror for good cause after the trial begins.
    (3) Court Order for a Jury of 11. After the jury has retired to deliberate, the court may permit a jury of 11 persons to return a verdict, even without a stipulation by the parties, if the court finds good cause to excuse a juror.

(c) Nonjury Trial. In a case tried without a jury, the court must find the defendant guilty or not guilty. If a party requests before the finding of guilty or not guilty, the court must state its specific findings of fact in open court or in a written decision or opinion.

Rule 24. Trial Jurors

(a) Examination.

(1) In General. The court may examine prospective jurors or may permit the attorneys for the parties to do so.

(2) Court Examination. If the court examines the jurors, it must permit the attorneys for the parties to:

(A) ask further questions that the court considers proper; or

(B) submit further questions that the court may ask if it considers them proper.

(b) Peremptory Challenges. Each side is entitled to the number of peremptory challenges to prospective jurors specified below. The court may allow additional peremptory challenges to multiple defendants, and may allow the defendants to exercise those challenges separately or jointly.

(1) Capital Case. Each side has 20 peremptory challenges when the government seeks the death penalty.

(2) Other Felony Case. The government has 6 peremptory challenges and the defendant or defendants jointly have 10 peremptory challenges when the defendant is charged with a crime punishable by imprisonment of more than one year.

(3) Misdemeanor Case. Each side has 3 peremptory challenges when the defendant is charged with a crime punishable by fine, imprisonment of one year or less, or both.

(c) Alternate Jurors.

(1) In General. The court may impanel up to 6 alternate jurors to replace any jurors who are unable to perform or who are disqualified from performing their duties.

(2) Procedure.

(A) Alternate jurors must have the same qualifications and be selected and sworn in the same manner as any other juror.

(B) Alternate jurors replace jurors in the same sequence in which the alternates were selected. An alternate juror who replaces a juror has the same authority as the other jurors.

(3) Retaining Alternate Jurors. The court may retain alternate jurors after the jury retires to deliberate. The court must ensure that a retained alternate does not discuss the case with anyone until that alternate replaces a juror or is discharged. If an alternate replaces a juror after deliberations have begun, the court must instruct the jury to begin its deliberations anew.

(4) Peremptory Challenges. Each side is entitled to the number of additional peremptory challenges to prospective alternate jurors specified below. These additional challenges may be used only to remove alternate jurors.

(A) One or Two Alternates. One additional peremptory challenge is permitted when one or two alternates are impaneled.

(B) Three or Four Alternates. Two additional peremptory challenges are permitted when three or four alternates are impaneled.

(C) Five or Six Alternates. Three additional peremptory challenges are permitted when five or six alternates are impaneled.

Rule 26.2. Producing a Witness's Statement

(a) Motion to Produce. After a witness other than the defendant has testified on direct examination, the court, on motion of a party who did not call the witness, must order an attorney for the government or the defendant and the defendant's attorney to produce, for the examination and use of the moving party, any statement of the witness that is in their possession and that relates to the subject matter of the witness's testimony.

(b) Producing the Entire Statement. If the entire statement relates to the subject matter of the witness's testimony, the court must order that the statement be delivered to the moving party.

(c) Producing a Redacted Statement. If the party who called the witness claims that the statement contains information that is privileged or does not relate to the subject matter of the witness's testimony, the court must inspect the statement in camera. After excising any privileged or unrelated portions, the court must order delivery of the redacted statement to the moving party. If the defendant objects to an excision, the court must preserve the entire statement with the excised portion indicated, under seal, as part of the record.

(d) Recess to Examine a Statement. The court may recess the proceedings to allow time for a party to examine the statement and prepare for its use.

(e) Sanction for Failure to Produce or Deliver a Statement. If the party who called the witness disobeys an order to produce or deliver a statement, the court must strike the witness's testimony from the record. If an attorney for the government disobeys the order, the court must declare a mistrial if justice so requires.

(f) "Statement" Defined. As used in this rule, a witness's "statement" means:

(1) a written statement that the witness makes and signs, or otherwise adopts or approves;

(2) a substantially verbatim, contemporaneously recorded recital of the witness's oral statement that is contained in any recording or any transcription of a recording; or

(3) the witness's statement to a grand jury, however taken or recorded, or a transcription of such a statement.

(g) Scope. This rule applies at trial, at a suppression hearing under Rule 12, and to the extent specified in the following rules:

(1) Rule 5.1(h) (preliminary hearing);

(2) Rule 32(i)(2) (sentencing);

(3) Rule 32.1(e) (hearing to revoke or modify probation or supervised release);

(4) Rule 46(j) (detention hearing); and

(5) Rule 8 of the Rules Governing Proceedings under 28 U.S.C. §2255.

Rule 29.   Motion for a Judgment of Acquittal

(a) Before Submission to the Jury. After the government closes its evidence or after the close of all the evidence, the court on the defendant's motion must enter a judgment of acquittal of any offense for which the evidence is insufficient to sustain a conviction. The court may on its own consider whether the evidence is insufficient to sustain a conviction. If the court denies a motion for a judgment of acquittal at the close of the government's evidence, the defendant may offer evidence without having reserved the right to do so.

(b) Reserving Decision. The court may reserve decision on the motion, proceed with the trial (where the motion is made before the close of all the evidence), submit the case to the jury, and decide the motion either before the jury returns a verdict or after it returns a verdict of guilty or is discharged without having returned a verdict. If the court reserves decision, it must decide the motion on the basis of the evidence at the time the ruling was reserved.

(c) After Jury Verdict or Discharge.

(1) Time for a Motion. A defendant may move for a judgment of acquittal, or renew such a motion, within 14 days after a guilty verdict or after the court discharges the jury, whichever is later.

(2) Ruling on the Motion. If the jury has returned a guilty verdict, the court may set aside the verdict and enter an acquittal. If the jury has failed to return a verdict, the court may enter a judgment of acquittal.

(3) No Prior Motion Required. A defendant is not required to move for a judgment of acquittal before the court submits the case to the jury as a prerequisite for making such a motion after jury discharge.

(d) Conditional Ruling on a Motion for a New Trial.

(1) Motion for a New Trial. If the court enters a judgment of acquittal after a guilty verdict, the court must also conditionally determine whether any motion for a new trial should be granted if the judgment of acquittal is later vacated or reversed. The court must specify the reasons for that determination.

(2) Finality. The court's order conditionally granting a motion for a new trial does not affect the finality of the judgment of acquittal.

(3) Appeal.

(A) Grant of a Motion for a New Trial. If the court conditionally grants a motion for a new trial and an appellate court later reverses the judgment of acquittal, the trial court must proceed with the new trial unless the appellate court orders otherwise.

(B) Denial of a Motion for a New Trial. If the court conditionally denies a motion for a new trial, an appellee may assert that the denial was erroneous. If the appellate court later reverses the judgment of acquittal, the trial court must proceed as the appellate court directs.

Rule 29.1. Closing Argument

Closing arguments proceed in the following order:

(a) the government argues;

(b) the defense argues; and

(c) the government rebuts.

Rule 31. Jury Verdict

(a) Return. The jury must return its verdict to a judge in open court. The verdict must be unanimous.

(b) Partial Verdicts, Mistrial, and Retrial.

(1) Multiple Defendants. If there are multiple defendants, the jury may return a verdict at any time during its deliberations as to any defendant about whom it has agreed.

(2) Multiple Counts. If the jury cannot agree on all counts as to any defendant, the jury may return a verdict on those counts on which it has agreed.

(3) Mistrial and Retrial. If the jury cannot agree on a verdict on one or more counts, the court may declare a mistrial on those counts. The government may retry any defendant on any count on which the jury could not agree.

(c) Lesser Offense or Attempt. A defendant may be found guilty of any of the following:

(1) an offense necessarily included in the offense charged;

(2) an attempt to commit the offense charged; or

(3) an attempt to commit an offense necessarily included in the offense charged, if the attempt is an offense in its own right.

(d) Jury Poll. After a verdict is returned but before the jury is discharged, the court must on a party's request, or may on its own, poll the jurors individually. If the poll reveals a lack of unanimity, the court may direct the jury to deliberate further or may declare a mistrial and discharge the jury.

Rule 32. Sentencing and Judgment

(a) [Reserved.]

(b) Time of Sentencing.

(1) In General. The court must impose sentence without unnecessary delay.

(2) Changing Time Limits. The court may, for good cause, change any time limits prescribed in this rule.

(c) Presentence Investigation.

(1) Required Investigation.

(A) In General. The probation officer must conduct a presentence investigation and submit a report to the court before it imposes sentence unless:

(i) 18 U.S.C. §3593(c) or another statute requires otherwise; or

(ii) the court finds that the information in the record enables it to meaningfully exercise its sentencing authority under 18 U.S.C. §3553, and the court explains its finding on the record.

(B) Restitution. If the law permits restitution, the probation officer must conduct an investigation and submit a report that contains sufficient information for the court to order restitution.

(2) Interviewing the Defendant. The probation officer who interviews a defendant as part of a presentence investigation must, on request, give the defendant's attorney notice and a reasonable opportunity to attend the interview.

(d) Presentence Report.

(1) Applying the Advisory Sentencing Guidelines. The presentence report must:

(A) identify all applicable guidelines and policy statements of the Sentencing Commission;

(B) calculate the defendant's offense level and criminal history category;

(C) state the resulting sentencing range and kinds of sentences available;

(D) identify any factor relevant to:

(i) the appropriate kind of sentence, or

(ii) the appropriate sentence within the applicable sentencing range; and

(E) identify any basis for departing from the applicable sentencing range.

(2) Additional Information. The presentence report must also contain the following:

(A) the defendant's history and characteristics, including:

(i) any prior criminal record;

(ii) the defendant's financial condition; and

(iii) any circumstances affecting the defendant's behavior that may be helpful in imposing sentence or in correctional treatment;

(B) information that assesses any financial, social, psychological, and medical impact on any victim;

(C) when appropriate, the nature and extent of nonprison programs and resources available to the defendant;

(D) when the law provides for restitution, information sufficient for a restitution order;

(E) if the court orders a study under 18 U.S.C. §3552(b), any resulting report and recommendation;

(F) a statement of whether the government seeks forfeiture under Rule 32.2 and any other law; and

(G) any other information that the court requires, including information relevant to the factors under 18 U.S.C. §3553(a).

(3) Exclusions. The presentence report must exclude the following:

(A) any diagnoses that, if disclosed, might seriously disrupt a rehabilitation program;

(B) any sources of information obtained upon a promise of confidentiality; and

(C) any other information that, if disclosed, might result in physical or other harm to the defendant or others.

(e) Disclosing the Report and Recommendation.

(1) Time to Disclose. Unless the defendant has consented in writing, the probation officer must not submit a presentence report to the court or disclose its contents to anyone until the defendant has pleaded guilty or nolo contendere, or has been found guilty.

(2) Minimum Required Notice. The probation officer must give the presentence report to the defendant, the defendant's attorney, and an attorney for the government at least 35 days before sentencing unless the defendant waives this minimum period.

(3) Sentence Recommendation. By local rule or by order in a case, the court may direct the probation officer not to disclose to anyone other than the court the officer's recommendation on the sentence.

(f) Objecting to the Report.

(1) Time to Object. Within 14 days after receiving the presentence report, the parties must state in writing any objections, including objections to material information, sentencing guideline ranges, and policy statements contained in or omitted from the report.

(2) Serving Objections. An objecting party must provide a copy of its objections to the opposing party and to the probation officer.

(3) Action on Objections. After receiving objections, the probation officer may meet with the parties to discuss the objections. The probation officer may then investigate further and revise the presentence report as appropriate.

(g) Submitting the Report. At least 14 days before sentencing, the probation officer must submit to the court and to the parties the presentence report and an addendum containing any unresolved objections, the grounds for those objections, and the probation officer's comments on them.

(h) Notice of Possible Departure from Sentencing Guidelines. Before the court may depart from the applicable sentencing range on a ground not identified for departure either in the presentence report or in a party's prehearing submission, the court must give the parties reasonable notice that it is contemplating such a departure. The notice must specify any ground on which the court is contemplating a departure.

(i) Sentencing.

(1) In General. At sentencing, the court:

(A) must verify that the defendant and the defendant's attorney have read and discussed the presentence report and any addendum to the report;

(B) must give to the defendant and an attorney for the government a written summary of—or summarize in camera—any information excluded from the presentence report under Rule 32(d)(3) on which the court will rely in sentencing, and give them a reasonable opportunity to comment on that information;

(C) must allow the parties' attorneys to comment on the probation officer's determinations and other matters relating to an appropriate sentence; and

(D) may, for good cause, allow a party to make a new objection at any time before sentence is imposed.

(2) Introducing Evidence; Producing a Statement. The court may permit the parties to introduce evidence on the objections. If a witness testifies at sentencing, Rule 26.2(a)-(d) and (f) applies. If a party fails to comply with a Rule 26.2 order to produce a witness's statement, the court must not consider that witness's testimony.

(3) Court Determinations. At sentencing, the court:

(A) may accept any undisputed portion of the presentence report as a finding of fact;

(B) must—for any disputed portion of the presentence report or other controverted matter—rule on the dispute or determine that a ruling is unnecessary either because the matter will not affect sentencing, or because the court will not consider the matter in sentencing; and

(C) must append a copy of the court's determinations under this rule to any copy of the presentence report made available to the Bureau of Prisons.

(4) Opportunity to Speak.

(A) By a Party. Before imposing sentence, the court must:

(i) provide the defendant's attorney an opportunity to speak on the defendant's behalf;

(ii) address the defendant personally in order to permit the defendant to speak or present any information to mitigate the sentence; and

(iii) provide an attorney for the government an opportunity to speak equivalent to that of the defendant's attorney.

(B) By a Victim. Before imposing sentence, the court must address any victim of the crime who is present at sentencing and must permit the victim to be reasonably heard.

(C) By a Victim of a Felony Offense. Before imposing sentence, the court must address any victim of a felony offense, not involving violence or sexual abuse, who is present at sentencing and must permit the victim to speak or submit any information about the sentence. If the felony offense involved multiple victims, the court may limit the number of victims who will address the court.

(D) In Camera Proceedings. Upon a party's motion and for good cause, the court may hear in camera any statement made under Rule 32(i)(4).

(j) Defendant's Right to Appeal.

(1) Advice of a Right to Appeal.

(A) Appealing a Conviction. If the defendant pleaded not guilty and was convicted, after sentencing the court must advise the defendant of the right to appeal the conviction.

(B) Appealing a Sentence. After sentencing—regardless of the defendant's plea—the court must advise the defendant of any right to appeal the sentence.

(C) Appeal Costs. The court must advise a defendant who is unable to pay appeal costs of the right to ask for permission to appeal in forma pauperis.

(2) Clerk's Filing of Notice. If the defendant so requests, the clerk must immediately prepare and file a notice of appeal on the defendant's behalf.

(k) Judgment.

(1) In General. In the judgment of conviction, the court must set forth the plea, the jury verdict or the court's findings, the adjudication, and the sentence. If the defendant is found not guilty or is otherwise entitled to be discharged, the court must so order. The judge must sign the judgment, and the clerk must enter it.

(2) Criminal Forfeiture. Forfeiture procedures are governed by Rule 32.2.

Rule 33.   New Trial

(a) Defendant's Motion. Upon the defendant's motion, the court may vacate any judgment and grant a new trial if the interest of justice so requires. If the case was tried without a jury, the court may take additional testimony and enter a new judgment.

(b) Time to File.

(1) Newly Discovered Evidence. Any motion for a new trial grounded on newly discovered evidence must be filed within 3 years after the verdict or finding of guilty. If an appeal is pending, the court may not grant a motion for a new trial until the appellate court remands the case.

(2) Other Grounds. Any motion for a new trial grounded on any reason other than newly discovered evidence must be filed within 14 days after the verdict or finding of guilty.

Rule 41.   Search and Seizure

(a) Scope and Definitions.

(1) Scope. This rule does not modify any statute regulating search or seizure, or the issuance and execution of a search warrant in special circumstances.

(2) Definitions. The following definitions apply under this rule:

(A) "Property" includes documents, books, papers, any other tangible objects, and information.

(B) "Daytime" means the hours between 6:00 a.m. and 10:00 p.m. according to local time.

(C) "Federal law enforcement officer" means a government agent (other than an attorney for the government) who is engaged in enforcing the criminal laws and is within any category of officers authorized by the Attorney General to request a search warrant.

(D) "Domestic terrorism" and "international terrorism" have the meanings set out in 18 U.S.C. §2331.

(E) "Tracking device" has the meaning set out in 18 U.S.C. §3117(b).

(b) Venue for a Warrant Application. At the request of a federal law enforcement officer or an attorney for the government:

(1) a magistrate judge with authority in the district—or if none is reasonably available, a judge of a state court of record in the district—has authority to issue a warrant to search for and seize a person or property located within the district;

(2) a magistrate judge with authority in the district has authority to issue a warrant for a person or property outside the district if the person or property is located within the district when the warrant is issued but might move or be moved outside the district before the warrant is executed;

(3) a magistrate judge—in an investigation of domestic terrorism or international terrorism—with authority in any district in which activities related to the terrorism may have occurred has authority to issue a warrant for a person or property within or outside that district;

(4) a magistrate judge with authority in the district has authority to issue a warrant to install within the district a tracking device; the warrant may authorize use of the device to track the movement of a person or property located within the district, outside the district, or both; and

(5) a magistrate judge having authority in any district where activities related to the crime may have occurred, or in the District of Columbia, may issue a warrant for property that is located outside the jurisdiction of any state or district, but within any of the following:

(A) a United States territory, possession, or commonwealth;

(B) the premises—no matter who owns them—of a United States diplomatic or consular mission in a foreign state, including any appurtenant building, part of a building, or land used for the mission's purposes; or

(C) a residence and any appurtenant land owned or leased by the United States and used by United States personnel assigned to a United States diplomatic or consular mission in a foreign state.

(6) a magistrate judge with authority in any district where activities related to a crime may have occurred has authority to issue a

warrant to use remote access to search electronic storage media and to seize or copy electronically stored information located within or outside that district if:

(A) the district where the media or information is located has been concealed through technological means; or

(B) in an investigation of a violation of 18 U.S.C. § 1030(a)(5), the media are protected computers that have been damaged without authorization and are located in five or more districts.

(c) Persons or Property Subject to Search or Seizure. A warrant may be issued for any of the following:

(1) evidence of a crime;

(2) contraband, fruits of crime, or other items illegally possessed;

(3) property designed for use, intended for use, or used in committing a crime; or

(4) a person to be arrested or a person who is unlawfully restrained.

(d) Obtaining a Warrant.

(1) In General. After receiving an affidavit or other information, a magistrate judge—or if authorized by Rule 41(b), a judge of a state court of record—must issue the warrant if there is probable cause to search for and seize a person or property or to install and use a tracking device.

(2) Requesting a Warrant in the Presence of a Judge.

(A) Warrant on an Affidavit. When a federal law enforcement officer or an attorney for the government presents an affidavit in support of a warrant, the judge may require the affiant to appear personally and may examine under oath the affiant and any witness the affiant produces.

(B) Warrant on Sworn Testimony. The judge may wholly or partially dispense with a written affidavit and base a warrant on sworn testimony if doing so is reasonable under the circumstances.

(C) Recording Testimony. Testimony taken in support of a warrant must be recorded by a court reporter or by a suitable recording device, and the judge must file the transcript or recording with the clerk, along with any affidavit.

(3) Requesting a Warrant by Telephonic or Other Reliable Electronic Means. In accordance with Rule 4.1, a magistrate judge may issue a warrant based on information communicated by telephone or other reliable electronic means.

(e) Issuing the Warrant.

(1) In General. The magistrate judge or a judge of a state court of record must issue the warrant to an officer authorized to execute it.

(2) Contents of the Warrant.

(A) Warrant to Search for and Seize a Person or Property. Except for a tracking-device warrant, the warrant must identify the person or property to be searched, identify any person or property to be seized, and designate the magistrate judge to whom it must be returned. The warrant must command the officer to:

(i) execute the warrant within a specified time no longer than 14 days;

(ii) execute the warrant during the daytime, unless the judge for good cause expressly authorizes execution at another time; and

(iii) return the warrant to the magistrate judge designated in the warrant.

(B) Warrant Seeking Electronically Stored Information. A warrant under Rule 41(e)(2)(A) may authorize the seizure of electronic storage media or the seizure or copying of electronically stored information. Unless otherwise specified, the warrant authorizes a later review of the media or information consistent with the warrant. The time for executing the warrant in Rule 41(e)(2)(A) and (f)(1)(A) refers to the seizure or on-site copying of the media or information, and not to any later off-site copying or review.

(C) Warrant for a Tracking Device. A tracking-device warrant must identify the person or property to be tracked, designate the magistrate judge to whom it must be returned, and specify a reasonable length of time that the device may be used. The time must not exceed 45 days from the date the warrant was issued. The court may, for good cause, grant one or more extensions for a reasonable period not to exceed 45 days each. The warrant must command the officer to:

(i) complete any installation authorized by the warrant within a specified time no longer than 10 days;

(ii) perform any installation authorized by the warrant during the daytime, unless the judge for good cause expressly authorizes installation at another time; and

(iii) return the warrant to the judge designated in the warrant.

(f) Executing and Returning the Warrant.

(1) Warrant to Search for and Seize a Person or Property.

(A) Noting the Time. The officer executing the warrant must enter on it the exact date and time it was executed.

(B) Inventory. An officer present during the execution of the warrant must prepare and verify an inventory of any property seized. The officer must do so in the presence of another officer and the person from whom, or from whose premises, the property was taken. If either one is not present, the officer must prepare and verify the inventory in the presence of at least one other credible person. In a case involving the seizure of electronic storage media or the seizure or copying of electronically stored information, the inventory may be limited to describing the physical storage media that were seized or copied. The officer may retain a copy of the electronically stored information that was seized or copied.

(C) Receipt. The officer executing the warrant must give a copy of the warrant and a receipt for the property taken to the person from whom, or from whose premises, the property was taken or leave a copy of the warrant and receipt at the place where the officer took the property. For a warrant to use remote access to search electronic storage media and seize or copy electronically stored information, the officer must make reasonable efforts to serve a copy of the warrant and receipt on the person whose property was searched or who possessed the information that was seized or copied. Service may be accomplished by any means, including electronic means, reasonably calculated to reach that person.

(D) Return. The officer executing the warrant must promptly return it—together with a copy of the inventory—to the magistrate judge designated on the warrant. The officer may do so by reliable electronic means. The judge must, on request, give a copy of the inventory to the person from whom, or from whose premises, the property was taken and to the applicant for the warrant.

(2) Warrant for a Tracking Device.

(A) Noting the Time. The officer executing a tracking-device warrant must enter on it the exact date and time the device was installed and the period during which it was used.

(B) Return. Within 10 days after the use of the tracking device has ended, the officer executing the warrant must return it to the judge designated in the warrant. The officer may do so by reliable electronic means.

(C) Service. Within 10 days after the use of the tracking device has ended, the officer executing a tracking-device warrant must serve a copy of the warrant on the person who was tracked or whose property was tracked. Service may be accomplished by delivering a copy to the person who, or whose property, was tracked; or by leaving a copy at the person's residence or usual place of abode with an individual of suitable age and discretion who resides at that location and by mailing a copy to the person's last known address. Upon request of the government, the judge may delay notice as provided in Rule 41(f)(3).

(3) Delayed Notice. Upon the government's request, a magistrate judge—or if authorized by Rule 41(b), a judge of a state court of record—may delay any notice required by this rule if the delay is authorized by statute.

(g) Motion to Return Property. A person aggrieved by an unlawful search and seizure of property or by the deprivation of property may move for the property's return. The motion must be filed in the district where the property was seized. The court must receive evidence on any factual issue necessary to decide the motion. If it grants the motion, the court must return the property to the movant, but may impose reasonable conditions to protect access to the property and its use in later proceedings.

(h) Motion to Suppress. A defendant may move to suppress evidence in the court where the trial will occur, as Rule 12 provides.

(i) Forwarding Papers to the Clerk. The magistrate judge to whom the warrant is returned must attach to the warrant a copy of the return, of the inventory, and of all other related papers and must deliver them to the clerk in the district where the property was seized.

Rule 44. Right to and Appointment of Counsel

(a) Right to Appointed Counsel. A defendant who is unable to obtain counsel is entitled to have counsel appointed to represent the defendant at every stage of the proceeding from initial appearance through appeal, unless the defendant waives this right.

(b) Appointment Procedure. Federal law and local court rules govern the procedure for implementing the right to counsel.

(c) Inquiry into Joint Representation.

(1) Joint Representation. Joint representation occurs when:

(A) two or more defendants have been charged jointly under Rule 8(b) or have been joined for trial under Rule 13; and

(B) the defendants are represented by the same counsel or counsel who are associated in law practice.

(2) *Court's Responsibilities in Cases of Joint Representation.* The court must promptly inquire about the propriety of joint representation and must personally advise each defendant of the right to the effective assistance of counsel, including separate representation. Unless there is good cause to believe that no conflict of interest is likely to arise, the court must take appropriate measures to protect each defendant's right to counsel.

Rule 45.   Computing and Extending Time[a]

(a) Computing Time. The following rules apply in computing any time period specified in these rules, in any local rule or court order, or in any statute that does not specify a method of computing time.

(1) *Period Stated in Days or a Longer Unit.* When the period is stated in days or a longer unit of time:

(A) exclude the day of the event that triggers the period;

(B) count every day, including intermediate Saturdays, Sundays, and legal holidays; and

(C) include the last day of the period, but if the last day is a Saturday, Sunday, or legal holiday, the period continues to run until the end of the next day that is not a Saturday, Sunday, or legal holiday.

(2) *Period Stated in Hours.* When the period is stated in hours:

(A) begin counting immediately on the occurrence of the event that triggers the period;

---

[a] The Supreme Court has approved an amendment to Rule 45(c) that would bring this subsection into conformity with a proposed amendment to Rule 49 ("Serving and Filing Papers"). In the absence of some action by Congress, the amendment will take effect on December 1, 2018. Rule 45(c) would be amended as follows:

(c) Additional Time After Certain Kinds of Service. Whenever a party must or may act within a specified time after being served and service is made under ~~Federal Rule of Civil Procedure~~ 49(a)(4)(C), (D), and (E) ~~5(b)(2)(C)~~ (mailing), ~~(D)~~ (leaving with the clerk), or ~~(F)~~ (other means consented to), 3 days are added after the period would otherwise expire under subdivision (a).

(B) count every hour, including hours during intermediate Saturdays, Sundays, and legal holidays; and

(C) if the period would end on a Saturday, Sunday, or legal holiday, the period continues to run until the same time on the next day that is not a Saturday, Sunday, or legal holiday.

(3) Inaccessibility of the Clerk's Office. Unless the court orders otherwise, if the clerk's office is inaccessible:

(A) on the last day for filing under Rule 45(a)(1), then the time for filing is extended to the first accessible day that is not a Saturday, Sunday, or legal holiday; or

(B) during the last hour for filing under Rule 45(a)(2), then the time for filing is extended to the same time on the first accessible day that is not a Saturday, Sunday, or legal holiday.

(4) "Last Day" Defined. Unless a different time is set by a statute, local rule, or court order, the last day ends:

(A) for electronic filing, at midnight in the court's time zone; and

(B) for filing by other means, when the clerk's office is scheduled to close.

(5) "Next Day" Defined. The "next day" is determined by continuing to count forward when the period is measured after an event and backward when measured before an event.

(6) "Legal Holiday" Defined. "Legal holiday" means:

(A) the day set aside by statute for observing New Year's Day, Martin Luther King Jr.'s Birthday, Washington's Birthday, Memorial Day, Independence Day, Labor Day, Columbus Day, Veterans' Day, Thanksgiving Day, or Christmas Day;

(B) any day declared a holiday by the President or Congress; and

(C) for periods that are measured after an event, any other day declared a holiday by the state where the district court is located.

(b) Extending Time.

(1) In General. When an act must or may be done within a specified period, the court on its own may extend the time, or for good cause may do so on a party's motion made:

(A) before the originally prescribed or previously extended time expires; or

(B) after the time expires if the party failed to act because of excusable neglect.

(2) Exception. The court may not extend the time to take any action under Rule 35, except as stated in that rule.

(c) Additional Time After Certain Kinds of Service. Whenever a party must or may act within a specified time after being served and service is made under Rule 49(a)(4)(C), (D), and (E), 3 days are added after the period would otherwise expire under subdivision (a).

Rule 46.   Release from Custody; Supervising Detention

(a) Before Trial. The provisions of 18 U.S.C. §§3142 and 3144 govern pretrial release.

(b) During Trial. A person released before trial continues on release during trial under the same terms and conditions. But the court may order different terms and conditions or terminate the release if necessary to ensure that the person will be present during trial or that the person's conduct will not obstruct the orderly and expeditious progress of the trial.

(c) Pending Sentencing or Appeal. The provisions of 18 U.S.C. §3143 govern release pending sentencing or appeal. The burden of establishing that the defendant will not flee or pose a danger to any other person or to the community rests with the defendant.

(d) Pending Hearing on a Violation of Probation or Supervised Release. Rule 32.1(a)(6) governs release pending a hearing on a violation of probation or supervised release.

(e) Surety. The court must not approve a bond unless any surety appears to be qualified. Every surety, except a legally approved corporate surety, must demonstrate by affidavit that its assets are adequate. The court may require the affidavit to describe the following:

(1) the property that the surety proposes to use as security;

(2) any encumbrance on that property;

(3) the number and amount of any other undischarged bonds and bail undertakings the surety has issued; and

(4) any other liability of the surety.

(f) Bail Forfeiture.

(1) Declaration. The court must declare the bail forfeited if a condition of the bond is breached.

(2) Setting Aside. The court may set aside in whole or in part a bail forfeiture upon any condition the court may impose if:

(A) the surety later surrenders into custody the person released on the surety's appearance bond; or

(B) it appears that justice does not require bail forfeiture.

(3) Enforcement.

(A) Default Judgment and Execution. If it does not set aside a bail forfeiture, the court must, upon the government's motion, enter a default judgment.

(B) Jurisdiction and Service. By entering into a bond, each surety submits to the district court's jurisdiction and irrevocably appoints the district clerk as its agent to receive service of any filings affecting its liability.

(C) Motion to Enforce. The court may, upon the government's motion, enforce the surety's liability without an independent action. The government must serve any motion, and notice as the court prescribes, on the district clerk. If so served, the clerk must promptly mail a copy to the surety at its last known address.

(4) Remission. After entering a judgment under Rule 46(f)(3), the court may remit in whole or in part the judgment under the same conditions specified in Rule 46(f)(2).

(g) Exoneration. The court must exonerate the surety and release any bail when a bond condition has been satisfied or when the court has set aside or remitted the forfeiture. The court must exonerate a surety who deposits cash in the amount of the bond or timely surrenders the defendant into custody.

(h) Supervising Detention Pending Trial.

(1) In General. To eliminate unnecessary detention, the court must supervise the detention within the district of any defendants awaiting trial and of any persons held as material witnesses.

(2) Reports. An attorney for the government must report biweekly to the court, listing each material witness held in custody for more than 10 days pending indictment, arraignment, or trial. For each material witness listed in the report, an attorney for the government must state why the witness should not be released with or without a deposition being taken under Rule 15(a).

(i) Forfeiture of Property. The court may dispose of a charged offense by ordering the forfeiture of 18 U.S.C. §3142(c)(1)(B)(xi) property under 18 U.S.C. §3146(d), if a fine in the amount of the property's value would be an appropriate sentence for the charged offense.

(j) Producing a Statement.

(1) In General. Rule 26.2(a)-(d) and (f) applies at a detention hearing under 18 U.S.C. §3142, unless the court for good cause rules otherwise.

(2) Sanctions for Not Producing a Statement. If a party disobeys a Rule 26.2 order to produce a witness's statement, the court must not consider that witness's testimony at the detention hearing.

Rule 51.   Preserving Claimed Error

(a) Exceptions Unnecessary. Exceptions to rulings or orders of the court are unnecessary.

(b) Preserving a Claim of Error. A party may preserve a claim of error by informing the court—when the court ruling or order is made or sought—of the action the party wishes the court to take, or the party's objection to the court's action and the grounds for that objection. If a party does not have an opportunity to object to a ruling or order, the absence of an objection does not later prejudice that party. A ruling or order that admits or excludes evidence is governed by Federal Rule of Evidence 103.

Rule 52.   Harmless and Plain Error

(a) Harmless Error. Any error, defect, irregularity, or variance that does not affect substantial rights must be disregarded.

(b) Plain Error. A plain error that affects substantial rights may be considered even though it was not brought to the court's attention.

Wire and Electronic Communications Interception and Interception of Oral Communications Act

18 U.S.C. §2510. Definitions

As used in this chapter—

(1) "wire communication" means any aural transfer made in whole or in part through the use of facilities for the transmission of communications by the aid of wire, cable, or other like connection between the

point of origin and the point of reception (including the use of such connection in a switching station) furnished or operated by any person engaged in providing or operating such facilities for the transmission of interstate or foreign communications or communications affecting interstate or foreign commerce;

(2) "oral communication" means any oral communication uttered by a person exhibiting an expectation that such communication is not subject to interception under circumstances justifying such expectation, but such term does not include any electronic communication;

(3) "State" means any State of the United States, the District of Columbia, the Commonwealth of Puerto Rico, and any territory or possession of the United States;

(4) "intercept" means the aural or other acquisition of the contents of any wire, electronic, or oral communication through the use of any electronic, mechanical, or other device.

(5) "electronic, mechanical, or other device" means any device or apparatus which can be used to intercept a wire, oral, or electronic communication other than—

(a) any telephone or telegraph instrument, equipment or facility, or any component thereof,

(i) furnished to the subscriber or user by a provider of wire or electronic communication service in the ordinary course of its business and being used by the subscriber or user in the ordinary course of its business or furnished by such subscriber or user for connection to the facilities of such service and used in the ordinary course of its business; or

(ii) being used by a provider of wire or electronic communication service in the ordinary course of its business, or by an investigative or law enforcement officer in the ordinary course of his duties;

(b) a hearing aid or similar device being used to correct subnormal hearing to not better than normal;

(6) "person" means any employee, or agent of the United States or any State or political subdivision thereof, and any individual, partnership, association, joint stock company, trust, or corporation;

(7) "Investigative or law enforcement officer" means any officer of the United States or of a State or political subdivision thereof, who is empowered by law to conduct investigations of or to make arrests for offenses enumerated in this chapter, and any attorney authorized by law to prosecute or participate in the prosecution of such offenses;

(8) "contents," when used with respect to any wire, oral, or electronic communication, includes any information concerning the substance, purport, or meaning of that communication;

(9) "Judge of competent jurisdiction" means—

(a) a judge of a United States district court or a United States court of appeals; and

(b) a judge of any court of general criminal jurisdiction of a State who is authorized by a statute of that State to enter orders authorizing interceptions of wire, oral, or electronic communications;

(10) "communication common carrier" has the meaning given that term in section 3 of the Communications Act of 1934;

(11) "aggrieved person" means a person who was a party to any intercepted wire, oral, or electronic communication or a person against whom the interception was directed;

(12) "electronic communication" means any transfer of signs, signals, writing, images, sounds, data, or intelligence of any nature transmitted in whole or in part by a wire, radio, electromagnetic, photoelectronic or photooptical system that affects interstate or foreign commerce, but does not include—

(A) any wire or oral communication;

(B) any communication made through a tone-only paging device;

(C) any communication from a tracking device (as defined in section 3117 of this title); or

(D) electronic funds transfer information stored by a financial institution in a communications system used for the electronic storage and transfer of funds;

(13) "user" means any person or entity who—

(A) uses an electronic communication service; and

(B) is duly authorized by the provider of such service to engage in such use;

(14) "electronic communications system" means any wire, radio, electromagnetic, photooptical or photoelectronic facilities for the transmission of wire or electronic communications, and any computer facilities or related electronic equipment for the electronic storage of such communications;

(15) "electronic communication service" means any service which provides to users thereof the ability to send or receive wire or electronic communications;

(16) "readily accessible to the general public" means, with respect to a radio communication, that such communication is not—

(A) scrambled or encrypted;

(B) transmitted using modulation techniques whose essential parameters have been withheld from the public with the intention of preserving the privacy of such communication;

(C) carried on a subcarrier or other signal subsidiary to a radio transmission;

(D) transmitted over a communication system provided by a common carrier, unless the communication is a tone only paging system communication; or

(E) transmitted on frequencies allocated under part 25, subpart D, E, or F of part 74, or part 94 of the Rules of the Federal Communications Commission, unless, in the case of a communication transmitted on a frequency allocated under part 74 that is not exclusively allocated to broadcast auxiliary services, the communication is a two-way voice communication by radio;

(17) "electronic storage" means —

(A) any temporary, intermediate storage of a wire or electronic communication incidental to the electronic transmission thereof; and

(B) any storage of such communication by an electronic communication service for purposes of backup protection of such communication;

(18) "aural transfer" means a transfer containing the human voice at any point between and including the point of origin and the point of reception;

(19) "foreign intelligence information," for purposes of section 2517(6) of this title, means —

(A) information, whether or not concerning a United States person, that relates to the ability of the United States to protect against —

(i) actual or potential attack or other grave hostile acts of a foreign power or an agent of a foreign power;

(ii) sabotage or international terrorism by a foreign power or an agent of a foreign power; or

(iii) clandestine intelligence activities by an intelligence service or network of a foreign power or by an agent of a foreign power; or

(B) information, whether or not concerning a United States person, with respect to a foreign power or foreign territory that relates to —

(i) the national defense or the security of the United States; or

(ii) the conduct of the foreign affairs of the United States;

(20) "protected computer" has the meaning set forth in section 1030; and

(21) "computer trespasser"—

(A) means a person who accesses a protected computer without authorization and thus has no reasonable expectation of privacy in any communication transmitted to, through, or from the protected computer; and

(B) does not include a person known by the owner or operator of the protected computer to have an existing contractual relationship with the owner or operator of the protected computer for access to all or part of the protected computer.

18 U.S.C. §2511. Interception and Disclosure of Wire, Oral, or Electronic Communications Prohibited

(1) Except as otherwise specifically provided in this chapter any person who—

(a) intentionally intercepts, endeavors to intercept, or procures any other person to intercept or endeavor to intercept, any wire, oral, or electronic communication;

(b) intentionally uses, endeavors to use, or procures any other person to use or endeavor to use any electronic, mechanical, or other device to intercept any oral communication when—

(i) such device is affixed to, or otherwise transmits a signal through, a wire, cable, or other like connection used in wire communication; or

(ii) such device transmits communications by radio, or interferes with the transmission of such communication; or

(iii) such person knows, or has reason to know, that such device or any component thereof has been sent through the mail or transported in interstate or foreign commerce; or

(iv) such use or endeavor to use (A) takes place on the premises of any business or other commercial establishment the operations of which affect interstate or foreign commerce; or (B) obtains or is for the purpose of obtaining information relating to the operations of any business or other commercial establishment the operations of which affect interstate or foreign commerce; or

(v) such person acts in the District of Columbia, the Commonwealth of Puerto Rico, or any territory or possession of the United States;

(c) intentionally discloses, or endeavors to disclose, to any other person the contents of any wire, oral, or electronic communication, knowing or having reason to know that the information was obtained through the interception of a wire, oral, or electronic communication in violation of this subsection;

(d) intentionally uses, or endeavors to use, the contents of any wire, oral, or electronic communication, knowing or having reason to know that the information was obtained through the interception of a wire, oral, or electronic communication in violation of this subsection; or

(e)(i) intentionally discloses, or endeavors to disclose, to any other person the contents of any wire, oral, or electronic communication, intercepted by means authorized by sections 2511(2)(a)(ii), 2511(2)(b)-(c), 2511(2)(e), 2516, and 2518 of this chapter,

(ii) knowing or having reason to know that the information was obtained through the interception of such a communication in connection with a criminal investigation,

(iii) having obtained or received the information in connection with a criminal investigation, and

(iv) with intent to improperly obstruct, impede, or interfere with a duly authorized criminal investigation, shall be punished as provided in subsection (4) or shall be subject to suit as provided in subsection (5).

(2)(a)(i) It shall not be unlawful under this chapter for an operator of a switchboard, or an officer, employee, or agent of a provider of wire or electronic communication service, whose facilities are used in the transmission of a wire or electronic communication, to intercept, disclose, or use that communication in the normal course of his employment while engaged in any activity which is a necessary incident to the rendition of his service or to the protection of the rights or property of the provider of that service, except that a provider of wire communication service to the public shall not utilize service observing or random monitoring except for mechanical or service quality control checks.

(ii) Notwithstanding any other law, providers of wire or electronic communication service, their officers, employees, and agents, landlords, custodians, or other persons, are authorized to provide information, facilities, or technical assistance to persons authorized by law to intercept wire, oral, or electronic communications or to conduct electronic surveillance, as defined in section 101 of the Foreign Intelligence Surveillance Act of 1978, if such provider, its officers, employees, or agents, landlord, custodian, or other specified person, has been provided with—

(A) a court order directing such assistance or a court order pursuant to section 704 of the Foreign Intelligence Surveillance Act of 1978 signed by the authorizing judge, or

(B) a certification in writing by a person specified in section 2518(7) of this title or the Attorney General of the United States that no warrant or court order is required by law, that all statutory requirements have been met, and that the specified assistance is required, setting forth the period of time during which the provision of the information, facilities, or technical assistance is authorized and specifying the information, facilities, or technical assistance required. No provider of wire or electronic communication service, officer, employee, or agent thereof, or landlord, custodian, or other specified person shall disclose the existence of any interception or surveillance or the device used to accomplish the interception or surveillance with respect to which the person has been furnished a court order or certification under this chapter, except as may otherwise be required by legal process and then only after prior notification to the Attorney General or to the principal prosecuting attorney of a State or any political subdivision of a State, as may be appropriate. Any such disclosure, shall render such person liable for the civil damages provided for in section 2520. No cause of action shall lie in any court against any provider of wire or electronic communication service, its officers, employees, or agents, landlord, custodian, or other specified person for providing information, facilities, or assistance in accordance with the terms of a court order, statutory authorization, or certification under this chapter.

(iii) If a certification under subparagraph (ii)(B) for assistance to obtain foreign intelligence information is based on statutory authority, the certification shall identify the specific statutory provision and shall certify that the statutory requirements have been met.

(b) It shall not be unlawful under this chapter for an officer, employee, or agent of the Federal Communications Commission, in the normal course of his employment and in discharge of the monitoring responsibilities exercised by the Commission in the enforcement of chapter 5 of title 47 of the United States Code, to intercept a wire or electronic communication, or oral communication transmitted by radio, or to disclose or use the information thereby obtained.

(c) It shall not be unlawful under this chapter for a person acting under color of law to intercept a wire, oral, or electronic communication, where such person is a party to the communication or one of the parties to the communication has given prior consent to such interception.

(d) It shall not be unlawful under this chapter for a person not acting under color of law to intercept a wire, oral, or electronic communication where such person is a party to the communication or where one of the parties to the communication has given prior consent to such interception unless such communication is intercepted for the purpose of committing any criminal or tortious act in violation of the Constitution or laws of the United States or of any State.

(e) Notwithstanding any other provision of this title or section 705 or 706 of the Communications Act of 1934, it shall not be unlawful for an officer, employee, or agent of the United States in the normal course of his official duty to conduct electronic surveillance, as defined in section 101 of the Foreign Intelligence Surveillance Act of 1978, as authorized by that Act.

(f) Nothing contained in this chapter or chapter 121 or 206 of this title, or section 705 of the Communications Act of 1934, shall be deemed to affect the acquisition by the United States Government of foreign intelligence information from international or foreign communications, or foreign intelligence activities conducted in accordance with otherwise applicable Federal law involving a foreign electronic communications system, utilizing a means other than electronic surveillance as defined in section 101 of the Foreign Intelligence Surveillance Act of 1978, and procedures in this chapter or chapter 121 and the Foreign Intelligence Surveillance Act of 1978 shall be the exclusive means by which electronic surveillance, as defined in section 101 of such Act, and the interception of domestic wire, oral, and electronic communications may be conducted.

(g) It shall not be unlawful under this chapter or chapter 121 of this title for any person—

(i) to intercept or access an electronic communication made through an electronic communication system that is configured so that such electronic communication is readily accessible to the general public;

(ii) to intercept any radio communication which is transmitted—

(I) by any station for the use of the general public, or that relates to ships, aircraft, vehicles, or persons in distress;

(II) by any governmental, law enforcement, civil defense, private land mobile, or public safety communications system, including police and fire, readily accessible to the general public;

(III) by a station operating on an authorized frequency within the bands allocated to the amateur, citizens band, or general mobile radio services; or

(IV) by any marine or aeronautical communications system;

(iii) to engage in any conduct which—

(I) is prohibited by section 633 of the Communications Act of 1934; or

(II) is excepted from the application of section 705(a) of the Communications Act of 1934 by section 705(b) of that Act;

(iv) to intercept any wire or electronic communication the transmission of which is causing harmful interference to any lawfully operating station or consumer electronic equipment, to the extent necessary to identify the source of such interference; or

(v) for other users of the same frequency to intercept any radio communication made through a system that utilizes frequencies monitored by individuals engaged in the provision or the use of such system, if such communication is not scrambled or encrypted.

(h) It shall not be unlawful under this chapter—

(i) to use a pen register or a trap and trace device (as those terms are defined for the purposes of chapter 206 (relating to pen registers and trap and trace devices) of this title); or

(ii) for a provider of electronic communication service to record the fact that a wire or electronic communication was initiated or completed in order to protect such provider, another provider furnishing service toward the completion of the wire or electronic communication, or a user of that service, from fraudulent, unlawful or abusive use of such service.

(i) It shall not be unlawful under this chapter for a person acting under color of law to intercept the wire or electronic communications of a computer trespasser transmitted to, through, or from the protected computer, if—

    (I) the owner or operator of the protected computer authorizes the interception of the computer trespasser's communications on the protected computer;

    (II) the person acting under color of law is lawfully engaged in an investigation;

    (III) the person acting under color of law has reasonable grounds to believe that the contents of the computer trespasser's communications will be relevant to the investigation; and

    (IV) such interception does not acquire communications other than those transmitted to or from the computer trespasser.

    (j) It shall not be unlawful under this chapter for a provider of electronic communication service to the public or remote computing service to intercept or disclose the contents of a wire or electronic communication in response to an order from a foreign government that is subject to an executive agreement that the Attorney General has determined and certified to Congress satisfies section 2523.

    (3)(a) Except as provided in paragraph (b) of this subsection, a person or entity providing an electronic communication service to the public shall not intentionally divulge the contents of any communication (other than one to such person or entity, or an agent thereof) while in transmission on that service to any person or entity other than an addressee or intended recipient of such communication or an agent of such addressee or intended recipient.

    (b) A person or entity providing electronic communication service to the public may divulge the contents of any such communication—

    (i) as otherwise authorized in section 2511(2)(a) or 2517 of this title;

    (ii) with the lawful consent of the originator or any addressee or intended recipient of such communication;

    (iii) to a person employed or authorized, or whose facilities are used, to forward such communication to its destination; or

    (iv) which were inadvertently obtained by the service provider and which appear to pertain to the commission of a crime, if such divulgence is made to a law enforcement agency.

    (4)(a) Except as provided in paragraph (b) of this subsection or in subsection (5), whoever violates subsection (1) of this section shall be fined under this title or imprisoned not more than five years, or both.

(b) Conduct otherwise an offense under this subsection that consists of or relates to the interception of a satellite transmission that is not encrypted or scrambled and that is transmitted—

(i) to a broadcasting station for purposes of retransmission to the general public; or

(ii) as an audio subcarrier intended for redistribution to facilities open to the public, but not including data transmissions or telephone calls, is not an offense under this subsection unless the conduct is for the purposes of direct or indirect commercial advantage or private financial gain.

(5)(a)(i) If the communication is—

(A) a private satellite video communication that is not scrambled or encrypted and the conduct in violation of this chapter is the private viewing of that communication and is not for a tortious or illegal purpose or for purposes of direct or indirect commercial advantage or private commercial gain; or

(B) a radio communication that is transmitted on frequencies allocated under subpart D of part 74 of the rules of the Federal Communications Commission that is not scrambled or encrypted and the conduct in violation of this chapter is not for a tortious or illegal purpose or for purposes of direct or indirect commercial advantage or private commercial gain, then the person who engages in such conduct shall be subject to suit by the Federal Government in a court of competent jurisdiction.

(ii) In an action under this subsection—

(A) if the violation of this chapter is a first offense for the person under paragraph (a) of subsection (4) and such person has not been found liable in a civil action under section 2520 of this title, the Federal Government shall be entitled to appropriate injunctive relief; and

(B) if the violation of this chapter is a second or subsequent offense under paragraph (a) of subsection (4) or such person has been found liable in any prior civil action under section 2520, the person shall be subject to a mandatory $500 civil fine.

(b) The court may use any means within its authority to enforce an injunction issued under paragraph (ii)(A), and shall impose a civil fine of not less than $500 for each violation of such an injunction.

18 U.S.C. §2515.   Prohibition of Use as Evidence of Intercepted Wire or Oral Communications

Whenever any wire or oral communication has been intercepted, no part of the contents of such communication and no evidence derived therefrom may be received in evidence in any trial, hearing, or other proceeding in or before any court, grand jury, department, officer, agency, regulatory body, legislative committee, or other authority of the United States, a State, or a political subdivision thereof if the disclosure of that information would be in violation of this chapter.

Bail Reform Act of 1984 (as amended)

18 U.S.C. §3141.   Release and Detention Authority Generally

(a) Pending trial. A judicial officer authorized to order the arrest of a person under section 3041 of this title before whom an arrested person is brought shall order that such person be released or detained, pending judicial proceedings, under this chapter [18 U.S.C. §§ 3141 et seq.].

(b) Pending sentence or appeal. A judicial officer of a court of original jurisdiction over an offense, or a judicial officer of a Federal appellate court, shall order that, pending imposition or execution of sentence, or pending appeal of conviction or sentence, a person be released or detained under this chapter [18 U.S.C. §§ 3141 et seq.].

18 U.S.C. §3142.   Release or Detention of a Defendant Pending Trial

(a) In general. Upon the appearance before a judicial officer of a person charged with an offense, the judicial officer shall issue an order that, pending trial, the person be—

(1) Released on personal recognizance or upon execution of an unsecured appearance bond, under subsection (b) of this section;

(2) released on a condition or combination of conditions under subsection (c) of this section;

(3) temporarily detained to permit revocation of conditional release, deportation, or exclusion under subsection (d) of this section; or

(4) detained under subsection (e) of this section.

(b) Release on personal recognizance or unsecured appearance bond. The judicial officer shall order the pretrial release of the person on personal recognizance, or upon execution of an unsecured appearance bond in an amount specified by the court, subject to the condition that the person not commit a Federal, State, or local crime during the period of release, unless the judicial officer determines that such release will not reasonably assure the appearance of the person as required or will endanger the safety of any other person or the community.

(c) Release on conditions.

(1) If the judicial officer determines that the release described in subsection (b) of this section will not reasonably assure the appearance of the person as required or will endanger the safety of any other person or the community, such judicial officer shall order the pretrial release of the person—

(A) subject to the condition that the person not commit a Federal, State, or local crime during the period of release; and

(B) subject to the least restrictive further condition, or combination of conditions, that such judicial officer determines will reasonably assure the appearance of the person as required and the safety of any other person and the community, which may include the condition that the person—

(i) remain in the custody of a designated person, who agrees to assume supervision and to report any violation of a release condition to the court, if the designated person is able reasonably to assure the judicial officer that the person will appear as required and will not pose a danger to the safety of any other person or the community;

(ii) maintain employment, or, if unemployed, actively seek employment;

(iii) maintain or commence an educational program;

(iv) abide by specified restrictions on personal associations, place of abode, or travel;

(v) avoid all contact with an alleged victim of the crime and with a potential witness who may testify concerning the offense;

(vi) report on a regular basis to a designated law enforcement agency, pretrial services agency, or other agency;

(vii) comply with a specified curfew;

(viii) refrain from possessing a firearm, destructive device, or other dangerous weapon;

(ix) refrain from excessive use of alcohol, or any use of a narcotic drug or other controlled substance, as defined in section 102 of the Controlled Substances Act (21 U.S.C. § 802), without a prescription by a licensed medical practitioner;

(x) undergo available medical, psychological, or psychiatric treatment, including treatment for drug or alcohol dependency, and remain in a specified institution if required for that purpose;

(xi) execute an agreement to forfeit, upon failing to appear as required, property of a sufficient unencumbered value, including money, as is reasonably necessary to assure the appearance of the person as required, and shall provide the court with proof of ownership and the value of the property along with information regarding existing encumbrances as the judicial office may require;

(xii) execute a bail bond with solvent sureties; who will execute an agreement to forfeit in such amount as is reasonably necessary to assure appearance of the person as required and shall provide the court with information regarding the value of the assets and liabilities of the surety if other than an approved surety and the nature and extent of encumbrances against the surety's property; such surety shall have a net worth which shall have sufficient unencumbered value to pay the amount of the bail bond;

(xiii) return to custody for specified hours following release for employment, schooling, or other limited purposes; and

(xiv) satisfy any other condition that is reasonably necessary to assure the appearance of the person as required and to assure the safety of any other person and the community.

In any case that involves a minor victim under section 1201, 1591, 2241, 2242, 2244(a)(1), 2245, 2251, 2251A, 2252(a)(1), 2252(a)(2), 2252(a)(3), 2252A(a)(1), 2252A(a)(2), 2252A(a)(3), 2252A(a)(4), 2260, 2421, 2422, 2423, or 2425 of this title, or a failure to register offense under section 2250 of this title, any release order shall contain, at a minimum, a condition of electronic monitoring and each of the conditions specified at subparagraphs (iv), (v), (vi), (vii), and (viii).

(2) The judicial officer may not impose a financial condition that results in the pretrial detention of the person.

(3) The judicial officer may at any time amend the order to impose additional or different conditions of release.

(d) Temporary detention to permit revocation of conditional release, deportation, or exclusion. If the judicial officer determines that—

(1) such person—

(A) is, and was at the time the offense was committed, on—

(i) release pending trial for a felony under Federal, State, or local law;

(ii) release pending imposition or execution of sentence, appeal of sentence or conviction, or completion of sentence, for any offense under Federal, State, or local law; or

(iii) probation or parole for any offense under Federal, State, or local law; or

(B) is not a citizen of the United States or lawfully admitted for permanent residence, as defined in section 101(a)(20) of the Immigration and Nationality Act (8 U.S.C. § 1101(a)(20)); and

(2) the person may flee or pose a danger to any other person or the community; such judicial officer shall order the detention of the person, for a period of not more than ten days, excluding Saturdays, Sundays, and holidays, and direct the attorney for the Government to notify the appropriate court, probation or parole official, or State or local law enforcement official, or the appropriate official of the Immigration and Naturalization Service. If the official fails or declines to take the person into custody during that period, the person shall be treated in accordance with the other provisions of this section, notwithstanding the applicability of other provisions of law governing release pending trial or deportation or exclusion proceedings. If temporary detention is sought under paragraph (1)(B) of this subsection, the person has the burden of proving to the court such person's United States citizenship or lawful admission for permanent residence.

(e) Detention.

(1) If, after a hearing pursuant to the provisions of subsection (f) of this section, the judicial officer finds that no condition or combination of conditions will reasonably assure the appearance of the person as required and the safety of any other person and the community, such judicial officer shall order the detention of the person before trial.

(2) In a case described in subsection (f)(1) of this section, a rebuttable presumption arises that no condition or combination of conditions will reasonably assure the safety of any other person and the community if such judicial officer finds that—

(A) the person has been convicted of a Federal offense that is described in subsection (f)(1) of this section, or of a State or local offense that would have been an offense described in subsection (f)(1) of this section if a circumstance giving rise to Federal jurisdiction had existed;

(B) the offense described in paragraph (A) of this subsection was committed while the person was on release pending trial for a Federal, State, or local offense; and

(C) a period of not more than five years has elapsed since the date of conviction, or the release of the person from imprisonment, for the offense described in paragraph (A) of this subsection, whichever is later.

(3) Subject to rebuttal by the person, it shall be presumed that no condition or combination of conditions will reasonably assure the appearance of the person as required and the safety of the community if the judicial officer finds that there is probable cause to believe that the person committed—

(A) an offense for which a maximum term of imprisonment of ten years or more is prescribed in the Controlled Substances Act (21 U.S.C. §§ 801 et seq.), the Controlled Substances Import and Export Act (21 U.S.C. §§ 951 et seq.), or chapter 705 of title 46;

(B) an offense under section 924(c), 956(a), or 2332b of this title;

(C) an offense listed in section 2332b(g)(5)(B) of title 18, United States Code, for which a maximum term of imprisonment of 10 years or more is prescribed;

(D) an offense under chapter 77 of this title for which a maximum term of imprisonment of 20 years or more is prescribed; or

(E) an offense involving a minor victim under section 1201, 1591, 2241, 2242, 2244(a)(1), 2245, 2251, 2251A, 2252(a)(1), 2252(a)(2), 2252(a)(3), 2252A(a)(1), 2252A(a)(2), 2252A(a)(3), 2252A(a)(4), 2260, 2421, 2422, 2423, or 2425 of this title.

(f) Detention hearing. The judicial officer shall hold a hearing to determine whether any condition or combination of conditions set forth in subsection (c) of this section will reasonably assure the appearance of the person as required and the safety of any other person and the community—

(1) upon motion of the attorney for the Government, in a case that involves—

(A) a crime of violence;

(B) an offense for which the maximum sentence is life imprisonment or death;

(C) an offense for which a maximum term of imprisonment often years or more is prescribed in the Controlled Substances Act (21 U.S.C. §§ 801 et seq.), the Controlled Substances Import and Export Act (21 U.S.C. §§ 951 et seq.), or the Maritime Drug Law Enforcement Act (46 U.S.C. App. §§ 1901 et seq.); or

(D) any felony if the person has been convicted of two or more offenses described in subparagraphs (A) through (C) of this paragraph, or two or more State or local offenses that would have been offenses described in subparagraphs (A) through (C) of this paragraph if a circumstance giving rise to Federal jurisdiction had existed, or a combination of such offenses; or

(2) upon motion of the attorney for the Government or upon the judicial officer's own motion, in a case that involves—

(A) a serious risk that such person will flee; or

(B) a serious risk that the person will obstruct or attempt to obstruct justice, or threaten, injure, or intimidate, or attempt to threaten, injure, or intimidate, a prospective witness or juror.

The hearing shall be held immediately upon the person's first appearance before the judicial officer unless that person, or the attorney for the Government, seeks a continuance. Except for good cause, a continuance on motion of the person may not exceed five days (not including any intermediate Saturday, Sunday, or legal holiday), and a continuance on motion of the attorney for the Government may not exceed three days (not including any intermediate Saturday, Sunday, or legal holiday). During a continuance, the person shall be detained and the judicial officer, on motion of the attorney for the Government or sua sponte, may order that, while in custody, a person who appears to be a narcotics addict receive a medical examination to determine whether such person is an addict. At the hearing, the person has the right to be represented by counsel and, if financially unable to obtain adequate representation, to have counsel appointed. The person shall be afforded an opportunity to testify, to present witnesses, to cross-examine witnesses who appear at the hearing, and to present information by proffer or otherwise. The rules concerning admissibility of evidence in criminal trials do not apply to the presentation and consideration of information at the hearing. The facts the judicial officer uses to support a finding pursuant to subsection (e) that no condition or combination of conditions will reasonably assure the safety of any other person and the community shall be supported by clear and convincing evidence. The person may be detained pending completion of the hearing. The hearing may be reopened, before or after a determination by the judicial officer, at any time before trial if the judicial officer finds that information exists that was not known to the movant at the time of the hearing and that has a material bearing on the issue whether there are conditions of release that will reasonably assure the appearance of the person as required and the safety of any other person and the community.

(g) Factors to be considered. The judicial officer shall, in determining whether there are conditions of release that will reasonably assure the appearance of the person as required and the safety of any other person and the community, take into account the available information concerning—

(1) the nature and circumstances of the offense charged, including whether the offense is a crime of violence or involves a narcotic drug;

(2) the weight of the evidence against the person;

(3) the history and characteristics of the person, including—

(A) the person's character, physical and mental condition, family ties, employment, financial resources, length of residence in the community, community ties, past conduct, history relating to drug or alcohol abuse, criminal history, and record concerning appearance at court proceedings; and

(B) whether, at the time of the current offense or arrest, the person was on probation, on parole, or on other release pending trial, sentencing, appeal, or completion of sentence for an offense under Federal, State, or local law; and

(4) the nature and seriousness of the danger to any person or the community that would be posed by the person's release. In considering the conditions of release described in subsection (c)(1)(B)(xi) or (c)(1)(B)(xii) of this section, the judicial officer may, upon his own motion, or shall, upon the motion of the Government, conduct an inquiry into the source of the property to be designated for potential forfeiture or offered as collateral to secure a bond, and shall decline to accept the designation, or the use as collateral, of property that, because of its source, will not reasonably assure the appearance of the person as required.

(h) Contents of release order. In a release order issued under subsection (b) or (c) of this section, the judicial officer shall—

(1) include a written statement that sets forth all the conditions to which the release is subject, in a manner sufficiently clear and specific to serve as a guide for the person's conduct; and

(2) advise the person of—

(A) the penalties for violating a condition of release, including the penalties for committing an offense while on pretrial release;

(B) the consequences of violating a condition of release, including the immediate issuance of a warrant for the person's arrest; and

(C) sections 1503 of this title (relating to intimidation of witnesses, jurors, and officers of the court), 1510 (relating to obstruction of criminal investigations), 1512 (tampering with a witness, victim, or an informant), and 1513 (retaliating against a witness, victim, or an informant).

(i) Contents of detention order. In a detention order issued under subsection (e) of this section, the judicial officer shall—

(1) include written findings of fact and a written statement of the reasons for the detention;

(2) direct that the person be committed to the custody of the Attorney General for confinement in a corrections facility separate, to the extent practicable, from persons awaiting or serving sentences or being held in custody pending appeal;

(3) direct that the person be afforded reasonable opportunity for private consultation with counsel; and

(4) direct that, on order of a court of the United States or on request of an attorney for the Government, the person in charge of the corrections facility in which the person is confined deliver the person to a United States marshal for the purpose of an appearance in connection with a court proceeding.

The judicial officer may, by subsequent order, permit the temporary release of the person, in the custody of a United States marshal or another appropriate person, to the extent that the judicial officer determines such release to be necessary for preparation of the person's defense or for another compelling reason.

(j) Presumption of innocence. Nothing in this section shall be construed as modifying or limiting the presumption of innocence.

18 U.S.C. §3143. Release or Detention of a Defendant Pending Sentence or Appeal

(a) Release or detention pending sentence.

(1) Except as provided in paragraph (2), the judicial officer shall order that a person who has been found guilty of an offense and who is awaiting imposition or execution of sentence, other than a person for whom the applicable guideline promulgated pursuant to 28 U.S.C. § 994 does not recommend a term of imprisonment, be detained, unless the judicial officer finds by clear and convincing evidence that the person is not likely to flee or pose a danger to the safety of any other person or the community if released under section 3142(b) or (c). If the judicial officer makes such a finding, such judicial officer shall order the release of the person in accordance with section 3142(b) or (c).

(2) The judicial officer shall order that a person who has been found guilty of an offense in a case described in subparagraph (A), (B), or (C) of subsection (f)(1) of section 3142 and is awaiting imposition or execution of sentence be detained unless—

(A) (i) the judicial officer finds there is a substantial likelihood that a motion for acquittal or new trial will be granted; or

(ii) an attorney for the Government has recommended that no sentence of imprisonment be imposed on the person; and

(B) the judicial officer finds by clear and convincing evidence that the person is not likely to flee or pose a danger to any other person or the community.

(b) Release or detention pending appeal by the defendant.

(1) Except as provided in paragraph (2), the judicial officer shall order that a person who has been found guilty of an offense and sentenced to a term of imprisonment, and who has filed an appeal or a petition for a writ of certiorari, be detained, unless the judicial officer finds—

(A) by clear and convincing evidence that the person is not likely to flee or pose a danger to the safety of any other person or the community if released under section 3142(b) or (c) of this title; and

(B) that the appeal is not for the purpose of delay and raises a substantial question of law or fact likely to result in—

(i) reversal

(ii) an order for a new trial,

(iii) a sentence that does not include a term of imprisonment, or

(iv) a reduced sentence to a term of imprisonment less than the total of the time already served plus the expected duration of the appeal process.

If the judicial officer makes such findings, such judicial officer shall order the release of the person in accordance with section 3142(b) or (c) of this title, except that in the circumstance described in subparagraph (B)(iv) of this paragraph, the judicial officer shall order the detention terminated at the expiration of the likely reduced sentence.

(2) The judicial officer shall order that a person who has been found guilty of an offense in a case described in subparagraph (A), (B), or (C) of subsection (f)(1) of section 3142 and sentenced to a term of imprisonment, and who has filed an appeal or a petition for a writ of certiorari, be detained.

(c) Release or detention pending appeal by the government. The judicial officer shall treat a defendant in a case in which an appeal has been taken by the United States under section 3731 of this title, in accordance with section 3142 of this title, unless the defendant is otherwise subject to a release or detention order. Except as provided in subsection (b) of this section, the judicial officer, in a case in which an appeal has been taken by the United States under section 3742, shall—

(1) if the person has been sentenced to a term of imprisonment, order that person detained; and

(2) in any other circumstance, release or detain the person under section 3142.

18 U.S.C. §3144. Release or Detention of a Material Witness

If it appears from an affidavit filed by a party that the testimony of a person is material in a criminal proceeding, and if it is shown that it may become impracticable to secure the presence of the person by subpoena, a judicial officer may order the arrest of the person and treat the person in accordance with the provisions of section 3142 of this title. No material witness may be detained because of inability to comply with any condition of release if the testimony of such witness can adequately be secured by deposition, and if further detention is not necessary to prevent a failure of justice. Release of a material witness may be delayed for a reasonable period of time until the deposition of the witness can be taken pursuant to the Federal Rules of Criminal Procedure.

18 U.S.C. §3145.   Review and Appeal of a Release or Detention Order

(a) Review of a release order. If a person is ordered released by a magistrate [United States magistrate judge], or by a person other than a judge of a court having original jurisdiction over the offense and other than a Federal appellate court—

(1) the attorney for the Government may file, with the court having original jurisdiction over the offense, a motion for revocation of the order or amendment of the conditions of release; and

(2) the person may file, with the court having original jurisdiction over the offense, a motion for amendment of the conditions of release. The motion shall be determined promptly.

(b) Review of a detention order. If a person is ordered detained by a magistrate [United States magistrate judge], or by a person other than a judge of a court having original jurisdiction over the offense and other than a Federal appellate court, the person may file, with the court having original jurisdiction over the offense, a motion for revocation or amendment of the order. The motion shall be determined promptly.

(c) Appeal from a release or detention order. An appeal from a release or detention order, or from a decision denying revocation or amendment of such an order, is governed by the provisions of section 1291 of title 28 and section 3731 of this title. The appeal shall be determined promptly. A person subject to detention pursuant to section 3143(a)(2) or (b)(2), and who meets the conditions of release set forth in section 3143(a)(1) or (b)(1), may be ordered released, under appropriate conditions, by the judicial officer if it is clearly shown that there are exceptional reasons why such person's detention would not be appropriate.

18 U.S.C. §3146.   Penalty for Failure to Appear

(a) Offense. Whoever, having been released under this chapter [18 U.S.C. §§ 3141 et seq.] knowingly—

(1) fails to appear before a court as required by the conditions of release; or

(2) fails to surrender for service of sentence pursuant to a court order; shall be punished as provided in subsection (b) of this section.

(b) Punishment.

(1) The punishment for an offense under this section is—

(A) if the person was released in connection with a charge of, or while awaiting sentence, surrender for service of sentence, or appeal or certiorari after conviction for—

(i) an offense punishable by death, life imprisonment, or imprisonment for a term of 15 years or more, a fine under this title or imprisonment for not more than ten years, or both;

(ii) an offense punishable by imprisonment for a term of five years or more, a fine under this title or imprisonment for not more than five years, or both;

(iii) any other felony, a fine under this title or imprisonment for not more than two years, or both; or

(iv) a misdemeanor, a fine under this title or imprisonment for not more than one year, or both; and

(B) if the person was released for appearance as a material witness, a fine under this chapter [18 U.S.C. §§ 3141 et seq.] or imprisonment for not more than one year, or both.

(2) A term of imprisonment imposed under this section shall be consecutive to the sentence of imprisonment for any other offense.

(c) Affirmative defense. It is an affirmative defense to a prosecution under this section that uncontrollable circumstances prevented the person from appearing or surrendering, and that the person did not contribute to the creation of such circumstances in reckless disregard of the requirement to appear or surrender, and that the person appeared or surrendered as soon as such circumstances ceased to exist.

(d) Declaration of forfeiture. If a person fails to appear before a court as required, and the person executed an appearance bond pursuant to section 3142(b) of this title or is subject to the release condition set forth in clause (xi) or (xii) of section 3142(c)(1)(B) of this title, the judicial officer may, regardless of whether the person has been charged with an offense under this section, declare any property designated pursuant to that section to be forfeited to the United States.

18 U.S.C. §3147. Penalty for an Offense Committed While on Release

A person convicted of an offense committed while released under this chapter [18 U.S.C. §§ 3141 et seq.] shall be sentenced, in addition to the sentence prescribed for the offense, to—

(1) a term of imprisonment of not more than ten years if the offense is a felony; or

(2) a term of imprisonment of not more than one year if the offense is a misdemeanor.

A term of imprisonment imposed under this section shall be consecutive to any other sentence of imprisonment.

18 U.S.C. §3148.   Sanctions for Violation of a Release Condition

(a) Available sanctions. A person who has been released pursuant to the provisions of section 3142 of this title, and who has violated a condition of his release, is subject to a revocation of release, an order of detention, and a prosecution for contempt of court.

(b) Revocation of release. The attorney for the Government may initiate a proceeding for revocation of an order of release by filing a motion with the district court. A judicial officer may issue a warrant for the arrest of a person charged with violating a condition of release, and the person shall be brought before a judicial officer in the district in which such person's arrest was ordered for a proceeding in accordance with this section. To the extent practicable, a person charged with violating the condition of release that such person not commit a Federal, State, or local crime during the period of release, shall be brought before the judicial officer who ordered the release and whose order is alleged to have been violated. The judicial officer shall enter an order of revocation and detention if, after a hearing, the judicial officer—

(1) finds that there is—

(A) probable cause to believe that the person has committed a Federal, State, or local crime while on release; or

(B) clear and convincing evidence that the person has violated any other condition of release; and

(2) finds that—

(A) based on the factors set forth in section 3142(g) of this title, there is no condition or combination of conditions of release that will assure that the person will not flee or pose a danger to the safety of any other person or the community; or

(B) the person is unlikely to abide by any condition or combination of conditions of release.

If there is probable cause to believe that, while on release, the person committed a Federal, State, or local felony, a rebuttable presumption arises that no condition or combination of conditions will assure that the person will not pose a danger to the safety of any other person or the community. If the judicial officer finds that there are conditions of release that will assure that the person will not flee or pose a danger to the safety of any other person or the community, and that the person will abide by such conditions, the judicial officer shall treat the person in accordance with the provisions of section 3142 of this title and may amend the conditions of release accordingly.

(c) Prosecution for contempt. The judicial officer may commence a prosecution for contempt, under section 401 of this title, if the person has violated a condition of release.

18 U.S.C. §3149.   Surrender of an Offender by a Surety

A person charged with an offense, who is released upon the execution of an appearance bond with a surety, may be arrested by the surety, and if so arrested, shall be delivered promptly to a United States marshal and brought before a judicial officer. The judicial officer shall determine in accordance with the provisions of section 3148(b) whether to revoke the release of the person, and may absolve the surety of responsibility to pay all or part of the bond in accordance with the provisions of Rule 46 of the Federal Rules of Criminal Procedure. The person so committed shall be held in official detention until released pursuant to this chapter [18 U.S.C. §§ 3141 et seq.] or another provision of law.

18 U.S.C. §3150.   Applicability to a Case Removed from a State Court

The provisions of this chapter [18 U.S.C. §§ 3141 et seq.] apply to a criminal case removed to a Federal court from a State court.

Speedy Trial Act of 1974 (as amended)

18 U.S.C. §3161. Time Limits and Exclusions

(a) In any case involving a defendant charged with an offense, the appropriate judicial officer, at the earliest practicable time, shall, after consultation with the counsel for the defendant and the attorney for the Government, set the case for trial on a day certain, or list it for trial on a weekly or other short-term trial calendar at a place within the judicial district, so as to assure a speedy trial.

(b) Any information or indictment charging an individual with the commission of an offense shall be filed within thirty days from the date on which such individual was arrested or served with a summons in connection with such charges. If an individual has been charged with a felony in a district in which no grand jury has been in session during such thirty-day period, the period of time for filing of the indictment shall be extended an additional thirty days.

(c)(1) In any case in which a plea of not guilty is entered, the trial of a defendant charged in an information or indictment with the commission of an offense shall commence within seventy days from the filing date (and making public) of the information or indictment, or from the date the defendant has appeared before a judicial officer of the court in which such charge is pending, whichever date last occurs. If a defendant consents in writing to be tried before a magistrate [United States magistrate judge] on a complaint, the trial shall commence within seventy days from the date of such consent.

(2) Unless the defendant consents in writing to the contrary, the trial shall not commence less than thirty days from the date on which the defendant first appears through counsel or expressly waives counsel and elects to proceed pro se.

(d) (1) If any indictment or information is dismissed upon motion of the defendant, or any charge contained in a complaint filed against an individual is dismissed or otherwise dropped, and thereafter a complaint is filed against such defendant or individual charging him with the same offense or an offense based on the same conduct or arising from the same criminal episode, or an information or indictment is filed charging such defendant with the same offense or an offense based on the same conduct or arising from the same criminal episode, the provisions of subsections (b) and (c) of this section shall be applicable with respect to such subsequent complaint, indictment, or information, as the case may be.

(2) If the defendant is to be tried upon an indictment or information dismissed by a trial court and reinstated following an appeal, the trial shall commence within seventy days from the date the action occasioning the trial becomes final, except that the court retrying the case may extend the period for trial not to exceed one hundred and eighty days from the date the action occasioning the trial becomes final if the unavailability of witnesses or other factors resulting from the passage of time shall make trial within seventy days impractical. The periods of delay enumerated in section 3161(h) are excluded in computing the time limitations specified in this section. The sanctions of section 3162 apply to this subsection.

(e) If the defendant is to be tried again following a declaration by the trial judge of a mistrial or following an order of such judge for a new trial, the trial shall commence within seventy days from the date the action occasioning the retrial becomes final. If the defendant is to be tried again following an appeal or a collateral attack, the trial shall commence within seventy days from the date the action occasioning the retrial becomes final, except that the court retrying the case may extend the period for retrial not to exceed one hundred and eighty days from the date the action occasioning the retrial becomes final if unavailability of witnesses or other factors resulting from passage of time shall make trial within seventy days impractical. The periods of delay enumerated in section 3161(h) are excluded in computing the time limitations specified in this section. The sanctions of section 3162 apply to this subsection.

(f) Notwithstanding the provisions of subsection (b) of this section, for the first twelve-calendar-month period following the effective date of this section as set forth in section 3163(a) of this chapter[,] the time limit imposed with respect to the period between arrest and indictment by subsection (b) of this section shall be sixty days, for the second such twelve-month period such time limit shall be forty-five days and for the third such period such time limit shall be thirty-five days.

(g) Notwithstanding the provisions of subsection (c) of this section, for the first twelve-calendar-month period following the effective date of this section as set forth in section 3163(b) of this chapter, the time limit with respect to the period between arraignment and trial imposed by subsection (c) of this section shall be one hundred and eighty days, for the second such twelve-month period such time limit shall be one hundred and twenty days, and for the third such period such time limit with respect to the period between arraignment and trial shall be eighty days.

(h) The following periods of delay shall be excluded in computing the time within which an information or an indictment must be filed, or in computing the time within which the trial of any such offense must commence:

(1) Any period of delay resulting from other proceedings concerning the defendant, including but not limited to—

(A) delay resulting from any proceeding, including any examinations, to determine the mental competency or physical capacity of the defendant;

(B) delay resulting from trial with respect to other charges against the defendant;

(C) delay resulting from any interlocutory appeal;

(D) delay resulting from any pretrial motion, from the filing of the motion through the conclusion of the hearing on, or other prompt disposition of, such motion;

(E) delay resulting from any proceeding relating to the transfer of a case or the removal of any defendant from another district under the Federal Rules of Criminal Procedure;

(F) delay resulting from transportation of any defendant from another district, or to and from places of examination or hospitalization, except that any time consumed in excess of ten days from the date an order of removal or an order directing such transportation, and the defendant's arrival at the destination shall be presumed to be unreasonable;

(G) delay resulting from consideration by the court of a proposed plea agreement to be entered into by the defendant and the attorney for the Government; and

(H) delay reasonably attributable to any period, not to exceed thirty days, during which any proceeding concerning the defendant is actually under advisement by the court.

(2) Any period of delay during which prosecution is deferred by the attorney for the Government pursuant to written agreement with the defendant, with the approval of the court, for the purpose of allowing the defendant to demonstrate his good conduct.

(3)(A) Any period of delay resulting from the absence or unavailability of the defendant or an essential witness.

(B) For purposes of subparagraph (A) of this paragraph, a defendant or an essential witness shall be considered absent when his whereabouts are unknown and, in addition, he is attempting to avoid apprehension or prosecution or his whereabouts cannot be determined by due diligence. For purposes of such subparagraph, a defendant or an essential witness shall be considered unavailable whenever his whereabouts are known but his presence for trial cannot be obtained by due diligence or he resists appearing at or being returned for trial.

(4) Any period of delay resulting from the fact that the defendant is mentally incompetent or physically unable to stand trial.

(5) If the information or indictment is dismissed upon motion of the attorney for the Government and thereafter a charge is filed against the defendant for the same offense, or any offense required to be joined with that offense, any period of delay from the date the charge was dismissed to the date the time limitation would commence to run as to the subsequent charge had there been no previous charge.

(6) A reasonable period of delay when the defendant is joined for trial with a codefendant as to whom the time for trial has not run and no motion for severance has been granted.

(7)(A) Any period of delay resulting from a continuance granted by any judge on his own motion or at the request of the defendant or his counsel or at the request of the attorney for the Government, if the judge granted such continuance on the basis of his findings that the ends of justice served by taking such action outweigh the best interest of the public and the defendant in a speedy trial. No such period of delay resulting from a continuance granted by the court in accordance with this paragraph shall be excludable under this subsection unless the court sets forth, in the record of the case, either orally or in writing, its reasons for finding that the ends of justice served by the granting of such continuance outweigh the best interests of the public and the defendant in a speedy trial.

(B) The factors, among others, which a judge shall consider in determining whether to grant a continuance under subparagraph (A) of this paragraph in any case are as follows:

(i) Whether the failure to grant such a continuance in the proceeding would be likely to make a continuation of such proceeding impossible, or result in a miscarriage of justice.

(ii) Whether the case is so unusual or so complex, due to the number of defendants, the nature of the prosecution, or the existence of novel questions of fact or law, that it is unreasonable to expect adequate preparation for pretrial proceedings or for the trial itself within the time limits established by this section.

(iii) Whether, in a case in which arrest precedes indictment, delay in the filing of the indictment is caused because the arrest occurs at a time such that it is unreasonable to expect return and filing of the indictment within the period specified in section 3161(b) or because the facts upon which the grand jury must base its determination are unusual or complex.

(iv) Whether the failure to grant such a continuance in a case that, taken as a whole, is not so unusual or so complex as to fall within clause (ii), would deny the defendant reasonable time to obtain counsel, would unreasonably deny the defendant or the Government continuity of counsel, or would deny counsel for the defendant or the attorney for the Government the reasonable time necessary for effective preparation, taking into account the exercise of due diligence.

(C) No continuance under subparagraph (A) of this paragraph shall be granted because of general congestion of the court's calendar, or lack of diligent preparation or failure to obtain available witnesses on the part of the attorney for the Government.

(8) Any period of delay, not to exceed one year, ordered by a district court upon an application of a party and a finding by a preponderance of the evidence that an official request, as defined in section 3292 of this title, has been made for evidence of any such offense and that it reasonably appears, or reasonably appeared at the time the request was made, that such evidence is, or was, in such foreign country.

(i) If trial did not commence within the time limitation specified in section 3161 because the defendant had entered a plea of guilty or nolo contendere subsequently withdrawn to any or all charges in an indictment or information, the defendant shall be deemed indicted with respect to all charges therein contained within the meaning of section 3161 on the day the order permitting withdrawal of the plea becomes final.

(j)(1) If the attorney for the Government knows that a person charged with an offense is serving a term of imprisonment in any penal institution, he shall promptly—

(A) undertake to obtain the presence of the prisoner for trial; or

(B) cause a detainer to be filed with the person having custody of the prisoner and request him to so advise the prisoner and to advise the prisoner of his right to demand trial.

(2) If the person having custody of such prisoner receives a detainer, he shall promptly advise the prisoner of the charge and of the prisoner's right to demand trial. If at any time thereafter the prisoner informs the person having custody that he does demand trial, such person shall cause notice to that effect to be sent promptly to the attorney for the Government who caused the detainer to be filed.

(3) Upon receipt of such notice, the attorney for the Government shall promptly seek to obtain the presence of the prisoner for trial.

(4) When the person having custody of the prisoner receives from the attorney for the Government a properly supported request for temporary custody of such prisoner for trial, the prisoner shall be made available to that attorney for the Government (subject, in cases of interjurisdictional transfer, to any right of the prisoner to contest the legality of his delivery).

(k)(1) If the defendant is absent (as defined by subsection (h)(3)) on the day set for trial, and the defendant's subsequent appearance before the court on a bench warrant or other process or surrender to the court occurs more than twenty-one days after the day set for trial, the defendant shall be deemed to have first appeared before a judicial officer of the court in which the information or indictment is pending within the meaning of subsection (c) on the date of the defendant's subsequent appearance before the court.

(2) If the defendant is absent (as defined by subsection (h)(3)) on the day set for trial, and the defendant's subsequent appearance before the court on a bench warrant or other process or surrender to the court occurs not more than twenty-one days after the day set for trial, the time limit required by subsection (c), as extended by subsection (h), shall be further extended by twenty-one days.

18 U.S.C. §3162. Sanctions

(a)(1) If, in the case of any individual against whom a complaint is filed charging such individual with an offense, no indictment or information is filed within the time limit required by section 3161(b) as extended by section 3161(h) of this chapter, such charge against that individual contained in such complaint shall be dismissed or otherwise dropped. In determining whether to dismiss the case with or without prejudice, the court shall consider, among others, each of the following factors: the seriousness of the offense; the facts and circumstances of the case which led to the dismissal; and the impact of a reprosecution on the administration of this chapter [18 U.S.C. §§ 3161 et seq.] and on the administration of justice.

(2) If a defendant is not brought to trial within the time limit required by section 3161(c) as extended by section 3161(h), the information or indictment shall be dismissed on motion of the defendant. The defendant shall have the burden of proof of supporting such motion but the Government shall have the burden of going forward with the evidence in connection with any exclusion of time under subparagraph 3161(h)(3).

In determining whether to dismiss the case with or without prejudice, the court shall consider, among others, each of the following factors: the seriousness of the offense; the facts and circumstances of the case which led to the dismissal; and the impact of a reprosecution on the administration of this chapter [18 U.S.C. §§ 3161 et seq.] and on the administration of justice. Failure of the defendant to move for dismissal prior to trial or entry of a plea of guilty or nolo contendere shall constitute a waiver of the right to dismissal under this section.

(b) In any case in which counsel for the defendant or the attorney for the Government

(1) knowingly allows the case to be set for trial without disclosing the fact that a necessary witness would be unavailable for trial;

(2) files a motion solely for the purpose of delay, which he knows is totally frivolous and without merit;

(3) makes a statement for the purpose of obtaining a continuance that he knows to be false and that is material to the granting of a continuance; or

(4) otherwise willfully fails to proceed to trial without justification consistent with section 3161 of this chapter, the court may punish any such counsel or attorney, as follows:

(A) in the case of an appointed defense counsel, by reducing the amount of compensation that otherwise would have been paid to such counsel pursuant to section 3006A of this title in an amount not to exceed 25 per centum thereof;

(B) in the case of a counsel retained in connection with the defense of a defendant, by imposing on such counsel a fine of not to exceed 25 per centum of the compensation to which he is entitled in connection with his defense of such defendant;

(C) by imposing on any attorney for the Government a fine of not to exceed $250;

(D) by denying any such counsel or attorney for the Government the right to practice before the court considering such case for a period of not to exceed 90 days; or

(E) by filing a report with an appropriate disciplinary committee.

The authority to punish provided for by this subsection shall be in addition to any other authority or power available to such court.

(c) The court shall follow procedures established in the Federal Rules of Criminal Procedure in punishing any counsel or attorney for the Government pursuant to this section.

18 U.S.C. §3164. Persons Detained or Designated As Being of High Risk

(a) The trial or other disposition of cases involving—

(1) a detained person who is being held in detention solely because he is awaiting trial, and

(2) a released person who is awaiting trial and has been designated by the attorney for the Government as being of high risk, shall be accorded priority.

(b) The trial of any person described in subsection (a)(1) or (a)(2) of this section shall commence not later than ninety days following the beginning of such continuous detention or designation of high risk by the attorney for the Government. The periods of delay enumerated in section 3161(h) are excluded in computing the time limitation specified in this section.

(c) Failure to commence trial of a detainee as specified in subsection (b), through no fault of the accused or his counsel, or failure to commence trial of a designated releasee as specified in subsection (b), through no fault of the attorney for the Government, shall result in the automatic review by the court of the conditions of release. No detainee, as defined in subsection (a), shall be held in custody pending trial after the expiration of such ninety-day period required for the commencement of his trial. A designated releasee, as defined in subsection (a), who is found by the court to have intentionally delayed the trial of his case shall be subject to an order of the court modifying his nonfinancial conditions of release under this title to insure that he shall appear at trial as required.

18 U.S.C. §3173.   Sixth Amendment Rights

No provision of this chapter [18 U.S.C. §§ 3161 et seq.] shall be interpreted as a bar to any claim of denial of speedy trial as required by amendment VI of the Constitution.

Jencks Act

18 U.S.C. §3500.   Demands for Production of Statements and Reports of Witnesses

(a) In any criminal prosecution brought by the United States, no statement or report in the possession of the United States which was made by a Government witness or prospective Government witness (other than the defendant) shall be the subject of subpena, discovery, or inspection until said witness has testified on direct examination in the trial of the case.

(b) After a witness called by the United States has testified on direct examination, the court shall, on motion of the defendant, order the United States to produce any statement (as hereinafter defined) of the witness in the possession of the United States which relates to the subject matter as to which the witness has testified. If the entire contents of any such statement relate to the subject matter of the testimony of the witness, the court shall order it to be delivered directly to the defendant for his examination and use.

(c) If the United States claims that any statement ordered to be produced under this section contains matter which does not relate to the subject matter of the testimony of the witness, the court shall order the United States to deliver such statement for the inspection of the court in camera. Upon such delivery the court shall excise the portions of such statement which do not relate to the subject matter of the testimony of the witness. With such material excised, the court shall then direct delivery of such statement to the defendant for his use. If, pursuant to such procedure, any portion of such statement is withheld from the defendant and the defendant objects to such withholding, and the trial is continued to an adjudication of the guilt of the defendant, the entire text of such statement shall be preserved by the United States and, in the event the defendant appeals, shall be made available to the appellate court for the purpose of determining the correctness of the ruling of the trial judge. Whenever any statement is delivered to a defendant pursuant to this section, the court in its discretion, upon application of said defendant, may recess proceedings in the trial for such time as it may determine to be reasonably required for the examination of such statement by said defendant and his preparation for its use in the trial.

(d) If the United States elects not to comply with an order of the court under subsection (b) or (c) hereof to deliver to the defendant any such statement, or such portion thereof as the court may direct, the court shall strike from the record the testimony of the witness, and the trial shall proceed unless the court in its discretion shall determine that the interests of justice require that a mistrial be declared.

(e) The term "statement," as used in subsections (b), (c), and (d) of this section in relation to any witness called by the United States, means—

(1) a written statement made by said witness and signed or otherwise adopted or approved by him;

(2) a stenographic, mechanical, electrical, or other recording, or a transcription thereof, which is a substantially verbatim recital of an oral statement made by said witness and recorded contemporaneously with the making of such oral statement; or

(3) a statement, however taken or recorded, or a transcription thereof, if any, made by said witness to a grand jury.

Criminal Appeals Act of 1970 (as amended)

18 U.S.C. §3731.   Appeal by United States

In a criminal case an appeal by the United States shall lie to a court of appeals from a decision, judgment, or order of a district court dismissing an indictment or information or granting a new trial after verdict or judgment, as to any one or more counts, or any part thereof, except that no appeal shall lie where the double jeopardy clause of the United States Constitution prohibits further prosecution.

An appeal by the United States shall lie to a court of appeals from a decision or order of a district court suppressing or excluding evidence or requiring the return of seized property in a criminal proceeding, not made after the defendant has been put in jeopardy and before the verdict or finding on an indictment or information, if the United States attorney certifies to the district court that the appeal is not taken for purpose of delay and that the evidence is a substantial proof of a fact material in the proceeding.

An appeal by the United States shall lie to a court of appeals from a decision or order, entered by a district court of the United States, granting the release of a person charged with or convicted of an offense, or denying a motion for revocation of, or modification of the conditions of, a decision or order granting release.

The appeal in all such cases shall be taken within thirty days after the decision, judgment, or order has been rendered and shall be diligently prosecuted.

The provisions of this section shall be liberally construed to effectuate its purposes.

Crime Victims' Rights Act

18 U.S.C. §3771.   Crime Victims' Rights

(a) Rights of crime victims.—A crime victim has the following rights:

(1) The right to be reasonably protected from the accused.

(2) The right to reasonable, accurate, and timely notice of any public court proceeding, or any parole proceeding, involving the crime or of any release or escape of the accused.

(3) The right not to be excluded from any such public court proceeding, unless the court, after receiving clear and convincing evidence, determines that testimony by the victim would be materially altered if the victim heard other testimony at that proceeding.

(4) The right to be reasonably heard at any public proceeding in the district court involving release, plea, sentencing, or any parole proceeding.

(5) The reasonable right to confer with the attorney for the Government in the case.

(6) The right to full and timely restitution as provided in law.

(7) The right to proceedings free from unreasonable delay.

(8) The right to be treated with fairness and with respect for the victim's dignity and privacy.

(9) The right to be informed in a timely manner of any plea bargain or deferred prosecution agreement.

(10) The right to be informed of the rights under this section and the services described in section 503(c) of the Victims' Rights and Restitution Act of 1990 (42 U.S.C. 10607(c)) and provided contact information for the Office of the Victims' Rights Ombudsman of the Department of Justice.

(b) Rights afforded.—

(1) In general.—In any court proceeding involving an offense against a crime victim, the court shall ensure that the crime victim is afforded the rights described in subsection (a). Before making a determination described in subsection (a)(3), the court shall make every effort to permit the fullest attendance possible by the victim and shall consider reasonable alternatives to the exclusion of the victim from the criminal proceeding. The reasons for any decision denying relief under this chapter shall be clearly stated on the record.

(2) Habeas corpus proceedings.—

(A) In general.—In a Federal habeas corpus proceeding arising out of a State conviction, the court shall ensure that a crime victim is afforded the rights described in paragraphs (3), (4), (7), and (8) of subsection (a).

(B) Enforcement.—

(i) In general.—These rights may be enforced by the crime victim or the crime victim's lawful representative in the manner described in paragraphs (1) and (3) of subsection (d).

(ii) Multiple victims.—In a case involving multiple victims, subsection (d)(2) shall also apply.

(C) Limitation.—This paragraph relates to the duties of a court in relation to the rights of a crime victim in Federal habeas corpus proceedings arising out of a State conviction, and does not give rise to any obligation or requirement applicable to personnel of any agency of the Executive Branch of the Federal Government.

(D) Definition.—For purposes of this paragraph, the term "crime victim" means the person against whom the State offense is committed or, if that person is killed or incapacitated, that person's family member or other lawful representative.

(c) Best efforts to accord rights.—

(1) Government.—Officers and employees of the Department of Justice and other departments and agencies of the United States engaged in the detection, investigation, or prosecution of crime shall

make their best efforts to see that crime victims are notified of, and accorded, the rights described in subsection (a).

(2) Advice of attorney.—The prosecutor shall advise the crime victim that the crime victim can seek the advice of an attorney with respect to the rights described in subsection (a).

(3) Notice.—Notice of release otherwise required pursuant to this chapter shall not be given if such notice may endanger the safety of any person.

(d) Enforcement and limitations.—

(1) Rights.—The crime victim or the crime victim's lawful representative, and the attorney for the Government may assert the rights described in subsection (a). A person accused of the crime may not obtain any form of relief under this chapter.

(2) Multiple crime victims.—In a case where the court finds that the number of crime victims makes it impracticable to accord all of the crime victims the rights described in subsection (a), the court shall fashion a reasonable procedure to give effect to this chapter that does not unduly complicate or prolong the proceedings.

(3) Motion for relief and writ of mandamus.—The rights described in subsection (a) shall be asserted in the district court in which a defendant is being prosecuted for the crime or, if no prosecution is underway, in the district court in the district in which the crime occurred. The district court shall take up and decide any motion asserting a victim's right forthwith. If the district court denies the relief sought, the movant may petition the court of appeals for a writ of mandamus. The court of appeals may issue the writ on the order of a single judge pursuant to circuit rule or the Federal Rules of Appellate Procedure. The court of appeals shall take up and decide such application forthwith within 72 hours after the petition has been filed, unless the litigants, with the approval of the court, have stipulated to a different time period for consideration. In deciding such application, the court of appeals shall apply ordinary standards of appellate review. In no event shall proceedings be stayed or subject to a continuance of more than five days for purposes of enforcing this chapter. If the court of appeals denies the relief sought, the reasons for the denial shall be clearly stated on the record in a written opinion.

(4) Error.—In any appeal in a criminal case, the Government may assert as error the district court's denial of any crime victim's right in the proceeding to which the appeal relates.

(5) Limitation on relief.—In no case shall a failure to afford a right under this chapter provide grounds for a new trial. A victim may make a motion to re-open a plea or sentence only if—

(A) the victim has asserted the right to be heard before or during the proceeding at issue and such right was denied;

(B) the victim petitions the court of appeals for a writ of mandamus within 14 days; and

(C) in the case of a plea, the accused has not pled to the highest offense charged. This paragraph does not affect the victim's right to restitution as provided in title 18, United States Code.

(6) No cause of action.—Nothing in this chapter shall be construed to authorize a cause of action for damages or to create, to enlarge, or to imply any duty or obligation to any victim or other person for the breach of which the United States or any of its officers or employees could be held liable in damages. Nothing in this chapter shall be construed to impair the prosecutorial discretion of the Attorney General or any officer under his direction.

(e) Definitions.—For the purposes of this chapter:

(1) Court of appeals.—The term "court of appeals" means—

(A) the United States court of appeals for the judicial district in which a defendant is being prosecuted; or

(B) for a prosecution in the Superior Court of the District of Columbia, the District of Columbia Court of Appeals.

(2) Crime victim.—

(A) In general.—The term "crime victim" means a person directly and proximately harmed as a result of the commission of a Federal offense or an offense in the District of Columbia.

(B) Minors and certain other victims.—In the case of a crime victim who is under 18 years of age, incompetent, incapacitated, or deceased, the legal guardians of the crime victim or the representatives of the crime victim's estate, family members, or any other persons appointed as suitable by the court, may assume the crime victim's rights under this chapter, but in no event shall the defendant be named as such guardian or representative.

(3) District court; court.—The terms "district court" and "court" include the Superior Court of the District of Columbia.

(f) Procedures to promote compliance.—

(1) Regulations.—Not later than 1 year after the date of enactment of this chapter, the Attorney General of the United States shall promulgate regulations to enforce the rights of crime victims and

to ensure compliance by responsible officials with the obligations described in law respecting crime victims.

(2) Contents.—The regulations promulgated under paragraph (1) shall—

(A) designate an administrative authority within the Department of Justice to receive and investigate complaints relating to the provision or violation of the rights of a crime victim;

(B) require a course of training for employees and offices of the Department of Justice that fail to comply with provisions of Federal law pertaining to the treatment of crime victims, and otherwise assist such employees and offices in responding more effectively to the needs of crime victims;

(C) contain disciplinary sanctions, including suspension or termination from employment, for employees of the Department of Justice who willfully or wantonly fail to comply with provisions of Federal law pertaining to the treatment of crime victims; and

(D) provide that the Attorney General, or the designee of the Attorney General, shall be the final arbiter of the complaint, and that there shall be no judicial review of the final decision of the Attorney General by a complainant.

Habeas Corpus Act of 1867 (as amended by Antiterrorism and Effective Death Penalty Act of 1996)

28 U.S.C. §2241. Power to Grant Writ

(a) Writs of habeas corpus may be granted by the Supreme Court, any justice thereof, the district courts, and any circuit judge within their respective jurisdictions. The order of a circuit judge shall be entered in the records of the district court of the district wherein the restraint complained of is had.

(b) The Supreme Court, any justice thereof, and any circuit judge may decline to entertain an application for a writ of habeas corpus and may transfer the application for hearing and determination to the district court having jurisdiction to entertain it.

(c) The writ of habeas corpus shall not extend to a prisoner unless—

(1) He is in custody under or by color of the authority of the United States or is committed for trial before some court thereof; or

(2) He is in custody for an act done or omitted in pursuance of an Act of Congress, or an order, process, judgment or decree of a court or judge of the United States; or

(3) He is in custody in violation of the Constitution or laws or treaties of the United States; or

(4) He, being a citizen of a foreign state and domiciled therein, is in custody for an act done or omitted under any alleged right, title, authority, privilege, protection, or exemption claimed under the commission, order or sanction of any foreign state, or under color thereof, the validity and effect of which depend upon the law of nations; or

(5) It is necessary to bring him into court to testify or for trial.

(d) Where an application for a writ of habeas corpus is made by a person in custody under the judgment and sentence of a State court of a State which contains two or more Federal judicial districts, the application may be filed in the district court for the district wherein such person is in custody or in the district court for the district within which the State court was held which convicted and sentenced him and each of such district courts shall have concurrent jurisdiction to entertain the application. The district court for the district wherein such an application is filed in the exercise of its discretion and in furtherance of justice may transfer the application to the other district court for hearing and determination.

(e) [**NOTE**—This provision, which was added to the statute as part of the Detainee Treatment Act of 2005 and which purported to deny access to habeas corpus for aliens detained by the U.S. Department of Defense at Guantanamo Bay as alleged "enemy combatants," was held unconstitutional by the U.S. Supreme Court in Boumediene v. Bush, 553 U.S. 723 (2008). See the main casebook, Chapter 17, pages 1652-1653, for further discussion of *Boumediene.*—EDS.]

28 U.S.C. §2242. Application

Application for a writ of habeas corpus shall be in writing signed and verified by the person for whose relief it is intended or by someone acting in his behalf.

It shall allege the facts concerning the applicant's commitment or detention, the name of the person who has custody over him and by virtue of what claim or authority, if known.

It may be amended or supplemented as provided in the rules of procedure applicable to civil actions.

If addressed to the Supreme Court, a justice thereof, or a circuit judge, it shall state the reasons for not making application to the district court of the district in which the applicant is held.

28 U.S.C. §2243. Issuance of Writ; Return; Hearing; Decision

A court, justice, or judge entertaining an application for a writ of habeas corpus shall forthwith award the writ or issue an order directing the respondent to show cause why the writ should not be granted, unless it appears from the application that the applicant or person detained is not entitled thereto.

The writ, or order to show cause, shall be directed to the person having custody of the person detained. It shall be returned within three days unless for good cause additional time, not exceeding twenty days, is allowed.

The person to whom the writ or order is directed shall make a return certifying the true cause of the detention.

When the writ or order is returned a day shall be set for hearing, not more than five days after the return unless for good cause additional time is allowed.

Unless the application for the writ and the return present only issues of law, the person to whom the writ is directed shall be required to produce at the hearing the body of the person detained.

The applicant or the person detained may, under oath, deny any of the facts set forth in the return or allege any other material facts.

The return and all suggestions made against it may be amended, by leave of court, before or after being filed.

The court shall summarily hear and determine the facts and dispose of the matter as law and justice require.

28 U.S.C. §2244. Finality of Determination

(a) No circuit or district judge shall be required to entertain an application for a writ of habeas corpus to inquire into the detention of a person pursuant to a judgment of a court of the United States if it appears that the legality of such detention has been determined by a judge or court of the United States on a prior application for a writ of habeas corpus, except as provided in section 2255.

(b)(1) A claim presented in a second or successive habeas corpus application under section 2254 that was presented in a prior application shall be dismissed.

(2) A claim presented in a second or successive habeas corpus application under section 2254 that was not presented in a prior application shall be dismissed unless—

(A) the applicant shows that the claim relies on a new rule of constitutional law, made retroactive to cases on collateral review by the Supreme Court, that was previously unavailable; or

(B)(i) the factual predicate for the claim could not have been discovered previously through the exercise of due diligence; and

(ii) the facts underlying the claim, if proven and viewed in light of the evidence as a whole, would be sufficient to establish by clear and convincing evidence that, but for constitutional error, no reasonable factfinder would have found the applicant guilty of the underlying offense.

(3)(A) Before a second or successive application permitted by this section is filed in the district court, the applicant shall move in the appropriate court of appeals for an order authorizing the district court to consider the application.

(B) A motion in the court of appeals for an order authorizing the district court to consider a second or successive application shall be determined by a three-judge panel of the court of appeals.

(C) The court of appeals may authorize the filing of a second or successive application only if it determines that the application makes a prima facie showing that the application satisfies the requirements of this subsection.

(D) The court of appeals shall grant or deny the authorization to file a second or successive application not later than 30 days after the filing of the motion.

(E) The grant or denial of an authorization by a court of appeals to file a second or successive application shall not be appealable and shall not be the subject of a petition for rehearing or for a writ of certiorari.

(4) A district court shall dismiss any claim presented in a second or successive application that the court of appeals has authorized to be filed unless the applicant shows that the claim satisfies the requirements of this section.

(c) In a habeas corpus proceeding brought in behalf of a person in custody pursuant to the judgment of a State court, a prior judgment of the Supreme Court of the United States on an appeal or review by a writ of certiorari at the instance of the prisoner of the decision of such State court, shall be conclusive as to all issues of fact or law with respect to an asserted denial of a Federal right which constitutes ground for discharge in a habeas corpus proceeding, actually adjudicated by the Supreme Court therein, unless the applicant for the writ of habeas corpus shall plead and the court shall find the existence of a material and controlling fact which did not appear in the record of the proceeding in the Supreme Court and the court shall further find that the applicant for the writ of habeas corpus could not have caused such fact to appear in such record by the exercise of reasonable diligence.

(d)(1) A one-year period of limitation shall apply to an application for a writ of habeas corpus by a person in custody pursuant to the judgment of a State court. The limitation period shall run from the latest of—

(A) the date on which the judgment became final by the conclusion of direct review or the expiration of the time for seeking such review;

(B) the date on which the impediment to filing an application created by State action in violation of the Constitution or laws of the United States is removed, if the applicant was prevented from filing by such State action;

(C) the date on which the constitutional right asserted was initially recognized by the Supreme Court, if the right has been newly recognized by the Supreme Court and made retroactively applicable to cases on collateral review; or

(D) the date on which the factual predicate of the claim or claims presented could have been discovered through the exercise of due diligence.

(2) The time during which a properly filed application for State post-conviction or other collateral review with respect to the pertinent judgment or claim is pending shall not be counted toward any period of limitation under this subsection.

28 U.S.C. §2253. Appeal

(a) In a habeas corpus proceeding or a proceeding under section 2255 before a district judge, the final order shall be subject to review, on appeal, by the court of appeals for the circuit in which the proceeding is held.

(b) There shall be no right of appeal from a final order in a proceeding to test the validity of a warrant to remove to another district or place for commitment or trial a person charged with a criminal offense against the United States, or to test the validity of such person's detention pending removal proceedings.

(c)(1) Unless a circuit justice or judge issues a certificate of appealability, an appeal may not be taken to the court of appeals from—

(A) the final order in a habeas corpus proceeding in which the detention complained of arises out of process issued by a State court; or

(B) the final order in a proceeding under section 2255.

(2) A certificate of appealability may issue under paragraph (1) only if the applicant has made a substantial showing of the denial of a constitutional right.

(3) The certificate of appealability under paragraph (1) shall indicate which specific issue or issues satisfy the showing required by paragraph (2).

28 U.S.C. §2254. State Custody; Remedies in Federal Courts

(a) The Supreme Court, a Justice thereof, a circuit judge, or a district court shall entertain an application for a writ of habeas corpus in behalf of a person in custody pursuant to the judgment of a State court only on the ground that he is in custody in violation of the Constitution or laws or treaties of the United States.

(b)(1) An application for a writ of habeas corpus on behalf of a person in custody pursuant to the judgment of a State court shall not be granted unless it appears that—

(A) the applicant has exhausted the remedies available in the courts of the State; or

(B) (i) there is an absence of available State corrective process; or

(ii) circumstances exist that render such process ineffective to protect the rights of the applicant.

(2) An application for a writ of habeas corpus may be denied on the merits, notwithstanding the failure of the applicant to exhaust the remedies available in the courts of the State.

(3) A State shall not be deemed to have waived the exhaustion requirement or be estopped from reliance upon the requirement unless the State, through counsel, expressly waives the requirement.

(c) An applicant shall not be deemed to have exhausted the remedies available in the courts of the State, within the meaning of this section, if he has the right under the law of the State to raise, by any available procedure, the question presented.

(d) An application for a writ of habeas corpus on behalf of a person in custody pursuant to the judgment of a State court shall not be granted with respect to any claim that was adjudicated on the merits in State court proceedings unless the adjudication of the claim—

(1) resulted in a decision that was contrary to, or involved an unreasonable application of, clearly established Federal law, as determined by the Supreme Court of the United States; or

(2) resulted in a decision that was based on an unreasonable determination of the facts in light of the evidence presented in the State court proceeding.

(e)(1) In a proceeding instituted by an application for a writ of habeas corpus by a person in custody pursuant to the judgment of a State court, a determination of a factual issue made by a State court shall be presumed to be correct. The applicant shall have the burden of rebutting the presumption of correctness by clear and convincing evidence.

(2) If the applicant has failed to develop the factual basis of a claim in State court proceedings, the court shall not hold an evidentiary hearing on the claim unless the applicant shows that—

(A) the claim relies on—

(i) a new rule of constitutional law, made retroactive to cases on collateral review by the Supreme Court, that was previously unavailable; or

(ii) a factual predicate that could not have been previously discovered through the exercise of due diligence; and

(B) the facts underlying the claim would be sufficient to establish by clear and convincing evidence that but for constitutional error, no reasonable factfinder would have found the applicant guilty of the underlying offense.

(f) If the applicant challenges the sufficiency of the evidence adduced in such State court proceeding to support the State court's determination of a factual issue made therein, the applicant, if able, shall produce that part of the record pertinent to a determination of the sufficiency of the evidence to support such determination. If the applicant, because of indigency or other reason is unable to produce such part of the record, then the State shall produce such part of the record and the Federal court shall direct the State to do so by order directed to an appropriate State official. If the State cannot provide such pertinent part of the record, then the court shall determine under the existing facts and circumstances what weight shall be given to the State court's factual determination.

(g) A copy of the official records of the State court, duly certified by the clerk of such court to be a true and correct copy of a finding, judicial opinion, or other reliable written indicia showing such a factual determination by the State court shall be admissible in the Federal court proceeding.

(h) Except as provided in section 408 of the Controlled Substance Acts [21 U.S.C. § 848], in all proceedings brought under this section, and any subsequent proceedings on review, the court may appoint counsel for an applicant who is or becomes financially unable to afford counsel, except as provided by a rule promulgated by the Supreme Court pursuant to statutory authority. Appointment of counsel under this section shall be governed by section 3006A of title 18.

(i) The ineffectiveness or incompetence of counsel during Federal or State collateral post-conviction proceedings shall not be a ground for relief in a proceeding arising under section 2254.

Collateral Review for Federal Prisoners

28 U.S.C. §2255. Federal Custody; Remedies on Motion Attacking Sentence

(a) A prisoner in custody under sentence of a court established by Act of Congress claiming the right to be released upon the ground that the sentence was imposed in violation of the Constitution or laws of the United States, or that the court was without jurisdiction to impose such sentence, or that the sentence was in excess of the maximum authorized by law, or is otherwise subject to collateral attack, may move the court which imposed the sentence to vacate, set aside or correct the sentence.

(b) Unless the motion and the files and records of the case conclusively show that the prisoner is entitled to no relief, the court shall cause notice thereof to be served upon the United States attorney, grant a prompt hearing thereon, determine the issues and make findings of fact and conclusions of law with respect thereto. If the court finds that the judgment was rendered without jurisdiction, or that the sentence imposed was not authorized by law or otherwise open to collateral attack, or that there has been such a denial or infringement of the constitutional rights of the prisoner as to render the judgment vulnerable to collateral attack, the court shall vacate and set the judgment aside and shall discharge the prisoner or resentence him or grant a new trial or correct the sentence as may appear appropriate.

(c) A court may entertain and determine such motion without requiring the production of the prisoner at the hearing.

(d) An appeal may be taken to the court of appeals from the order entered on the motion as from the final judgment on application for a writ of habeas corpus.

(e) An application for a writ of habeas corpus in behalf of a prisoner who is authorized to apply for relief by motion pursuant to this section, shall not be entertained if it appears that the applicant has failed to apply for relief, by motion, to the court which sentenced him, or that such court has denied him relief, unless it also appears that the remedy by motion is inadequate or ineffective to test the legality of his detention.

(f) A one-year period of limitation shall apply to a motion under this section. The limitation period shall run from the latest of—

(1) the date on which the judgment of conviction becomes final;

(2) the date on which the impediment to making a motion created by governmental action in violation of the Constitution or laws of the United States is removed, if the movant was prevented from making a motion by such governmental action;

(3) the date on which the right asserted was initially recognized by the Supreme Court, if that right has been newly recognized by the Supreme Court and made retroactively applicable to cases on collateral review; or

(4) the date on which the facts supporting the claim or claims presented could have been discovered through the exercise of due diligence.

(g) Except as provided in section 408 of the Controlled Substances Act [21 U.S.C. § 848], in all proceedings brought under this section, and any subsequent proceedings on review, the court may appoint counsel, except as provided by a rule promulgated by the Supreme Court pursuant to statutory authority. Appointment of counsel under this section shall be governed by section 3006A of title 18.

(h) A second or successive motion must be certified as provided in section 2244 by a panel of the appropriate court of appeals to contain—

(1) newly discovered evidence that, if proven and viewed in light of the evidence as a whole, would be sufficient to establish by clear and convincing evidence that no reasonable factfinder would have found the movant guilty of the offense; or

(2) a new rule of constitutional law, made retroactive to cases on collateral review by the Supreme Court, that was previously unavailable.

Foreign Intelligence Surveillance Act

50 U.S.C. §1861. Access to Certain Business Records for Foreign Intelligence and International Terrorism Investigations

(a) Application for order; conduct of investigation generally

(1) Subject to paragraph (3), the Director of the Federal Bureau of Investigation or a designee of the Director (whose rank shall be no lower than Assistant Special Agent in Charge) may make an application for an order requiring the production of any tangible things (including books, records, papers, documents, and other items) for an investigation to obtain foreign intelligence information not concerning a United States person or to protect against international terrorism or clandestine intelligence activities, provided that such investigation of a United States person is not conducted solely upon the basis of activities protected by the first amendment to the Constitution.

(2) An investigation conducted under this section shall

(A) be conducted under guidelines approved by the Attorney General under Executive Order 12333 (or a successor order); and

(B) not be conducted of a United States person solely upon the basis of activities protected by the first amendment to the Constitution of the United States.

(3) In the case of an application for an order requiring the production of library circulation records, library patron lists, book sales records, book customer lists, firearms sales records, tax return records, educational records, or medical records containing information that would identify a person, the Director of the Federal Bureau of Investigation may delegate the authority to make such application

to either the Deputy Director of the Federal Bureau of Investigation or the Executive Assistant Director for National Security (or any successor position). The Deputy Director or the Executive Assistant Director may not further delegate such authority.

(b) Recipient and contents of application. Each application under this section—

(1) shall be made to—

(A) a judge of the court established by section 1803 (a) of this title; or

(B) a United States Magistrate Judge under chapter 43 of Title 28, who is publicly designated by the Chief Justice of the United States to have the power to hear applications and grant orders for the production of tangible things under this section on behalf of a judge of that court; and

(2) shall include—

(A) a specific selection term to be used as the basis for the production of the tangible things sought;

(B) in the case of an application other than an application described in subparagraph (C) (including an application for the production of call detail records other than in the manner described in subparagraph (C)), a statement of facts showing that there are reasonable grounds to believe that the tangible things sought are relevant to an authorized investigation (other than a threat assessment) conducted in accordance with subsection (a) (2) to obtain foreign intelligence information not concerning a United States person or to protect against international terrorism or clandestine intelligence activities, such things being presumptively relevant to an authorized investigation if the applicant shows in the statement of the facts that they pertain to—

(i) a foreign power or an agent of a foreign power;

(ii) the activities of a suspected agent of a foreign power who is the subject of such authorized investigation; or

(iii) an individual in contact with, or known to, a suspected agent of a foreign power who is the subject of such authorized investigation;

(C) in the case of an application for the production on an ongoing basis of call detail records created before, on, or after the date of the application relating to an authorized investigation (other than a threat assessment) conducted in accordance with subsection (a)(2) to protect against international terrorism, a statement of facts showing that—

(i) there are reasonable grounds to believe that the call detail records sought to be produced based on the specific selection term required under subparagraph (A) are relevant to such investigation; and

(ii) there is a reasonable, articulable suspicion that such specific selection term is associated with a foreign power engaged in international terrorism or activities in preparation therefor, or an agent of a foreign power engaged in international terrorism or activities in preparation therefor; and

(D) an enumeration of the minimization procedures adopted by the Attorney General under subsection (g) that are applicable to the retention and dissemination by the Federal Bureau of Investigation of any tangible things to be made available to the Federal Bureau of Investigation based on the order requested in such application.

(c) Ex parte judicial order of approval

(1) Upon an application made pursuant to this section, if the judge finds that the application meets the requirements of subsections (a) and (b) and that the minimization procedures submitted in accordance with subsection (b)(2)(D) meet the definition of minimization procedures under subsection (g), the judge shall enter an ex parte order as requested, or as modified, approving the release of tangible things. Such order shall direct that minimization procedures adopted pursuant to subsection (g) be followed.

(2) An order under this subsection—

(A) shall describe the tangible things that are ordered to be produced with sufficient particularity to permit them to be fairly identified, including each specific selection term to be used as the basis for the production;

(B) shall include the date on which the tangible things must be provided, which shall allow a reasonable period of time within which the tangible things can be assembled and made available;

(C) shall provide clear and conspicuous notice of the principles and procedures described in subsection (d);

(D) may only require the production of a tangible thing if such thing can be obtained with a subpoena duces tecum issued by a court of the United States in aid of a grand jury investigation or with any other order issued by a court of the United States directing the production of records or tangible things;

(E) shall not disclose that such order is issued for purposes of an investigation described in subsection (a); and

(F) in the case of an application described in subsection (b)(2)(C), shall—

(i) authorize the production on a daily basis of call detail records for a period not to exceed 180 days;

(ii) provide that an order for such production may be extended upon application under subsection (b) and the judicial finding under paragraph (1) of this subsection;

(iii) provide that the Government may require the prompt production of a first set of call detail records using the specific selection term that satisfies the standard required under subsection (b)(2)(C)(ii);

(iv) provide that the Government may require the prompt production of a second set of call detail records using session-identifying information or a telephone calling card number identified by the specific selection term used to produce call detail records under clause (iii);

(v) provide that, when produced, such records be in a form that will be useful to the Government;

(vi) direct each person the Government directs to produce call detail records under the order to furnish the Government forthwith all information, facilities, or technical assistance necessary to accomplish the production in such a manner as will protect the secrecy of the production and produce a minimum of interference with the services that such person is providing to each subject of the production; and

(vii) direct the Government to—

(I) adopt minimization procedures that require the prompt destruction of all call detail records produced under the order that the Government determines are not foreign intelligence information; and

(II) destroy all call detail records produced under the order as prescribed by such procedures.

(3) No order issued under this subsection may authorize the collection of tangible things without the use of a specific selection term that meets the requirements of subsection (b)(2).

(4) A denial of the application made under this subsection may be reviewed as provided in section 1803 of this title.

(d) Nondisclosure

(1) No person shall disclose to any other person that the Federal Bureau of Investigation has sought or obtained tangible things pursuant to an order issued or an emergency production required under this section, other than to

(A) those persons to whom disclosure is necessary to comply with such order or such emergency production;

(B) an attorney to obtain legal advice or assistance with respect to the production of things in response to the order or the emergency production; or

(C) other persons as permitted by the Director of the Federal Bureau of Investigation or the designee of the Director.

(2) (A) A person to whom disclosure is made pursuant to paragraph (1) shall be subject to the nondisclosure requirements applicable to a person to whom an order or emergency production is directed under this section in the same manner as such person.

(B) Any person who discloses to a person described in subparagraph (A), (B), or (C) of paragraph (1) that the Federal Bureau of Investigation has sought or obtained tangible things pursuant to an order or emergency production under this section shall notify such person of the nondisclosure requirements of this subsection.

(C) At the request of the Director of the Federal Bureau of Investigation or the designee of the Director, any person making or intending to make a disclosure under subparagraph (A) or (C) of paragraph (1) shall identify to the Director or such designee the person to whom such disclosure will be made or to whom such disclosure was made prior to the request.

(e) Liability for good faith disclosure; waiver

(1) No cause of action shall lie in any court against a person who—

(A) produces tangible things or provides information, facilities, or technical assistance in accordance with an order issued or an emergency production required under this section; or

(B) otherwise provides technical assistance to the Government under this section or to implement the amendments made to this section by the USA FREEDOM Act of 2015.

(2) A production or provision of information, facilities, or technical assistance described in paragraph (1) shall not be deemed to constitute a waiver of any privilege in any other proceeding or context.

(f) Judicial review of FISA orders

(1) In this subsection—

(A) the term "production order" means an order to produce any tangible thing under this section; and

(B) the term "nondisclosure order" means an order imposed under subsection (d).

(2)(A)(i) A person receiving a production order may challenge the legality of the production order or any nondisclosure order imposed in connection with the production order by filing a petition with the pool established by section 1803(e)(1) of this title.

(ii) The presiding judge shall immediately assign a petition under clause (i) to 1 of the judges serving in the pool established by section 1803(e)(1) of this title. Not later than 72 hours after the assignment of such petition, the assigned judge shall conduct an initial review of the petition. If the assigned judge determines that the petition is frivolous, the assigned judge shall immediately deny the petition and affirm the production order or nondisclosure order. If the assigned judge determines the petition is not frivolous, the assigned judge shall promptly consider the petition in accordance with the procedures established under section 1803(e)(2) of this title.

(iii) The assigned judge shall promptly provide a written statement for the record of the reasons for any determination under this subsection. Upon the request of the Government, any order setting aside a nondisclosure order shall be stayed pending review pursuant to paragraph (3).

(B) A judge considering a petition to modify or set aside a production order may grant such petition only if the judge finds that such order does not meet the requirements of this section or is otherwise unlawful. If the judge does not modify or set aside the production order, the judge shall immediately affirm such order, and order the recipient to comply therewith.

(C)(i) A judge considering a petition to modify or set aside a nondisclosure order may grant such petition only if the judge finds that there is no reason to believe that disclosure may endanger the national security of the United States, interfere with a criminal, counterterrorism, or counterintelligence investigation, interfere with diplomatic relations, or endanger the life or physical safety of any person.

(ii) If the judge denies a petition to modify or set aside a nondisclosure order, the recipient of such order shall be precluded for a period of 1 year from filing another such petition with respect to such nondisclosure order.

(D) Any production or nondisclosure order not explicitly modified or set aside consistent with this subsection shall remain in full effect.

(3) A petition for review of a decision under paragraph (2) to affirm, modify, or set aside an order by the Government or any person receiving such order shall be made to the court of review established under section 1803(b) of this title, which shall have jurisdiction to consider such petitions. The court of review shall provide for the record a written statement of the reasons for its decision and, on petition by the Government or any person receiving such order for writ of certiorari, the record shall be transmitted under seal to the Supreme Court of the United States, which shall have jurisdiction to review such decision.

(4) Judicial proceedings under this subsection shall be concluded as expeditiously as possible. The record of proceedings, including petitions filed, orders granted, and statements of reasons for decision, shall be maintained under security measures established by the Chief Justice of the United States, in consultation with the Attorney General and the Director of National Intelligence.

(5) All petitions under this subsection shall be filed under seal. In any proceedings under this subsection, the court shall, upon request of the Government, review ex parte and in camera any Government submission, or portions thereof, which may include classified information.

(g) Minimization procedures

(1) In general

The Attorney General shall adopt, and update as appropriate, specific minimization procedures governing the retention and dissemination by the Federal Bureau of Investigation of any tangible things, or information therein, received by the Federal Bureau of Investigation in response to an order under this subchapter.

(2) Defined

In this section, the term "minimization procedures" means—

(A) specific procedures that are reasonably designed in light of the purpose and technique of an order for the production of tangible things, to minimize the retention, and prohibit the dissemination, of nonpublicly available information concerning unconsenting United States persons consistent with the need of the United States to obtain, produce, and disseminate foreign intelligence information;

(B) procedures that require that nonpublicly available information, which is not foreign intelligence information, as defined in section 1801(e)(1) of this title, shall not be disseminated in a manner that identifies any United States person, without such person's consent, unless such person's identity is necessary to understand foreign intelligence information or assess its importance; and

(C) notwithstanding subparagraphs (A) and (B), procedures that allow for the retention and dissemination of information that is evidence of a crime which has been, is being, or is about to be committed and that is to be retained or disseminated for law enforcement purposes.

(3) Rule of construction

Nothing in this subsection shall limit the authority of the court established under section 1803(a) of this title to impose additional, particularized minimization procedures with regard to the production, retention, or dissemination of nonpublicly available information concerning unconsenting United States persons, including additional, particularized procedures related to the destruction of information within a reasonable time period.

(h) Use of information

Information acquired from tangible things received by the Federal Bureau of Investigation in response to an order under this subchapter concerning any United States person may be used and disclosed by Federal officers and employees without the consent of the United States person only in accordance with the minimization procedures adopted pursuant to subsection (g). No otherwise privileged information acquired from tangible things received by the Federal Bureau of Investigation in accordance with the provisions of this subchapter shall lose its privileged character. No information acquired from tangible things received by the Federal Bureau of Investigation in response to an order under this subchapter may be used or disclosed by Federal officers or employees except for lawful purposes.

(i) Emergency authority for production of tangible things

(1) Notwithstanding any other provision of this section, the Attorney General may require the emergency production of tangible things if the Attorney General—

(A) reasonably determines that an emergency situation requires the production of tangible things before an order authorizing such production can with due diligence be obtained;

(B) reasonably determines that the factual basis for the issuance of an order under this section to approve such production of tangible things exists;

(C) informs, either personally or through a designee, a judge having jurisdiction under this section at the time the Attorney General requires the emergency production of tangible things that the decision has been made to employ the authority under this subsection; and

(D) makes an application in accordance with this section to a judge having jurisdiction under this section as soon as practicable, but not later than 7 days after the Attorney General requires the emergency production of tangible things under this subsection.

(2) If the Attorney General requires the emergency production of tangible things under paragraph (1), the Attorney General shall require that the minimization procedures required by this section for the issuance of a judicial order be followed.

(3) In the absence of a judicial order approving the production of tangible things under this subsection, the production shall terminate when the information sought is obtained, when the application for the order is denied, or after the expiration of 7 days from the time the Attorney General begins requiring the emergency production of such tangible things, whichever is earliest.

(4) A denial of the application made under this subsection may be reviewed as provided in section 1803 of this title.

(5) If such application for approval is denied, or in any other case where the production of tangible things is terminated and no order is issued approving the production, no information obtained or evidence derived from such production shall be received in evidence or otherwise disclosed in any trial, hearing, or other proceeding in or before any court, grand jury, department, office, agency, regulatory body, legislative committee, or other authority of the United States, a State, or a political subdivision thereof, and no information concerning any United States person acquired from such production shall subsequently be used or disclosed in any other manner by Federal officers or employees without the consent of such person, except with the approval of the Attorney General if the information indicates a threat of death or serious bodily harm to any person.

(6) The Attorney General shall assess compliance with the requirements of paragraph (5).